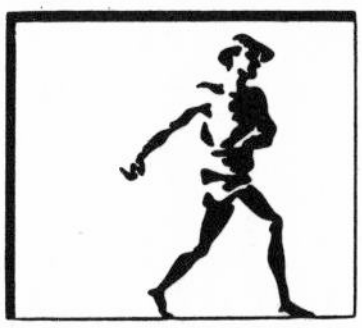

Foreword by Amby Burfoot,
Winner 1968 Boston Marathon

MARATHONING

Bill Rodgers
with Joe Concannon

Simon and Schuster
NEW YORK

Copyright © 1980 by Bill Rodgers and Joe Concannon
All rights reserved
including the right of reproduction
in whole or in part in any form
Published by Simon and Schuster
A Division of Gulf & Western Corporation
Simon & Schuster Building
Rockefeller Center
1230 Avenue of the Americas
New York, New York 10020

SIMON AND SCHUSTER and colophon are
trademarks of Simon and Schuster

Designed by Stanley S. Drate
Manufactured in the United States of America
Printed by Murray Printing Company
Bound by Book Press

1 2 3 4 5 6 7 8 9 10

Library of Congress Cataloging in Publication Data

Rodgers, Bill, date.
 Marathoning.

 Autobiographical.
 1. Rodgers, Bill, date. 2. Runners (Sports)—
United States—Biography. 3. Marathon running.
I. Concannon, Joe, joint author. II. Title.
GV697.R58A35   796.4'26 [B]   79-26049
ISBN 0-671-25087-6

Acknowledgments

Throughout the fifteen years I have been a runner I have found many good friends and running partners. These particular friends and runners will always have my gratitude: first, my running partners in high school, my brother Charlie, Jim (Jason) Kehoe—still a running partner and best friend—Jimmy and Ray Hall, and special thanks to Coach Frank O'Rourke of Newington High School. During my collegiate years I was fortunate enough to meet, run, and become friends with Amby Burfoot, America's finest marathoner in the middle 1960s and a great teacher of distance running. I thank Jeff Galloway for help during my freshman year, Coach Elmer Swanson of Wesleyan University for his understanding of athletes as persons with post-collegiate athletic potential—and all my Cardinal teammates. As a member of the Greater Boston Track Club I am most indebted to Coach Billy Squires, Coach Bob Sevene, Coach Jack McDonald, Don Ricciato, Dick Mahoney, Chuck Riley, Scott Graham, Vinnie Fleming, Greg Meyer, Randy Thomas, Bob Hodge, Tom Grilk, Larry Newman, and Pat Lynch. For his friendship and support I thank Tommy Leonard, perhaps the most inspirational force in New England road racing. In recent years I have enjoyed friendship and runs with Rob and Patti Yahn, Lois Dowd, and Robin Clayton and thank them for their high spirits and support. Without their help and understanding of the sport, Bill Rodgers & Company, our clothing line, would never have developed. Similarly the Bill Rodgers Running Centers would not function so well without the guidance and hard work of Charlie Rodgers, Russell McCarter, Joe Notar, Mark Murray, and all the staff members.

I want to thank those race directors and sponsors who love the sport and have demonstrated it by designing their races primarily for the runners' benefit. In particular, Will Cloney of the BAA has shown an intelligent and thoughtful regard for the runners who race Boston. Eiichi Shibuya of the JAAF has been a great force in keeping the Fukuoka Marathon the magnificent race it is, and Fred Lebow of the New York City Marathon has worked hard to create the finest contemporary mass marathon in the world. There are many race directors who were kind to me and I will remember their thoughtfulness; I want to thank Rudy and Marilyn Straub, Hugh Stobbs, Jim Lillstrom, John Carroll, and Rich Sherman.

Pepsi-Cola, through its National Diet Pepsi ten-thousand meter series, and Perrier, Inc., are two companies at the forefront in helping to develop the sport of running and I'm grateful for their efforts.

There are several trainers, podiatrists, and other medical professionals I want to thank for their help. Buddy Evans of Bentley College, Lloyd Smith, D.P.M. at St. Elizabeth's Hospital, Jock Semple of the BAA, and Dr. Robert Leach of University Hospital.

Sincere thanks must go to those spectators who cheered for and supported me in victory and defeat and those runners with whom I've shared many of the most enjoyable times of my life running.

In many ways, this book is akin to a long-distance run, a product of global travel. In fact, actual work on the manuscript was done in Japan, Hawaii, California, Arizona, Michigan,

New Hampshire, and Connecticut but, above all, in a second-floor apartment in Melrose, Massachusetts, and in a basement apartment in Brighton, Massachusetts.

Since the conversations and thoughts remembered from so many runs are incorporated into the pages of the book, it is safe to say that anyone who either tagged along or pushed ahead on any of those runs played a role in the story. They are inherently part of it.

In particular, the authors would like to thank Joanne Melanson Cronin, who transcribed the tapes; Bill Lally of Connections Publications, who cleaned up some sloppy copy; Mary Hazard, who typed the manuscript; and Peter Schwed of Simon and Schuster, whose editorial wisdom made it a better book.

A special thanks to Ellen Rodgers, for her advice, counsel, encouragement, and indulgence and, after some long work sessions, for dinner.

Of course, I deeply appreciate the support and understanding that my sisters, Martha and Linda, and my parents, Mr. and Mrs. Charles A. Rodgers, have always given me.

BILL RODGERS
Melrose, Massachusetts

For Ellen

B.R.

To my mother Mary who,
in a lifetime as an educator,
started many on the right road.

J.C.

Contents

Foreword

The first time I saw Bill Rodgers I rooted hard for him to trip and falter or maybe slip on a rain-slicked leaf. He was a high school senior in Newington, Connecticut, then, trying his best to decimate the rest of the cross-country runners in the state-championship race. And doing a pretty good job of it, too. Among his closest pursuers, however, was my brother Gary, only a tenth-grader. Naturally, I was pulling for a family win, especially since Gary was a green kid, a clear underdog.

Even in those days Bill had cultivated the tactic of breaking away from the field in mid-race. I countered by finding a position out on the back nine of the golf course and waiting there for the runners to churn past. By that point, Bill had a fifty-yard lead over the second group, which included my brother. Undaunted, I held my ground and yelled, "C'mon Gary! You can catch him! Rodgers is dying."

In 1965 it seemed a reasonable thing to yell. Today I don't think I'd want to try it out.

I never dreamed that this same Rodgers would be attending my college a year later, that we would train together nearly every day, that we would eventually decide to become roommates. Or that after his freshman season, we'd be competing against each other in varsity cross-country and track.

When that happened I found myself once again rooting for Rodgers to lose races. We considered ourselves more teammates than rivals, to be sure, but I still remember training extra hard at times just to "keep the soph in his place." During the winter of 1967–68, when I was gearing up for the Boston Marathon, I regularly went out for twenty-five-mile training runs on Sunday mornings. It was almost impossible to drag Bill out of bed early enough to go the whole distance—he had always been out carousing in bars and dancing spots the night before—but he would usually join me for the final ten-mile loop. The arrangement worked well for both of us. Bill got in some needed distance training and I suffered no loss of face when he managed to stay with me through the ten miles.

I remember clearly, though, the one Sunday morning when Bill actually forced himself up early enough to cover the whole route with me. I guess that "psyched" me a bit, because from the start we ran faster than my norm, covering the first 15 miles at a 6:30-per-mile pace, Bill wafting easily at my shoulder. As we crossed campus to begin the last 10, which consisted of a virtually unbroken string of hills, I stepped up the pace and we dropped to 6:00-minute miles. Eight miles later Bill was still there, light as a feather and floating just as effortlessly. That was a little more than I could take. After all, I had been training about 120 miles a week; Bill maybe a third that. I had done numerous 25-milers; he had almost never been beyond 10. Deciding that justice must prevail, I announced my intention to do a "pick-up" over the final 2 miles. He was welcome to tag along if he pleased. With that, I pushed it hard all the way back to the dorm, knocking off a couple of 5:15 miles. Bill staggered in roughly 2 minutes later.

Sweet victory. And the first intimation of a prodigious marathoning talent.

After graduating from Wesleyan in 1968, I saw and heard

little of Bill Rodgers for several years. In the early 70s, while competing in Connecticut races, I would occasionally see him at roadside, looking a bit forlorn, his soft blond hair lapping comfortably at his shoulders. I wrote a support letter for his Conscientious Objector application to Selective Service, and I later heard that he had moved to Boston to do "alternative duty" in a hospital there.

Then in February 1973 I decided to run a Boston Marathon tune-up race over the first twenty miles of the famous course. Warming up beside the Hopkinton Green, I spotted Bill, in a torn green sweatshirt and patched khakis, doing the same. We greeted each other warmly and I allowed as to how it was "great to see you out running a little again." Forty-nine minutes and some odd seconds later, while Bill dogged my footsteps as we passed the ten-mile checkpoint, I was wishing him back in his smoke-filled bars. I held Bill off that day, but was astounded that he ran 1:44 for twenty miles in his first race in more than three years.

For the next two years Bill ran successfully on the New England roads, with the same ups and downs most distance runners experience. Then in March 1975 came a breakthrough: third place in the International Cross-country Championship in Morocco, the highest an American has ever finished in this Olympic-caliber event, and a virtually unthinkable performance for a New England road racer coming off the slush-covered winter training roads. Something was up.

Deciding to find out what, I traveled to Boston to visit Bill and his girl friend Ellen Lalone, to do an interview for Runner's World magazine. Most of the interview was conducted in the living room—if that's what you can call a six-foot by ten-foot chamber with a tiny window at one end—of her three-room basement apartment in Jamaica Plain. While Bill and I chatted, Ellen tended spaghetti in the kitchen.

Over the years I've learned that the best gauge of a runner's condition is his own perceived effort. When the runner feels relaxed and "easy" while the stopwatch hums a high-speed tune, then the runner is reaching a peak. That evening Bill said about his Morocco race: "I went into the lead at about three miles and really felt good—not fatigued at all. It didn't feel fast at that point and I kept expecting people to go past me." Two eventually did, but the rest of the world ate his dust. I realized by his description that higher peaks lay ahead for Bill.

Three weeks later, running the Boston Marathon, I stopped at every familiar face to ask, "How's Bill doing?"

At every point I heard the same—"He's with the leaders"— and got more and more excited. Near eighteen miles I saw Greater Boston Track Club coach Bill Squires and asked my question. "He's a quarter mile ahead," Squires screamed back at me, "and a minute under the course record pace."

I spent the rest of the race begging people to drive me to the Prudential Center so I could see Bill finish, but to no avail. "We can't make it," they'd all tell me. "Never be able to get through all the traffic in time." Soon after reaching the Pru under my own power I came upon a lonely-looking Ellen and—gallantry substituting for strength—grabbed her by the hand to lead a blustery charge through the police and press to get her to Bill's side.

I didn't get the full story from Bill until the next day. By then most of Boston had discovered a new hometown hero (no Boston area resident had won the marathon since "Old John" Kelley managed it in 1945), and cameras and microphones were probing every inch of Bill's life.

What came from all the stories, amazingly, was that the 2:09:55 American record felt easy to Bill. You had to believe him, too, when you considered the nonchalant pauses for water and to retie his shoelaces. And at the same time you had to wonder: If a 2:09:55 was easy, what did the future hold?

The answer is now part of running's history, part open still to speculation.

The question people most often ask me is, "Did you know

way back in 1965 that Bill Rodgers was going to become such a great distance runner?" The answer is simple and monosyllabic: "No." Certainly I recognized his running talent, as did others, and certainly we saw his genuine love for running, but those qualities alone do not translate into a 2:09 marathoner. There's also that small matter of consistent, day-in-and-day-out, never-ending twenty-mile training runs. In the 1960s, this kind of application was not part of Bill's running philosophy. Not that he was slouch; he worked very hard on occasion . . . but on occasion he lost his training shoes under the bed for a week or two at a time.

It seems to me that you could quite simply (and perhaps too simplistically) graph Bill Rodgers' psychological and running development over the last fifteen years. In high school, coming from a tight family and an authoritarian coach, he did everything as told and became a state champion. In college, with no one to issue orders, he drifted along—in shape some seasons, out of shape other seasons. After college, facing the overwhelming presence of the Vietnam War, Bill, like many, "dropped out," directionless and searching. Several years later, while working off his military requirement, he began to find himself, met a solid woman, and started off on a return to fitness and running.

That's the framework. All the between-the-lines color rests in the pages ahead.

And one more thing—a note to Bill: I'm finally rooting for you these days.

AMBY BURFOOT
New London, Connecticut

MARATHONING

1
Beginning

The earliest entry in the first running diary I ever kept is dated September 8, 1963, and it indicates I set a Personal Record for the mile with a time of 5:10. I was fifteen. It wasn't in the diary, but I remember I had run a 5:20 mile in a Parks and Recreation Department meet one month earlier in my hometown of Newington, Connecticut, to establish my previous low.

I often thumb through the pages of that little brown notebook. I paid a dime for it. It covers the formative years, and it's all so unstructured. I was a sophomore in high school and there are days when the only notations in the diary say, "Rainy. No running. Went to block dance." Sometimes people tend to make running too complicated.

The course I ran was around the block from my family home in Newington, a suburban community about ten miles south of Hartford. It was two laps to the mile and I usually ran five laps. I read some of the entries in the diary and I laugh. "Too cold to run," for September 26. "Pouring rain. Can't run," for September 28. I was a fair-weather runner.

I just began running on a semi-consistent basis. I was no more than a part-time runner in high school and college. The cross-country program that I was beginning at Newington High School was a very informal thing. It wasn't even a varsity sport. It was an intramural activity.

We had three meets with other high schools, and our coach used to reward us with ice cream cones after the race. It always seemed I had excuses not to run. It's all there in the diary. I had to get a haircut. I had a cold. I might run five hundred yards in a gym class. I never did more than two or three miles.

People were not involved in this tremendous motivational urge to go out and run long distances in 1963. People considered me to be extreme and almost fanatical for just going out in the neighborhood and running a few times around the block. Two miles was a long distance for a high school runner. It was long for any runner.

Imagine. I ran one 5:10 mile. I contrast that with my top marathons when I run a 4:57 or 4:58 pace for twenty-six consecutive miles. It's a very different approach today. I had a very, very slow start as a runner. People start so fast and push themselves so hard today. Maybe too fast and too hard. I think that's why so many are injured.

I have to credit Frank O'Rourke, my coach at Newington High School, for knowing how to get the best out of me. My training was based on the interval method. Probably 90 percent of my workouts involved intervals. I did repeat 220s, 440s, 880s, and occasionally miles on the track. I ended up my high school career with PRs (Personal Records) of 2:07 in the 880, 4:28.8 in the mile and 9:36 in the two-mile.

I looked at running then as a purely fun thing to do. I was pretty good at it; consequently, I was excited about it. I was close to the school record for the mile. I just loved the sport. I enjoyed the feeling of running, and it's something that's stayed with me.

My parents were neutral. They were happy I was running

and involved in it. They knew there were positive effects. They were not the sort of parents who pushed me and forced me to strive for a higher goal as a runner. They figured it was a temporary thing. I'd get out of high school, go on to college, and concentrate on my studies. That's the way it would be.

Why am I a top runner now? Why did I get seriously involved in running? I can't put my finger on one specific thing. I became a runner because it suited my personality. It suited me as an individual. There may be a lot of different reasons, but, somehow, they all came together.

It wasn't because I wasn't good in any other sports. It wasn't because I thought I had a special talent for it. The primary reason was that I enjoyed it, physically and psychologically. The feeling of moving along the way I did when I ran was something I enjoyed.

I'm also impatient. I couldn't sit in a classroom and tediously take notes all day. I'm the type of person who likes to be outside. I like the outdoors. People who spend all day inside an office or a house are missing out on life.

I was always very active when I was ten or twelve. I was into hiking, camping, hunting with a bow and arrow, and fishing. I'd go out with my brother, Charlie, and the neighborhood kids and we'd put in a lot of miles. Just walking. You read about the Kenyan schoolchildren running to and from school. That's the way we were. We were always moving.

We were also juvenile semi-delinquent-type kids. We'd always be running away from people. We used to sneak on the Stanley Public Golf Course in nearby New Britain, find golf balls on the edge of the course, and take off with them. We'd go fishing in a private pond and someone would always be chasing us away. We'd go out into the cornfields and eat the farmer's corn or run away with some of his other crops.

One time, Jim (Jason) Kehoe, another friend, and I, went hunting with our BB guns in a nearby public park—Stanley Park in New Britain, Connecticut. We were having a grand time chasing squirrels and ducks until a police car suddenly appeared. We split in three different directions, but I must have set a personal record for running through bushes, prickers, etc., as I did not get caught but ended up safely waist deep in the nearby pond hidden by reeds. My two friends were caught.

A favorite pastime of mine was to chase butterflies, and I still have part of my collection on the wall of our apartment. We used to make nets with pillowcases and broomsticks. I had a large butterfly and moth collection with polyphemous and cecropia moths, tiger swallowtails, question mark, red admiral, and red-spotted purple butterflies.

I can still remember one particular instance when a friend of mine was poised to catch a beautiful tiger swallowtail butterfly. I was about eighty yards away and I did this incredible sprint just to beat him out. I threw myself on top of it. It was really a bit unfair to my friend because our unwritten law was first come, first served, and he'd been on the spot.

We'd spend hours in the middle of summer running back and forth in this huge field in Newington. I love the sensation that running through the fields and running on grass gives me. It's a very natural thing and it brings back a lot of memories. It was a big factor in my conditioning when I was young.

I was also active in different sports. I played baseball, basketball, tennis, and badminton. I swam. I can remember playing touch football when I was about twelve with Jason, and I often used to be the guy who ran a lot with the ball. His father had been a top high school miler in the late 1930s and early 1940s and he was always telling me how I would be a good runner someday. I prided myself on my ability to take the football and run away from people.

So, running always seemed to fit me very well. I think I get a lot of it from my mother, who ran her first serious road race in the 1979 Bonne Bell in Boston. We're similar in terms of personality. She has a lot of energy. I have a lot of energy. I have to use it up. If I didn't I'd be an insomniac. I'd rather use it up outside running than sitting in a classroom listening to lectures.

That is something that has come up at frequent junctures in my life. I went to Wesleyan University in Middletown, Connecticut, and I well remember another student in my class who weighed about 350 pounds. He hated the thought of exercise. He felt the mind was superior to the body. I seemed to be at the other end of the spectrum.

We two went back and forth on the mind-body dichotomy. We argued about which one was superior to the other, the mind to the body or vice-versa. He used to write these thirty-, forty-, or-fifty-page papers on Plato and Kant. We used to throw oranges at each other. We were friends, but we certainly were two very different people.

He was the epitome of pure mind and I was the epitome of pure body. I was the jock. I used to get out there and do intervals on the Wesleyan track. I was at the very bottom of my class. He was near the top, but he was obese. I think there has to be an even mix. In some ways, Wesleyan was a good school. But as far as I was concerned, too many people were too carried away with the intellectual side of life in general.

It's cyclical. Today, people are taking more of an interest in their physical well-being. It's your body after all, and you're stuck with it for life. So you'd better use your mind intelligently, as well as intellectually, and work at developing a good body. People are beginning to realize the truth of this.

What is intelligence? Is it people with Ph.D.'s who are working on sending people to the moon? Sure, but is that all there is to intelligence? I think it is at least as intelligent to take care of yourself physically so you'll be around longer to enjoy yourself.

All of this relates to the marathon and why it fits my personality. It slows me down, for one thing. I have all this energy to use up, and this is something I can put all of it into.

You can see very tangible results from the effort you put into a marathon.

There is nothing wishy-washy about the marathon. There's nothing abstract about it. You go up there, you get your time, you get your results. It's a very clear-cut, pure sort of thing. I saw a man at the start of the Boston Marathon one year. He had a T-shirt on with the word "Dare" printed across the front. It struck me as appropriate. That's what marathon running is.

My whole feeling, in terms of racing, is that you have to be very bold. You sometimes have to be aggressive and gamble. If you're going to win fairly consistently, you have to get out there and gamble and hope the moves you make are right. ,

This is also true of your training. Sometimes you might put in a little higher mileage in one week, and some of the people in your club might be beating you in the middle of the week because of it. You're gambling that the end result will justify it. You're going to make mistakes. Everyone does. Running can be a very frustrating sport. It can be very disheartening.

The beginning runners all want to know what the secrets are. You can tell people to drink fruit juices. You can tell them to drink water so they don't dehydrate. A lot of times a person just has to go out there and experience it. Learn what running is all about through the experience. You have to go through the physical experience. You can't simply be told about it.

When I was a teenager, the situation in Southeast Asia had barely started to heat up. It was a gentle time, a time that was in marked contrast to what it would be like on the college campus before the decade was over. There was no great motivation to excel, and no pressure to run.

Still, I religiously noted my progress in my diary. I lowered my PR in the mile to 5:06 on October 3. I ran the 2.2 mile cross-country course in Goodwin Park in Hartford the next afternoon in 11:48.8. I was down to a 5:04.5 mile by October 17, and, on

November 4, I noted I had decided "to give up daily running until track begins."

I said earlier that the unstructured nature of my first diary indicated an unstructured approach to running. I think much of that underscores the reasons that I have been able to compete successfully beyond the age of thirty. Running is fun and nobody should be pushed into it too early.

There are plenty of stories about preteenagers running in marathons. I read that a boy of five ran a marathon and finished it. An eight-year-old runner from Missouri ran the 1977 New York City Marathon in 3:00:31. I am suitably impressed, but I question the wisdom of it.

I do not feel kids of that age should be running marathons. There are, of course, parallels in age-group programs in swimming. But swimmers reach their peaks by the time they are twenty. Runners at any distance are still approaching their peaks at that age, and marathon runners are mere infants at twenty.

There is a tremendous pounding on the feet from running on asphalt, and the human skeletal system isn't mature until the late teens or early twenties. That is time enough to start thinking about the marathon. The East Germans have done a lot of research on it, and they have confirmed that you should be about that age before you start doing a lot of hard, anaerobic running, that is speed work, on the track. (I casually describe aerobic running as running at a slower pace, at which you're able to carry on a conversation. Anaerobic running is more intense, over short distances. Intervals, or fartlek workouts, are anaerobic efforts.)

I think even people who are sixteen or seventeen, and run a marathon, do not really understand the race and are running it under certain misconceptions. Some of them might think it's fun, but it's also very grueling if you are out there a long time. Adults should advise young people and coach them in the right way.

If somebody under twelve wants to run, it should be a part of his or her daily activity. I mentioned how the Kenyan schoolchildren run to school. John Treacy, who won the International Cross-Country Championship in 1978 in Glasgow and in 1979 in Limerick, Ireland, used to run five miles to and from school in his native Ireland.

Running is a healthy activity for the young. Since children are unusually active, their hearts haven't suffered any cholesterol damage. They are generally healthy. They don't smoke. The proper running of a marathon centers on two factors: The first is psychological and the second is physical.

I do not believe somebody twelve or under has any understanding of what running a marathon is all about. How much awareness of the difficulties can such a youngster have? I don't think an individual should simply go out and run unless there is an understanding of why he or she is out there.

It stands to reason that I don't believe parents should be trying to force their kids to run marathons. If a kid just decided to run one because he read about it in a magazine or newspaper, I think the sensible thing for the parents to do would be to talk him out of it.

If they want to get involved in marathon running, they can still do it in a systematic way. If they want to be good, this is the way to do it. There is no short cut to running the marathon and being good at it. It's important to educate people and eliminate the myths about running.

The best way to start racing at high school age is with shorter distances of between two to six miles, maybe a ten-mile race at the most. It should be very much of a fun thing. In college, there is ample time to begin the serious training. If your ultimate goal is the marathon and you really want to excel at it, you must realize you will not be at your best when you are twenty. You may not be at your best until twenty-five, thirty or even thirty-five.

Training for cross-country is similar to training for the

marathon or road racing. It's important to build a base. You must get in your daily easy mileage. Most of your mileage has to be easy running. This is particularly true for someone who is just beginning to train for the sport.

For someone who is fifteen or sixteen, a maximum of thirty to thirty-five miles a week during the first year is plenty. Most of that should be gentle running. You should incorporate stretching into it as well and, if you're concentrating on cross-country, some anaerobic work is advisable once a week.

In cross-country, there are hills and rough terrain, and you should train over the same terrain you will race on. This means running in the woods and on golf courses. What you have to do is develop a base and incorporate the anaerobic work into your training. It's a very hard sport. It can be extremely fatiguing. You should make sure you are properly rested before actual cross-country competition.

Anaerobic work is speed work on the track. It is important for cross-country. Do some repeat quarter miles, half miles, and maybe some three-quarter miles or miles. Any long-distance runner can benefit from it. I think this combination will give you that extra edge.

Each runner should be in touch with his coach on a daily basis. The coach should ask the runner if he or she is tired or aches. "How much have you run the day before?" If it's a Monday, the coach should ask if the runner put in any work on Sunday. "Are you tight in certain spots? Is the potential for injury there? How do you feel emotionally toward a specific workout?"

But a runner must always retain his individuality as a runner. Never get caught up too much with the pack or with a coach. You have to think for yourself. Take the advice of the coach and select what is valuable for you. Let it filter through, be selective, and discard the rest. You must know yourself and what is right for you. Of course, this knowledge will develop as your career progresses.

The use of weights can be an important part of training for cross-country. Since most distances for a high school runner vary from two to four miles, a lot of strength is required, in particular quadriceps strength. This strength, in the front area of the thigh just above the knee, can be best developed through hill training and light weight repetitions. There is not much published on cross-country running in the United States, and I can't claim to be a real authority on it. All I can do is pass along my own feelings as a runner.

What appeals to me is that it is a less restricted, much more natural sport than organized ones with rules. You run through the woods and fields, over streams and around trees, much the same way our ancestors did thousands of years ago. This is why it is appealing to younger runners. It seems to have less of an appeal to older people. I guess many feel that they shouldn't be out there doing that sort of thing anymore. They feel they have to act grown-up.

When you are young, you can get away with it. The unrestraining nature of it is such that you don't have to stick to a track and do lap after lap. You can get bored doing track work. But you begin cross-country racing in September, when it's warm, and you finish in the colder parts of the country in November, when there's frequently snow on the ground. That's the diversity of cross-country. That aspect of change is appealing in many ways. It's fun running through the woods and over streams. There are many links for me with my own childhood, when I was out hunting or hiking or chasing butterflies.

I believe it is safe to wager that cross-country running and racing will grow in the United States in the next five to ten years. It will be a direct outgrowth of the interest in road running. It will also grow in popularity because of the low cost factor and the anticipated decline of football in the public schools. I expect that corporations will become more intensely involved as sponsors of cross-country meets with large fields, much as they now get behind the big road races.

The most important thing for the beginning runner is attitude. You have to possess an understanding of what you want from the sport. The primary thing someone is going to get out of running is the satisfaction of it. That is only going to come if you stick with it for a period of time.

This means you have to go at it comfortably. You can't be forcing yourself. You shouldn't set your expectations too high. You shouldn't set your daily mileage level beyond reason. Beware of copying other training programs to the letter. You shouldn't try to go at it too fast and say, for example, "I'm going to run a 6:50 mile a month from now."

For people who are just starting out in running at an older age, it is important to evaluate your physical condition and level of activity in recent years. If you are over thirty-five and you haven't been athletically involved in a cardiovascular sport in several years, it's advisable to take a stress test, given by medical people who understand running and sports. This will determine your fitness and your cardio-respiratory capacity.

One thing that is helpful in the beginning stages is to run with some people who can give you information and who will also run at a comfortable pace for the group. Running together makes it more bearable to go out when the weather is inclement and you'd rather stay indoors. Assistance from someone else can play a big part as you make running a part of your life style. The social aspects of running are not to be underestimated.

Sometimes you simply do not feel like running. Act accordingly. There are times when it is good not to run if you are not in the mood. You don't want to be telling yourself, "Oh, I've got to get out there."

I think of my first course around the block in Newington. It's good to pick out a short course, maybe a quarter to a half mile long. Your goal might be to finish the course as slowly as possible. Once you finish it that first time, you can increase the distance. Just run as slowly as is comfortable. It takes months to develop your base of endurance before you start thinking about improving your speed.

The whole idea at first is being able to run the distance. You may feel slow as you see other people passing you. What you have to realize is that they may have been at it much longer than you have. Everybody has to begin somewhere. Even the top runners in the world started at scratch. It was three years before I ran as far as seven miles. I never ran farther than two or three miles my first year. If you work up that far, you're on the right track. Not only will that distance become easier to run the more you do it, but you will be providing yourself some hefty health benefits.

I realize many beginning runners start out because they want to lose weight. You will lose weight by running. What happens is that your metabolism changes. The lighter you are, the easier it is on your bones and the fewer the injuries. The two go hand in hand. You might want to work out a diet with your doctor before you start. Let him know that you have a running program in mind, and he may be able to help you with it as well.

The beautiful part of it is that there is no age limit on running. It is the ageless sport. I talk to people all the time who are taking it up after years of inactivity. There was a seventy-eight-year-old woman, Ruth Rothfarb, who ran in the Bonne Bell race in Boston in 1979. We also have a New England institution named Johnny Kelley. He is still going strong in his seventies. Clarence DeMar, who died in his early seventies some years ago of cancer, competed in the Boston Marathon and other road races until his late sixties.

In 1977 I ran with a gentleman named Marty Cavanagh in the Baltimore Marathon over a very difficult course. I won in

2:14:22, and Marty finished in over four hours. I met him at the party following the awards ceremony and he was pretty energetic. In fact, he was quite wild for an eighty-year-old man. He drank great quantities of beer and, in general, was a regular fireball.

The most difficult part, when you decide to make running a part of your life style, is the basic initial commitment. Everybody says, "I don't have the time." It's up to you to say, "I do have the time." For me, beginning to run when I was a student was an ideal situation. However, I've also trained as much as 130 miles per week during periods when I worked at a full-time job. It ultimately becomes second nature. It becomes a habit, a routine part of your daily life.

2
Quitting

The decade of the 1960s evolved into a time of turmoil for the young, one of indecision and anxiety. When I enrolled at Wesleyan in September 1966, the war in Vietnam was escalating and the college campus was entering into a state of unrest.

By the time I was a senior, in 1970, I had quit running. Why? There was a variety of reasons, but the primary one was that the military draft was fast approaching. I'd applied for conscientious objector status, but I was told I wasn't going to get it for a year, if at all.

It was a time of not knowing where I was headed and, obviously, this worried me. I was not willing to go to Vietnam. I was prepared to leave the country if I had to. I was against the war—politically, morally. I felt it was definitely a mistake on the part of the United States. I didn't support the government. I was not going to go to war. I was planning to go to New Zealand, and I had sent away for information on freighters. It was a big, abstract fantasy, but that was what I had in mind.

There was the student strike at Wesleyan. Some seven

hundred colleges in the United States went on strike and closed down. It was a pretty unusual time, and not the moment for getting heavily involved in athletics. There were bigger things in the wind. Whether or not I was going to be running a two-mile at a Wesleyan track meet was not what I was thinking about. The Vietnam war was. There was no way in the world I was going to go over there and participate in an unconscionable war.

What the college student today has to deal with is "Hey, where am I going to get a job?" My concern was "Hey, I'm likely to have to leave my family and friends forever." In this country just then, you were frequently hated if you were against the war. People came down hard on you. I was fairly radical, politically. I still am.

I also felt my running career had been coming to a close. I'd started smoking cigarettes. Now I support anti-smoking legislation. There was no running boom back in 1970. I figured I'd just be like most people. I'd get out of college and quit my sport. There were very few track clubs, very few opportunities for the graduate.

So, many things came together. I'd run an 8:58 two mile in December 1969, and breaking nine minutes in the two mile was a goal. Once I did that, I felt I'd accomplished what I'd set out to do. I'd been running for seven years. It wasn't always intense, but it was pretty consistent.

I gradually phased myself out of running. When I left Wesleyan, I stayed out of it for a few years. I was still very interested in running but I just stopped being a participant. If there was a track meet on television, I'd watch it. It was like another world. I'd pick up a paper and say, "Good grief, Dan Moynihan ran an 8:47-4:07 double at Tufts. I used to run against him." It was easy, in 1970, to get out of running, and I did.

The longest I'd ever run in high school was twelve miles, in late spring of my senior year. Consequently, I didn't have much of a distance base, and that limited what progress I could make. I'd hit a certain point, level off, and go stale. I had won the high school division in the annual Manchester, Connecticut, five-miler on Thanksgiving Day when I was seventeen. I placed eighteenth overall, out of perhaps two hundred runners. It was one of the few road races in the state, and it represented my peak performance at a long distance at that time.

When I arrived at Wesleyan, I found the atmosphere very different. There was a heavy emphasis on academics. The students were not very involved in athletics, and running was not very popular. There were times when we were unable to field five men in freshman cross-country and we'd lose our meets by default.

Also, the running program at Wesleyan was considerably more relaxed and informal than it had been at Newington High School. Even though the coach, Elmer Swanson, had as much desire for us to win, he simply went about it in a more relaxed manner than my high school coach had. His approach was not as direct or as blunt.

I often felt this ended up working to my benefit, as well as to the benefit of a lot of runners at Wesleyan. When I was in high school, I was willing to work hard for a coach I liked. When I went to Wesleyan, the demands of a part-time job, the academic situation, and trying to run made it difficult to excel. Running became of less importance to me, even though my motivation was still fairly strong.

Athletic competition was minimal. We ran mostly against comparable small colleges such as Trinity and Williams. I did well. I won most of my dual-meet races as a freshman. I finished third in the freshmen division of the IC4A cross-country race in New York in 1966, and fourth in the New England Cross-Country Championships.

There was also a major difference in my training. It went along with my whole change in attitude toward running. I became more relaxed. This is probably due to meeting a runner named Amby Burfoot at Wesleyan. He started me doing long, slow distances when I arrived.

I had never run over ten or twelve miles in high school, as I mentioned. Amby tried to get me out doing ten- to fifteen-mile runs on the weekends. Generally, we would go between seven to ten miles once a day, but on Sundays he would try to get me to go a full fifteen miles, an incredible distance, as far as I was concerned.

I remember the first time I tried it. I didn't make it. My legs cramped in the last miles and I had to walk in. But Amby finally worked me up to the stage where I once actually completed a twenty-five-mile training run in my freshman year. If I had extended myself for one more mile, I would have run under three hours for the marathon distance. I surged ahead of Amby at eighteen miles and I felt great. I was reduced to a walk by twenty-two miles. That was my first introduction to the wall. I'll talk about "the wall" that marathoners hit a little later. After we ran together for a while, Amby started telling me I'd be a good marathoner.

His influence on me was really major. Coach Swanson allowed me to train under him, and he became a second coach for me. I just followed Amby everywhere for two years. We'd go out for a run and I would fall right in behind him. All of his workouts were at a 6:30 or 7:00 pace per mile. It's slow by contemporary standards. But he also did mileage weeks of between 100 to 140 miles, and that was pretty high in 1966, 1967, and 1968. We also trained in every kind of weather condition and over rough terrain. We usually kept our pace fairly steady, whether we were going uphill or on the flats.

I generally did anywhere from thirty-five to seventy-five miles per week when I was in college, my PR being ninety-six miles in my senior year. When Amby was around to influence me in the right direction, I did seventy-five. When he wasn't around, I tended to drop off. "You'd be a good runner if you ever became serious about it," Amby always told me.

My social life started to interfere with my training during my freshman year. I used to go out to parties and started drinking alcohol for the first time. I drank gin and beer. I got drunk for the first time as a freshman. All of these were new experiences. I was settling into a different life style. Friday and Saturday nights were for parties, dances, and having fun. The rest of the week was mostly work, relieved by my running.

I also had to contend with the fact that college was much more demanding academically than high school had been. It all added up to a change in attitude, and part of it was that running became purely fun. I was putting in more distance, but it was slower. It fitted into my life style at Wesleyan, and I was having too good a time to worry about changing it.

When Amby was graduated in 1968, my training really fell off sharply. That was the first year since I had started running that I didn't improve either my mile or two-mile time. I ran a 4:18.8 mile as a sophomore and a 9:23 two-mile. In my junior year, I could only do 9:27 in the two-mile and I can't even remember what I did in the mile, but I know it was considerably slower. In fact, my PR in the mile is still 4:18.8.

It points up how significant the influence of one person can be. Having someone to follow is really important. It makes training easier, and improvement goes with it. Amby tried to impress upon me that consistency was the most important thing. "Train, don't strain" was our motto. It's an overworked cliché, but I can assure you the advice is sound. The effect is still there. Being persistent and running at a moderately hard pace will bring bigger rewards ultimately than attempting to find success through short, violent workouts.

Amby was my roommate in 1968 when he won the Boston Marathon, and my scrapbooks are filled with newspaper accounts and pictures of the victory. I was unaware that, at twenty-one, he was one of the youngest ever to win Boston. I didn't realize that a person of twenty-one was a baby in the world of marathoning. The win certainly impressed me, but I didn't understand the mystique of the marathon or road running in general. All I knew was that he was one of the few

Americans to win the Boston Marathon since the end of World
War II. I had been equally impressed when Amby ran an 8:45
two-mile behind George Young on the indoor track circuit the
winter prior to his Boston win.

I used to go home in the summers, relax, go to the beach, to
dances, to the movies. If I felt the urge, I might run five miles
every third or fourth day. Amby had tried to get me to run five
miles every day. I didn't have the motivation to do it. I was
still a part-time runner, someone who enjoyed it but was still
unwilling to take the next step. When I went out with my
friends to play poker or go to a dance, we might do some
smoking and drinking. I enjoyed both and was not about to
give them up for running.

I was always in awe of Amby and I still am, in many ways. I
learned so much from him. He was the best marathoner in the
country and one of the best in the world in 1968. He went to
the Fukuoka International Marathon in Japan in December,
1968, and finished sixth in 2:14:28.8. Tom Fleming had the
same time in 1977 at Fukuoka and finished fourth. Amby was a
versatile distance runner, winning the IC4A and New England
Championships several times and graduating from Wesleyan
undefeated in dual-meet competition.

Amby taught me a lot about running. He taught me how to
build up my mileage slowly, how to train for consistency and
moderation. He taught me how to build up endurance with
long-distance runs and moderate interval speed work. "Don't
over-race," he always said, and "Get a lot of sleep." He always
emphasized getting a lot of rest when preparing for a race.

He would occasionally give me information and advice, but
never in a preaching manner. It was always in a joking way.
"Hey, Rodgers, you still drinking a bottle of gin a night?"
Through running he let me discover the good and bad of
distance running on my own. He managed to get me out to
train when the weather was bad. When it was cold in the
winter, he showed me how to alleviate the wind-chill factor by
wearing several layers of light clothing, a wool hat, and

mittens. I discovered running over snow can be an exhilarating experience.

Some of our runs would be almost like long hikes. We might go out for a fifteen-mile run and part of it would be a five-mile loop around a lake where the terrain was rocky. We'd go along cliffs. We'd walk and climb up over the barriers and rocks. It was really the essence of cross-country running.

That was a fantastic time. We were oriented toward running in the woods and out in the country. The countryside was beautiful, once you left the city of Middletown. So running once again became an experience I related to those good, positive things of my youth. It was relaxing. I am not embarrassed to say that I felt like a kid running in those days. Our runs were sort of uncharted adventures.

In high school, I had concentrated on working on the track and beating people there. My focus now was no longer that intense. I had other things in my life that were more important than running. It was still significant, but I was doing it because I enjoyed it.

Everybody has his or her own level to find. You have to be totally self-motivated in a sport like running in order to reach a world-class level. If you get into it because it's trendy, you may not continue it. If you are motivated by peripheral reasons, running will not become a permanent part of your life.

You find your own level in running as you go through life. There was one level of importance for me in high school, another in college. After I left Wesleyan, it disappeared entirely. It came back and, finally, I approached running at the highest level of all.

We all go through changes in attitude. I have always felt I knew what running has meant for me at any one time. I never had any difficulty understanding that. It was just that it underwent changes over the years. Having quit one time, I know more than ever how important it is for me.

The top athletes have to be very self-motivated. In the beginning, it is hard to get out there on your own and take those first steps. It can be difficult to make it a part of your life style. There are certain people who will never be able to do it. The motivation isn't there.

Yet we read that there are an estimated twenty-five million people in the United States who are out there running. What were they doing before? Where did that motivation come from? I think it shows there always have been that many people who have had it in them. The seed was simply allowed to sprout.

They saw their peers doing it and they learned more about it through books, magazines, and television programs. Seventy-year-old men found out there were world records for seventy-year-old men in the mile. They found their level. They started to aim for it. They became good at it. There are examples like this for all age groups.

I mentioned that a 78-year-old woman finished the ten-thousand-meter Bonne Bell race in Boston. I competed along with an 80-year-old man one year in the Maryland Marathon. I read about Larry Lewis, who was 105, who ran six miles every day before he went to work as a waiter. It shows that age is not a limit. Sex is not a limit. Running is open to everybody.

Throughout my senior year at Wesleyan, I wrestled with a decision to quit or not. I can remember running in some cross-country races in the morning and smoking cigarettes in the evening. I can remember in the middle of my senior year at Wesleyan thinking, "It's going to be one thing or the other." Was there to be running after college? There wasn't too much opportunity. Everything seemed to come together and my decision became very clear cut. Quit.

The urge to run is an individual thing. Before you really give it up, give it as many chances as you can. Learn as much as you can about it and yourself, and make it something easy and comfortable. But if you begin a running program and later quit, even that becomes a learning experience. It was for me. I didn't realize what I was losing when I quit.

You determine how much time you want to put into it. I was

a part-time runner. Eventually I became a full-time runner. It's presently my life and my business. The whole reason I run has never been for money. I run because I love to run. It's a very, very simple thing.

Two years passed before I felt I wanted to run again. I know many other runners who have gone through the same situation. They went through high school and college and ran with a certain degree of success. When they were graduated from college, they entered a critical time of their lives and running lost its sense of importance.

High school and college is often not the real world. You leave and that fact hits you with a lot of force. You have been living in a fantasy world. Life is not always that way. You find you have to adapt to the real world. Once you have adapted, if you have been a runner who quit, it's easy to fit running back into your life.

I have discovered that running is something I want to do forever. There's a long time ahead and it's important to think of the future. I never used to think of it that much. In high school and college I took life one year at a time, and that seemed the way to go. On the other hand, today I'm intimidated by Johnny Kelley. He's seventy-two. He's run 48 Bostons and 105 total marathons. I tease him and tell him I'm going to run more Bostons than he has, but I'm realistic enough to know that there are some records that will never be broken.

You are never too old to begin running. I'm not alone when I maintain that there are other options open to older persons besides golf and shuffleboard. There is always time on your side. Speak to the person who is thirty, forty, fifty, sixty, seventy, or eighty. "I'm too old," he'll say. "Why should I begin?" This is the wrong attitude. You always have to give it a try. If you quit, try it again. You may want to quit again. That's OK. Just keep giving it a fair chance. I don't mean to proselytize. Any anaerobic exercise is good for you. I just happen to think running is about the best way to exercise.

3
Returning

Some people say, "I'm a painter." Well, I'm a runner. It comes from within. What started me running again? The primary reason was that I finally came to realize I was a runner. It was always a part of my personality. It fitted me so well. Although I had quit the physical experience of running, I had never quit being a runner at heart.

I moved to Boston and ended up working at Peter Bent Brigham Hospital. It was a selective service job, a consequence of my status as a conscientious objector to the Vietnam war. I was given a choice: Find a meaningful job on my own or the selective service would assign me one someplace within the United States. I might have ended up in Alaska chopping trees for the Forestry Service.

Given the restrictions and the opportunity to pick out something for myself, I was lucky enough to find a job at the hospital. Jason Kehoe, my boyhood friend from Newington, worked there and helped me locate it. We shared an apartment in Boston, near the Fens in the Back Bay section of the city.

I was an escort messenger. I carried samples of blood, the mail, various medical supplies. I transported patients from one area to another. I had to take dead bodies to the morgue. All of it added up to an upsetting emotional experience. It may have been work that had to be done by someone, but you couldn't help feeling that you were being dumped upon. There was no self-esteem.

We were poorly paid. My take home pay was seventy-five dollars per week. I was basically a servant for the government. My impression was that they wanted to treat me as poorly as they could because I did not want to go to war. The doctors and a large percentage of the medical personnel are part of a caste system. The doctors didn't treat the nurses too well. The nurses' aides were below that. We escort messengers were at the very bottom, particularly those of us who were there because of the selective service. There were quite a few of us in that category.

All of this combined to put me back into something that I was able to get some satisfaction out of by doing very well— running. I had experienced some success in it before and some success, with its concomitant positive side effects, was something I needed now. So I started going over to the YMCA on Huntington Avenue, near where I lived. I had a membership there and I started running a little bit. I spent just as much time doing calisthenics, lifting weights, and getting back some of my muscle strength.

I also met Ellen, my wife. She worked at the hospital next to Peter Bent Brigham and I met her at a bar in Boston. We both smoked cigarettes at the time and neither of us was thinking too much about athletics.

We seemed to take to each other from the start. It stabilized my life. She had an influence on me that became a significant part of my running development. I have often been motivated by people, either abstractly or in a very real sense. Ellen motivated me to run and to improve at it.

I was always motivated whenever I saw Abebe Bikila on television. He was the great Ethiopian runner who won two gold medals in the Olympic Marathon. Seeing him run is forever etched in my mind. Amby Burfoot seemed to me almost a reincarnation of Bikila, a living, in-the-flesh person I could identify with. He inspired me more than I can ever put in words.

For a couple of years, I was down, aimless, unmotivated, and without direction. I had a job I didn't like and my entire environment was depressing. The only fun I had was going out to the bars in Boston. That was my escape, but it was a fleeting thing. Going back to running finally gave me a permanent sense of satisfaction, and meeting up with Ellen stabilized it. Those were the critical factors in my return to real life.

I also had a ten-speed bicycle and it was stolen. I bought it when I moved to Boston and I used to ride it to work. Subsequently I bought a motorcycle and it, too, was stolen. I hated riding the trolley cars. I was too impatient to sit on one through all the stops, and I couldn't stand waiting around for one to come along. I'd rather get going and run. I'd rather run than walk. So I ended up running a mile and a half to and from work. It was the Kenyan schoolchildren revisited.

It was now the spring of 1972, almost two years since I had left Wesleyan. It was more than two years since I had run the 8:57 two-miler. I was running at the Y and I met a few people who said they were training for the Boston Marathon. I remember telling them, "Yeah, I used to be a distance runner. I knew a guy who won the Boston Marathon." They were pretty awe-struck by that.

I started to get more and more involved in running. I'd been running indoors and I worked up to the point where I could do ten miles. I probably ran about three or four times a week. On Saturdays, before I went out to hit the bars and smoke my half pack of cigarettes, I would do my long run to prepare me for this orgy of gin and vodka and smoking in the bars.

In order to do ten miles on the track at the Y, I had to go 125 laps. It could be pretty boring. I can remember losing my sense of direction on that little track—it's so easy to be caught up in the momentum of movement on a small, banked track. But I finally went outside to run, and I found I had lost my feeling of being comfortable and secure in the open air with thousands of people around. I had never trained in a big city and I felt weird as I ran on the congested streets near Northeastern University and the Boston Y. I was glad to get past the couple of city blocks I had to cover to get to the Fens, where there were open spaces and garden areas.

Once I was finally out there, it was like the earlier days all over again. One of the great things about running is getting outside. You should never stay on an indoor track too long. If you want to enjoy running, go outdoors. Even if it is winter, running is to be done in the open air. I can see going inside on a few extremely bad days in the depths of winter, but, on the whole, forget it.

One of the really significant things about running is being in touch with the weather: the cold, the heat—the bad weather, the beautiful weather. All outside running can be good, but there's nothing like running on a beautiful day. I started getting used to those great feelings again—among the most simple things in the world, and most people miss out on them completely.

If my life had become more stable, my economic situation was pretty bleak. After I was fired from my job at Peter Bent Brigham because I was trying to set up a union, I found myself out of work for a year. I finally found a part-time job at the Fernald School, a state institution for the retarded and the emotionally disturbed.

Later I enrolled in graduate school at Boston College to work for a degree in Special Education and, after eighteen months at the Fernald School, I quit to concentrate on my academic work. I was existing on food stamps. I lived in a run-down apartment. There is no way to describe my situation as anything but poverty-stricken. I had no time to work full time, so I took small part-time jobs. I can remember mowing grass for my landlord. He paid me something like $1.65 an hour. He was the perfect example of someone who was completely uninterested in what I was trying to achieve as an amateur athlete, although he was a very wealthy man who could have used publicity in his business.

It's ironic to think of that time. I went on to set the American record (2:09:55) that same year in the Boston Marathon in April, 1975. I look at the contrast. I look at Joe Namath signing a Brut contract for two million dollars. Here I was with an athletic achievement equivalent to anything he had ever done and I was living on food stamps.

It epitomized the American view toward amateur athletics. I have always recognized a very visible dichotomy. Every four years during the Olympics, people's interest in the amateur athlete picks up, and a few articles are written about him. And that's it. When are we going to start to give adequate attention and financial support to the amateur athlete? The media and television exposure is given to the professional athlete because pro sports are a money-making venture. Even though there have been some changes since 1976, the neglect of the amateur athlete is something the United States has yet to wake up to and confront head on.

Our Amateur Athletic Union has always had to be prodded and pushed to help athletes. The AAU does not go out and try to make things easier for us. AAU officials have never gone out of their way to help athletes on their own. Frank Shorter had to go to the AAU and say, "I'd like to do this. I'd like to open a store." He had to do it himself. That's still very true today. The AAU seems to react to pressure. But will the AAU initiate policies that are beneficial to the athlete? No. It's part of our system, part of the hypocrisy that permeates amateur athletics in the United States.

Unless there is money to be made from a sport, it is not going to receive coverage by the press, radio, or television. This, in turn, means the sport is not likely to be taught in the schools and there's not going to be a viable club system. For the United States to support its amateur athletes, there has to be some economic motive.

I can see it appearing more and more. You can see it in road running, where corporations can realize cheap sponsorship for their goods and inexpensive advertising for their products. The AAU gets some of those corporations' funds. The corporation receives favorable publicity. The reason the AAU is involved in road running is not because road running is a great sport and it's making a lot of people healthy. The AAU is involved in it because the corporations are in the act and it wants a slice of the financial cake. A large slice.

When the return came, it was complete. I had not run outside in nearly three years, since the fall of 1969. There is something about the early spring, when everything is returning to life. I felt the enthusiasm coming back, the incredible feeling I had when I used to run in the countryside of Connecticut.

One of the most important things about running is the relationship of man and woman to earth and nature. I think it is at the heart of why so many people are running. It is as simple as that. There is a little of the Thoreau in all of us.

As much as we become more increasingly involved in technology, science, and business, we should not lose that instinct, that feeling for the earth. Running is a very beautiful way to bring out those healthy feelings. Running is a very natural activity. If you get too caught up, you find yourself constantly seeking to make running something that it isn't. You should let it be what it is. A very simple activity.

You should almost let it happen to you. Just go out and run. Don't push it, let it be comfortable for you. Philosophically, it sounds almost Eastern oriented. On the other hand, realize you are working to obtain a little fitness. You should not do so little that it's meaningless, but you mustn't do so much that you become turned off by it. When you overdo it, you are in trouble.

Running has become too complicated for many people and they wind up turning sour on the sport, or losing the focus of their direction. Gerry Lindgren is an example. He was one of the greatest distance runners in the United States when he was in high school. He set age-group records. He ran tremendous mileage. He defeated the Russians as a schoolboy in the ten-thousand-meter race, which was not a strong American event. He was a great athlete. I consider Lindgren one of the elite of American distance runners.

He was unaware of the scientific aspects of running when he was young. He just loved to run and run and run. He went to college and he started to have the pressure put on him. Aim for a certain record. Beat a certain runner. It all piled up. He worried about anaerobic oxygen debt—which occurs when an athlete's muscles begin to function less effectively and lactic acid starts building up in the muscle tissue. He consequently developed ulcers and he never returned to the level he had attained at an age well before he should have reached his peak.

You often read about the Kenyan runners and the statements they make about why the American and European runners tighten up: that they worry too much about the other competitors; that they worry too much about individual times in a race, or about their splits—that is, the times given to runners at specific distances throughout the race. They refuse to let the pure naturalness of running take over. There are times when you have to run on your emotions. If you have too many things on your mind, how can you concentrate? Indeed, how can you run?

Sometimes your emotions are controlled. There are other times when you simply let them go. An accomplished runner is one who knows when he has control of a race and of himself. He knows and understands when to let go and run. The sport can become too technical.

Recently there has been an overwhelming amount of literature on running. There is an avalanche of it. About 10 percent of it is worth reading. I think the important thing is to talk with knowledgeable, experienced runners. Talk to people who have been running five, ten, fifteen years or more. They have learned through their own personal experience.

Some of what is on the market today is valuable. Much of it is repetitive. It isn't worth your time to read it. As I said before, it all depends upon what you want to get out of running. Before you buy a book, talk to the experienced runner, someone in a running store who will be able to tell you what the book is about.

If you want to learn about fitness, read some of the books by Dr. Kenneth Cooper entitled *Aerobics*, or *The Aerobics Way*, or *Aerobics for Women*. If you want to become involved in competition, you might want a systematic approach to running and racing such as *Jog, Run, Race*, by Joe Henderson. If you want something on the philosophy of running, read Dr. George Sheehan's book *Running and Being*. I think the best all-around book on running is Jim Fixx's *The Complete Book of Running*.

A lot of the books have material dealing with sports medicine and training techniques. Frequently, it is no more than concepts or ideas or approaches in the minds of a few individuals or researchers. They write without having much to base their research on. It is opinion.

You have to be careful in separating the wheat from the chaff. You can pick up information by reading the top magazines on running, *The Runner* and *Runner's World*. You still must remember to read intelligently. It all comes down to learning on your own. Everybody has to pay his or her dues and make some mistakes here and there. The best way to keep them to a minimum is by consulting the experienced runner, someone who has been there.

4
Approaching the Marathon

The whole world was tuned in to the troubled Munich Olympics in the summer of 1972. There was the drama of athletic competition, the tragedy of the Israeli team members who were kidnapped, taken hostage, and murdered. Out of it came the grim reminder of the uneasy alliance of nationalism, politics, and sports.

I watched the Games on television with Ellen. I remember Erich Segal, the author, marathoner, and Dartmouth classics professor, interviewing Frank Shorter. I watched Shorter win the gold medal and it had an interesting effect on me. I guess the best way to describe it was shocking.

Even though I did not know Frank, and I was not following the sport that closely, it was astonishing to see an American win the Olympic Marathon. Americans simply didn't win medals in the marathon. Then again, we were contemporaries. When I was a freshman at Wesleyan, Frank was a sophomore at Yale. In 1966, I won a freshman cross-country race against Yale and Amby beat Frank in the varsity cross-country race. It all somehow seemed intertwined.

No American had won the Olympic gold medal in the marathon since 1908, when Johnny Hayes did it—and he won amidst the controversy of Dorando Pietri's "assisted finish." (Pietri was first into the stadium, but he staggered and couldn't make it to the finish line on his own. Olympic officials helped him across the line as first finisher, but he was later disqualified and second-placer Hayes took the gold medal. Pietri was awarded a special gold medal.)

We were also to find out, as a country, that not only a few of the elite of athletes can run the marathon. Anybody can run the marathon, with proper training. Even if you don't train for it you can still do it, but it's not advisable. It proved to a lot of Americans that we are tougher than we thought we were. We could go out there and compete in a very, very difficult athletic event that we hadn't thought Americans could be good at.

I was running about thirty-five or forty miles a week, but my last competitive race had been in December 1969, when I ran the 8:58.8 two-mile and placed fourth at the Coast Guard Relays. As I mentioned, I thought I had closed the book on my competitive running career when I moved to Boston, started smoking, and began to live a casual life.

Once I returned, in 1972, I started to run longer distances. I noted in my diary how I'd averaged close to 100 miles per week from October 17, 1972 to January 1, 1973. One week, I was as high as 124 miles. I quit smoking. My breathing and ease of running improved and, on New Year's Day, I ran ten laps around Jamaica Pond near Boston, a total of 16 miles. For the week, I had run 104 miles.

You know that I was fired from my job at Peter Bent Brigham. This was in the fall of 1972, after I'd been working there for eighteen months. I was involved with another worker in trying to establish a union. We wrote slogans and put them up in elevators and inside offices and storerooms.

The hospital officials brought in a handwriting expert and confronted the two of us with a statement that he had picked us out as the guilty ones. The other guy denied it, and I just laughed. They gave us our pay for one week and said, "Get out." I was fired, an unemployed conscientious objector.

We stormed down to the personnel office at Peter Bent Brigham with about thirty other workers who were interested in forming a union. We confronted them with what had happened and said we wanted a hearing. The head of personnel came out and called in the Boston Police. I ended up fleeing the hospital before they arrived to drag me away.

I went back to the hospital about a week later and they were circulating papers with a description of me. I felt like a convicted criminal. The papers said if I were to be seen on the grounds of the hospital I was to be apprehended and the police should be called in. I'll always remember the description: It said I dressed in ragged clothes and I had long hair and a pony tail.

There was a mild recession in the United States at the time. Jobs were hard to find. I still had a six-month obligation to fulfill to the government as a conscientious objector. I was required to find a job for a nonprofit agency or foundation, such as a hospital.

I encountered a tremendous amount of opposition. I'd been fired and there was a recession. The government was unable to find me a job, but they were unrelenting. I still owed them six months of employment and they were determined that I was going to do it for them. I was discriminated against in a lot of places. I couldn't find a job in this country for one year. The government finally gave up, let me go, and changed my status to that of a permanent conscientious objector who had served his time.

The consequences were that I was unable to find a job for a year. I worked one night in Arby's Roast Beef Restaurant, but ran out because I couldn't stand the boring work and low pay—to say nothing of the ridiculous hats we were required to wear. I was fortunate, because Ellen supported me. She was working as a secretary in the cardiac ward at Children's Hospital in Boston and this enabled me to get through the year financially.

Running provides a sense of relief, gives you a feeling of psychological well-being. When I run now, I get away from the daily demands and pressures of my business interests. Ellen and I opened our first Bill Rodgers Running Center in Boston in November 1977. We used money we had saved from our teaching jobs which we had planned to use for a house. We now have another Bill Rodgers Running Center in Boston and one in Worcester, Massachusetts. All three stores sell primarily running clothing, shoes, and accessories. The stores also sponsor clinics, fun-runs, offer data on races, medical resources, and so forth, and serve as places where runners can share information and training runs.

When I ran during the time I worked at the hospital, and after I was fired, it took my mind off all the discomforting things that were going on in my life. I started to run about five miles every morning and another ten at night around Jamaica Pond. I started to point for the 1973 Boston Marathon. I was basing my training on what Amby Burfoot had done when we roomed together at Wesleyan in 1968 at the time he was getting ready for the marathon.

My objective was to do twenty miles per day. I couldn't reach it at first. But since I had been fired, I had all day to train, sleep, rest, and prepare for the marathon. I had met these people at the Boston YMCA who were aiming for the Boston Marathon too, and I told them how I used to be a good runner and how I thought I could do it again.

It's the same thing that motivates a lot of Americans. You have to prove you can do it. I've seen people running in cold weather marathons in February without any gloves or hats, in light shorts and shirts, feeling that they just have to finish a marathon. I had done something once, but sometimes people don't believe you. I felt I had to go out and give it a try, not only to convince other people, but myself as well.

I had run some pretty long distances when I was at Wesleyan. I went twenty-five miles that day with Amby. I knew I could go the distance and run it comfortably in respectable time. I don't think I ever thought I could be a really great runner. I hadn't been a great runner at Wesleyan.

The primary motivation was the same as it was when I first ran in high school. It's the same as it is now. I like to run. I like the training. Gold medals and everything else are the extras. The primary thing is getting out there and running every day, no matter how wealthy you are or how many gold medals you have. All you have to do is look at Frank Shorter, Lasse Viren, Marty Liquori. They have enough money and they have more than enough medals, but they are still out running.

Boston, 1973. My first marathon. I became very goal oriented, very conscious of my training. It should be pointed out that I had no assistance at the time from any club or any coach. The only encouragement and assistance I received was from Ellen, but that was considerable.

My training was slow, methodical, all at a pace of seven minutes per mile. I did no speed work. I decided to run a few races before Boston. I ran a twenty-mile race that February in Newton, a suburb of Boston. It was a freezing day, with temperatures in the twenties. I had no sweat pants, although I did have running shoes. I placed third in the time of 1:47:37, over a flat course. Amby had come up from Connecticut and he won the race. It was my first race since December 1969 and I ran it wearing blue jeans. I can still remember my legs cramping badly, the effect of my racing inactivity.

I ran the New England AAU Thirty-Kilometer Championship one month later. I was second in 1:34:13. I entered a twelve-mile handicap race in early April and won it in 59:17. I had made steady progress and I was enthusiastic about how well my preparation for Boston was coming along. I could smell success.

Sartorially, I was not your modern runner. Since I didn't own the normal running gear, I ran in blue jeans. I used to train dressed as the British runners once dressed, wearing dark socks. I was out of the 1950s, a road runner from the old school. I used to think of Dave Bedford of Great Britain, who dressed that way when he ran. I could identify with him.

About this time, I joined the Boston Athletic Association, the organization that sponsors and runs the Boston Marathon, and met Jock Semple. Everybody who has ever run Boston knows Jock, or knows of him. He gave me Number 38 for Boston, a low number that permitted me to start up front. He felt I was capable of doing fairly well.

On marathon day, the weather was hot. I have never had a love affair with running in really hot weather. It was seventy-eight degrees. Apart from the weather, I had conflicting feelings about what I wanted to get out of the race that proved to be my undoing. My goal was to run a 2:20 to 2:25 marathon. My primary goal, in my first marathon, should have been just to finish.

Before the race, Amby came up to me and said, "You should modify your approach. It's hot. You should add at least five minutes onto your time goal." I said, "Yeah, sure," and I went out and ran. I also remember him talking to me about Tom Fleming, a young college kid who had trained 160 miles a week. He wound up second to Jon Anderson, a college student from Oregon, who had also been a conscientious objector during Vietnam.

In your first marathon, as I've said, your goal should be just to be sure to finish. This was my mistake. I went out too hard, without the proper background to support me. I had been running for over a year. I'd done as much as 100 to 125 miles per week. I thought I knew all there was to know. I wanted to duel with the top runners, just as I always tried to in high school and college.

The first thing I learned from this race was not to drink too much. I started having trouble early in the race. I started cramping. So I started drinking, taking water from everybody who was offering it to me. I dropped out for the first time at seven miles, then dropped out another twenty times before I finally packed it in at Boston College, at twenty-one miles. I had learned what it means to pace yourself in a marathon.

The only thing I had to eat before the race was a cup of yogurt that morning. I noted in my diary that I must have lacked salt. I figured I should have sweated more than I did. It was a definite indication that something was going wrong. I was probably dehydrated. I may not have taken enough water before the race. I drank too much while running in the later stages of it. I came out of that race with the feeling I would never be a good distance runner.

I was unable to conceive of how someone could run a 2:16 marathon when the temperature was seventy-eight degrees. That's what Jon Anderson ran that April day. It impressed me then and I am still impressed by anybody who can run well when it is hot. I always seem to have my poorest races in the heat.

After Boston, I cut away for a while from doing any running and Ellen and I and a pet cat drove to California. I was hoping to move there in order to train in warmer weather and become more acclimatized to heat. Neither Ellen nor I could find a job in California. We didn't know anybody there. We didn't have a place to stay. We ended up staying two days in California and then driving back. Then we moved to Connecticut.

Since the Boston Marathon, my training had been either inconsistent or nonexistent. For the last two weeks of April and through the end of May, it simply stopped.

In June I began to do four or five miles every day. In July, I ran in an AAU track meet in Connecticut and came in second

with a 14:52 three-mile. I was living with my brother Charlie
in the city of New Britain and Ellen was living in the town of
Vernon, a few miles outside Hartford. I was doing a lot of slow-
hill runs. Occasionally, I'd go out on the track and do forty
laps for my ten miles. After moving back to Boston in early
August 1973 I ran a 14:32 three-mile and came in second to
Michael Burke, who also ran for the BAA. I was working up to
the hundred-mile weeks again.

After my bad run in Boston, I set my sights on a second
marathon. I had been fairly successful on the roads. I won a 10-
miler, a 10,000-meter race, and the National Twenty-Kilometer
Championship in Gloucester, Massachusetts. I had been doing
up to 120 miles in some weeks and I felt a marathon was
within my reach. I entered the Bay State Marathon in Framingham, Massachusetts in October 1973.

My goal was to finish. It was a flat course, with five loops of
about five miles each. I felt I could finish, if I was suitably
cautious, so I went out and I ran the first sixteen miles
comfortably. I chatted with Tom Derderian and Chuck Riley,
some racing friends. I was somewhere between fifteenth and
twentieth. It was a nice, cool day. I started to pick it up after
sixteen miles. I ran as hard as I could for the last ten miles,
slowly made up ground on the field, and won the race in
2:28:12.

I had eliminated the conflicting goals. If I had said, "I'm
going to run a 2:28," I might have missed it. I might not have
finished. Instead I ran it comfortably and I finished. And,
incidentally, I won. I had learned a little more about the
marathon. I knew I could run it faster because the first sixteen
miles of the race had been virtually a training run for me.

I learned that the marathon is a very long race, which, to be
run successfully, requires just the right balance of organization
and caution. I learned you have to be careful running that
distance. I learned you must know enough to pace yourself. I
ran it cautiously, because I had been defeated so badly in my

first marathon. This time, I just wanted to learn what it was like to finish the course. It was almost not a race. It only became a race over the final ten miles.

For most people who run marathons, it is and it should be that way. It's not a race, except a race within yourself. Can you finish it? Sometimes that becomes a difficult question for a marathoner. An Irish marathoner I know described such situations best. He likened them to "a crucifixion."

I ran my third marathon in Boston in 1974. I was still a novice. I learned even more lessons from this race. I finished fourteenth with a time of 2:19:34. I was in fourth place for the first nineteen miles, behind Neil Cusack, Tom Fleming, and Lucien Rosa. There was a slight tail wind. I hit Heartbreak Hill again and I cramped up.

That race taught me two more things. The first was I had not done enough speed work. I started out at about a 5:00-per-mile pace for the first eight or ten miles. That's a 2:11 marathon pace. I slowed to a 2:15 marathon pace, or 5:10 per mile, by eighteen miles. It was still too fast. I cramped up tremendously. In fact, I came to a complete halt on Heartbreak Hill for at least one or two minutes. Hamstring cramps. The lack of speed work was a major reason. The majority of my training had been at a very easy 7:00-per-mile pace.

The second thing I learned had to do with taking water. I didn't drink any at all until after the ten-mile mark. It's very important to take water before you start and in the first miles of the marathon. If you don't take any in the first five or six miles of a marathon, you will dehydrate. Taking a few sips of water every few miles is good policy in cool weather, but it's absolutely essential for most marathoners in hot, seventy-degree weather.

Your blood is going to the surface of your skin, particularly in hot weather. Water cools your body down. It acts as a refrigerant. The sweat cools off the outer layer of your skin. You need water to keep your blood viscosity at the proper level, to keep your cell tissue functioning properly, and to keep your cells in a proper balance.

If you lose too much water, your inner body temperature tends to go up. In hot weather, it can lead to a heat stroke. What you want to do is to minimize some of the possible later difficulties by being careful early in the race. The first miles, to me, are the most critical ones in the marathon.

Some people say the marathon does not begin until twenty miles. That's when you hit the wall. The real truth is that the first few miles are the most important ones of the race. People who make mistakes in the early miles by going out too hard or by not taking enough water are the ones who aren't going to win the race, or, perhaps even finish it.

On a cool day, under sixty degrees, one might take water only every three or four miles or so. In hot weather, sixty degrees and up, I would recommend several good swallows every mile if possible—in addition to drinking a few swallows every five minutes or so in the hour prior to the race.

By now, the marathon had become my race. I entered the New York City Marathon on September 29, 1974. This was before it became the mass marathon, before it was run through the five boroughs of the city, and before the organizers brought in an international field. It was run entirely within the confines of Central Park that year.

I entered with the intention of winning. First prize was a trip to Greece, to compete in the Athens Marathon over the original course from Marathon to Athens. I had run a 2:19:34 at Boston and the course record was 2:21:54, run the year before by Tom Fleming. If I broke 2:20, I figured I'd win.

Since the race was in Central Park, you had to do five loops and there was one pretty rugged hill. It was also more humid than I had bargained on. By twenty-one miles, I developed my usual hamstring cramps, and even though I had a three-minute lead, they were so tight I couldn't get rid of them. I eventually finished fifth in the time of 2:35:59, almost ten minutes behind winner Norb Sander. It remains my slowest completed marathon time.

I was still being educated. I reasoned that one of the reasons for my poor performance in the later stages of the race was that I had never trained consistently over distances of more than fifteen miles. I found out you need longer runs to build up the strength to combat heat, humidity, and a tough course like the one in Central Park.

Once again, I failed to drink enough water early in the race. I had made the same mistake. I hadn't checked the weather carefully enough. I went out and said, "I can beat these guys." What happened was, the course beat me. I didn't analyze the race carefully enough. I wasn't smart. You have to be smart to be successful at the marathon.

Ellen and I had driven to New York. After the race, I climbed into the car and I had cramps all over my body. Ellen drove home. All I could think of was quitting the marathon. I said to Ellen, "I'm not cut out to be a marathoner." I started to think of dropping down to ten thousand meters and concentrating on running that distance well.

I had tried Boston. I had dropped out in 1973. I developed the cramps in 1974, and faded to fourteenth. My fastest marathon was 2:19:34. That's not bad, but I always had these troubles with my hamstrings around twenty miles. I hadn't learned that it was probably dehydration and a lack of speed work that caused the problems. Those were things I still had to correct.

In order to be successful in the marathon, you have to know exactly what you want out of it. I frequently get letters from high school runners and people who are starting out later in life. They always have conflicting goals. They don't know what they really want out of the distance they're trying to run. The answers come from experience.

The important thing to remember is you can't succeed at

everything. You can't be good at the 880, the mile, and the marathon. You aim for a certain one. The classic example I know of is Amby Burfoot in 1968, when he was a senior at Wesleyan and was aiming for Boston.

He knew what he wanted. The Boston Marathon was his solitary goal. He put everything he had into it. Intercollegiate track meets were not very important. They played a very minor role in the total game plan. He used them as speed work. He still ran in them, but he adapted them to his major goal. He used them as stepping stones to the marathon. He refused to let them become anything he would have to expend any psychological energy on. He geared everything psychologically and physiologically for the Boston Marathon.

This is something you ought to realize when you are in high school. It's not a good time to concentrate on the marathon. Concentrate on the events you will be running most of the time during the school year. I say this because, physiologically, teenagers are too young to handle the consistent high mileage at a solid pace that is necessary to produce a world-class marathon time.

Pick out the mile, the two-mile. If you want to run a marathon, build up the minimum amounts of mileage. Run fifty, sixty, or seventy miles every week consistently for one year. After that, run a marathon for fun. But do not take it seriously. Run it after cross-country season, or before indoor and outdoor track arrives.

To understand the marathon is to run it a lot. I had a lot of failures in the marathon. I still have occasional failures in it. But I do know the race pretty well now. I know it better than a lot of people who think they know it because they have run it once or twice with some success. You can't really know it until you've felt the other side of it. That's the only way it's possible.

And that's the way you become a better runner. You ultimately become more consistent and able to deal with the pressures of high-level racing. It's true of anybody. You learn who your competitors are. You start recognizing people at races. You can recognize your abilities and levels at that given stage of your career. You recognize the type of pace that is necessary for you to run in that race. After a while, you start recognizing courses you've run in previous years. These are all factors that lead to better performances.

It's important to evaluate your marathons, uncover your weaknesses and your mistakes, and learn from them. Sometimes the sport is such that there are a lot of unanswered questions. You can't always determine why you did poorly. In general, though, you can if you go about it intelligently.

You cannot reach your maximum potential in a marathon until you are in your middle to late twenties or early thirties. There's about a ten-year span when you can be at your very best. There are exceptions to every rule. Jack Foster of New Zealand ran a 2:11 marathon when he was forty-one. Toshihiko Seko beat a world-class field to win the 1978 Fukuoka International Marathon when he was twenty-two, and he finished a strong second in the 1979 Boston Marathon. That's scary.

When you are still a teenager, your bones haven't matured enough to absorb the pounding and adapt to anaerobic and aerobic types of training. You must build your mileage up slowly over a period of years. This allows your muscle tissue to develop. You will be a better marathoner if you have a higher percentage of slow-twitch muscle fibers.

One's muscle tissue is composed of both fast-twitch muscle fibers, which enable a person to exercise most efficiently in short-term activities such as sprints, and slow-twitch muscle fibers, which enable a person to exercise most efficiently in long-term exercises such as cross-country skiing or marathons. Everyone is born with a predetermined amount of each, but the body can be trained so that maximum potential is derived from both types of muscle tissue. All the top marathoners in the world have a higher percentage of slow-twitch fibers. I do.

It is a fact that people with certain genetic backgrounds have better potential to be top distance runners.

Your heart muscle will develop and grow in size. My heart is about 25 percent larger than that of a normal person with the same height (5'9") and weight (128 lbs.). It's impossible over a short period of time, like one season, to develop your muscle tissue, your heart, your cardiovascular system, and the veins and capillaries in your body to their fullest capacities. It takes years. That's why I say you shouldn't worry if you don't do as well as you expected in your first marathon. You haven't reached your full potential.

Fatigue is a problem common both to beginners and world-caliber runners. If you've been running for five years and you run five miles a day, you're used to it. It probably doesn't tire you at all. It invigorates you. If you are just starting, it's a shock to your body and you're going to be tired. It should take you about a year to build up to thirty-five miles per week.

One method of coping with fatigue from your training is to get enough rest. Another is to make sure you take hot baths when your legs are aching. It helps the diffusion of blood through the muscle tissue and will accelerate the movement of lactic acid out of your system. Aspirin really helps reduce aching muscle soreness in your legs, whether from training or racing. Sometimes a gentle massage is in order. I am one of many runners who have often made the trip to see Jock Semple in his physiotherapy office at the Boston Garden. Sometimes we use the sauna and Jacuzzi at Boston College to ward off aches.

You should make sure you have an adequate diet. You should eat the right percentage of fats, proteins, and carbohydrates. The more you run, the more you will want carbohydrates. Carbohydrates I like are rice, macaroni (with cheese), and potatoes. I eat fruits like grapes, oranges, and melons, vegetables like beans, spinach, asparagus, breads and grains (muffins and toast), fruit juices like cranberry-grape, orange and lemonade. I also eat so-called junk foods like cookies, donuts, pastries, pies, candy, chips, and dips. I never worry about getting too much protein. You normally have enough protein in your diet just by eating the right foods.

One more problem that is common to beginners and to world-class runners is how to avoid boredom. The best way is to run with someone you know, a friend. Do not train with someone who is either more advanced than you are, or who is much slower than you are. You want someone who can train with you comparably. You don't want to be pushing each other too hard. I carry on my best conversations during long training runs and when I've had a few social drinks. People claim that I pick up the pace during runs as the conversations intensify.

Many runners do this and it supports my theory that running is a very emotional activity. For example, a good friend, Bob Sevene, is a miler and when we go on training runs if Filbert Bayi or some other top miler's name is mentioned, Bob begins talking more and picking up on running pace.

Do your best to enjoy your run. Since you are having a good time, you may as well do it with someone who is a friend. Changing the course you run is another way of reducing boredom. Some days, you should just skip it if you are feeling the pressures of running. Take the day off and come back refreshed the next day.

Sometimes a change of pace is good. Run a little bit faster. You might want to do little pickups during your run. If you have a three-mile course, run fast for one hundred yards. Do that seven or eight times. Make sure that whenever you are beginning to feel really tired, slow down and don't worry about it. Do what you please. Do what you want to do. This is for you.

If you want to walk, then walk. Forget about what the other runners might be saying. "Oh, he's got to walk." Everybody walks in the beginning. You have to build up slowly. If you pick out a three-mile course, run part of it and walk part of it.

When you run it for the first time without stopping, you will experience an incredible feeling of accomplishment.

It's good to pick out a course that is attractive. Pick one that has water fountains near it. You can stop and take a drink. Pick one that is away from traffic, cars, fumes, dogs, and too many people. Running is basically a time of tranquility. You get away from the BS of the world. You may find a beautiful place that you have missed in your life. You wake up to it when you're running. This happens a lot.

5
Excelling

The employment market finally opened up for me in the autumn of 1973. After one year without a job, I accepted a position at the Fernald School in Waltham, Massachusetts. I was an attendant, mopping floors, making up beds, feeding and transporting patients, and doing the most basic sort of work.

What was important was that I became involved. It was my first job in a long time. After two months as an attendant, I was promoted to a job where I was responsible for an experimental ward for the mentally retarded, where they were using behavior-modification techniques with the patients. I had the best of both worlds; a real responsibility and time to train.

There were seven men in the ward, ranging in age from eighteen to fifty-five. They were all moderately retarded, and we used the behavior-modification techniques to teach them learning skills. These were people who were largely forgotten by society, shunted off to the side by their families. This was something that significantly affected my life, and it had an impact on me that has carried over to my running.

There are always tie-ins that affect your attitude about life. I realized that here were people from all kinds of backgrounds who ended up in this institution. They were swept out of sight, out of mind. They were living in the most terrible conditions, in filth. They were fed the worst food. There were few relatives who chose to visit them. They were the forgotten people.

Yet, many of them were happy. The smallest thing made them incredibly happy. I remember one guy named Joe. He loved Tootsie Rolls. If you gave him a Tootsie Roll, you gave him happiness. When you think of it, you learn something through this about the world you live in. You have a new understanding of what life is all about. You don't get upset about so many trivial things.

I'd go out and train and run fairly hard and it didn't seem as hard anymore. I was seeing people who were in circumstances that were very hard. It had a balancing effect on my life. I think everybody should be in some situation like the one I was in. It was a learning experience. I suddenly felt very fortunate to be able to run, to be able to go out and move about freely.

I joined the Greater Boston Track Club in late 1973 and, in retrospect, it had a significant influence on my running career. Bill Squires was the coach, and he changed my training regimen. He started me doing longer intervals that were geared for the world-class marathon race pace of five minutes per mile. I also did one interval workout per week which was a radical step up from the year before, when I seldom did any speed work.

Jack McDonald, a former Boston College runner who is presently the head track coach there, organized the Greater Boston TC. He was ahead of his time, a guy who was bold enough to establish a club for the postgraduate runner who wanted to run but was pretty much out by himself in the cold. This was before the running boom had really hit.

It all seemed to come together in a relatively short time. Jack was a recent graduate of Boston College and he was helping

out around the athletic department. There was a track meet at
Harvard involving a combined Harvard and Yale team and a
similar team from Oxford and Cambridge in England.

John Hemery, whose brother Dave won the Olympic gold
medal in the intermediate hurdles in 1968, talked to some
people at Boston College and asked if they could get a team
together for a meet there. It became a project for Jack, and as a
result he had a lot of interaction with people from all around
New England. That convinced him there was a definite need
for a structured track-and-field club for people who wanted to
participate beyond college. So when I heard that a new club
was being formed and its base would be Boston College, near
the area I lived in, I signed up.

Bill Squires coached without pay. He was also coaching at
Boston State. I used to run over to Boston College from Jamaica
Plain and we'd train on the track there one or two nights a
week. I said to Bob Sevene, who was then the Bentley College
coach and a co-founder of the Greater Boston TC, that it was
rather dumb to be a member of the BAA when I was training
with all the Greater Boston guys. I never trained with the BAA
team members because we were all living far apart from each
other. Sevene helped me draft a letter to Jock Semple of the
BAA, telling him I was leaving his club.

The Greater Boston TC has evolved into more of a club for
road runners and marathoners. It still functions as a track club,
but road running is so strong in the New England area that all
of the top distance runners have gravitated toward Greater
Boston. Part of it, too, is that the state of traditional track for
the runner who has left college is not very well developed in
the United States, and many runners who might continue to
excel on the track move to the road because of the lack of top-
level track meets.

Squires was the primary catalyst, the coach who became a
dominating force. Sevene, who was returning to the indoor
circuit that winter for the first time in six years, was also a

major factor in the success of the club. He worked as an administrator, trainer, coach, and jack-of-all-trades for the club. Squires started me doing more anaerobic work and he pointed me toward the International Cross-Country Trials in Gainesville, Florida, in the winter of 1975, which would qualify the runners who would go to the actual World Cross-Country Championships in Morocco.

This anaerobic work was done indoors at Tufts University in Medford, Massachusetts, where our club was allowed access to the track for one or two hours, one or two days per week. Most of my track work consisted of ladders of different types. For example, we might go one-quarter, one-half, three-quarter miles at a sixty-eight-second pace with very comfortable, easy running rest periods between intervals. I think one of the unique aspects of Bill Squires and his track program is that he gives his athletes moderate workouts with longer-than-average rest intervals between hard efforts.

Everything was going fine until I became sick with the flu four or five days before the trials. I stayed in bed, did no running, took cold medications like aspirin, and drank plenty of fluids. The sickness broke just in time and I comfortably tied for fourth place with Gary Tuttle over the fifteen-kilometer cross-country course.

Frank Shorter won the trials, but he hadn't led the whole race. I actually ran stride for stride with him at about the three-mile mark, before he slowly pulled away. Frank seemed to be breathing really hard and I remember thinking, "Good grief, I'm in better shape than he is. I'm going to race this guy." That day it wasn't to be, but when we went on to Morocco, Frank placed twentieth and I was the bronze medalist. Even though Frank had an impacted wisdom tooth, which was a legitimate excuse for a race below his normal standard, I knew there would no longer be a domination of American distance running by one man.

I feel the World Cross-Country Championships are of the

same caliber as the Olympic Games, European Championships, or World Cup in track and field. I was very pleased with
that race. It was my first world-class race, my first defeat of
Shorter, and, I believe, the highest placing by an American
male in the history of the event. It still ranks with me as one of
the two top races of my career. (I consider my top race so far to
be my first Boston Marathon win in 1975.)

It was something of a shock both to Squires and myself. I
was an unknown, but I was only seven seconds behind the
winner, Ian Stewart of England. I'd run the best race of my life.
I knew I was in great shape, and, one month later, I set an
American record in the Boston Marathon. People considered
Boston to be my emergence as a world-class distance runner,
but the real truth was that it occurred a month earlier in Rabat,
Morocco.

The Greater Boston TC was made up of a lot of people like
me. I made a lot of very good friends through my associations
with the club. People like Scott Graham, Bob Sevene, Vinnie
Fleming, and Dick Mahoney were helpful in many ways. They
were the ones who would get me out on the tough days in the
winter and they helped make running a lot of fun. We did a lot
of things together. We'd travel to meets by car together, have
post-race and pre-race parties, scheme about how to win the
National Thirty-Kilometer and, in general, raise hell all over
the place.

I think all of it helped me turn adversity into success.
Although I was living in a situation bordering on poverty,
Ellen was helping me out financially and I had the encouragement and support of my friends in the club. All of these
became major factors in my running success. I could count on
help in trying to beat the odds.

To excel in the marathon involves some luck, tremendous
motivation, and, to some extent, fortunate heredity. By heredity I mean the physiology that I inherited: predominately slow-
twitch muscle fibers, no imbalances of great significance in

stride length or foot plant, and an efficient metabolism. I had the traits that would enable me to develop if I kept at it, and as long as I would be able to train without injury there was no doubt that I would run some fast times. This is true of most people with the same abilities.

A most important factor is to avoid injury. Most of my track workouts with the Greater Boston TC were fairly moderate. When I added those moderate track workouts to fairly arduous runs of between fifteen and twenty miles on the roads, it proved to be the right combination. If the training had been too intense, I might have been injured or become too broken-down or too sick to run. This happens to a lot of runners who train too hard.

So, I had this tremendous base and I worked for the necessary sharpness at the right time. I was twenty-seven. I was in graduate school, studying special education at Boston College. Don Ricciato, a Greater Boston TC teammate, had introduced me to the program, and there seemed to be a lot that could be done working in this area. My life was very stable and relatively non-taxing. I had met Ellen. I wasn't going out and getting smashed in bars all the time. I was doing the necessary speed work. Everything meshed at the opportune time.

To succeed in the marathon at a high level of competition you have to live in a very stable environment. You can't be running around doing ten different things. You can't be working too hard at a job. You need people to support you and help you out. If you don't have this kind of backing, you're not going to make it.

You have to find whatever it is that, with a little luck, will enable you to move up a step. What happened to me, initially, was that I won the National AAU Twenty-Kilometer Championship in Gloucester, Massachusetts, in October 1973. I later received a call from the AAU and was invited to run in the famed San Blas Half Marathon the following February in Puerto Rico.

I placed seventh. I led for ten thousand meters of the race, but somebody named Lasse Viren went by and beat me. This was a tremendously inspirational experience altogether, because I went out to restaurants with Viren and Neil Cusack, the Irish runner who won Boston in 1974. I was breaking bread with the top runners in the world, talking to them and learning how they trained and what their life styles were like. They were not living the way most U.S. runners do: They were unfamiliar with the forty-hour work week and were in training situations where their lives were stabilized. Often they received government support or economic assistance and grants from their fellow citizens or sponsors. They trained hard.

Viren, for example, did 150 miles every week in training. I saw how hard he trained and how much effort he put into his races. I learned about his background and how it enabled him to put in the time. He is a policeman in his hometown and receives a grant from the Finnish Sports Federation each year to enable him to train when and where it benefits him most. I understand that he was given the land he built his house on by his countrymen. Viren is a national hero in Finland.

I realized that if I was going to reach a similar level I would have to do the same thing. I made the commitment and I simply carried it through to Boston, 1975. This commitment meant that running had to come first. In America, that meant you gambled. There was little AAU backing, no government assistance, and only the supportive help of close friends. Of course, there is plenty of support for a Reggie Jackson, a Jack Nicklaus, or a Chris Evert. I'm proud that running meant more to me than money at that time, and still does. I'd rather have an Olympic medal than a million dollars. But isn't there any way one can try for both?

No matter at what level you find yourself, you can always find inspirational points. Just being there running is often inspirational for me. I've always loved running through the woods on a beautiful day. So many people have cut that sort of thing out of their lives. Once you forget it, I guess you don't miss it and maybe it was never there for you. Anyway, I was glad to have it back.

It all takes some time before running or any similar cardiovascular exercise becomes ingrained as part of your life style. You have to learn it for a while, just as you have to learn to brush your teeth. It becomes something that you habitually do. Fortunately, it's not like brushing your teeth. You get a lot more pleasure out of running.

I had been training twice a day since the end of 1973 and when April 1975 and the Boston Marathon rolled around, I was in pretty decent shape. Squires and I tried to play down my position. We talked it over and we thought I would run about a 2:15 or 2:16 marathon. We never anticipated a 2:09:55. Maybe you don't realize that a 5-or 6-minute difference in a race that goes more than two hours is as significant as it really is. Do a little mathematics. Five minutes is 300 seconds and 6 minutes is 360 seconds, and a marathon is 26 miles, 385 yards. So a 5-minute differential means running each and every mile about 12 seconds faster, and a 6-minute one means about 14 seconds faster per mile. That's *some* difference!

You try to size up the other runners. I knew Ron Hill, who set the Boston record in 1970, was in the field. His reputation intrigued me the most. He was an awe-inspiring figure, a giant among marathoners. He was the 1970 Commonwealth Games and European champion as well. I knew Jerome Drayton of Canada, who had won the Fukuoka Marathon in 1969 and was a former world-record holder for ten miles, was also coming.

I found myself running right next to Hill for the first five miles. It was tremendously challenging for me. It started my adrenaline flowing. Just to match strides with Hill for a while was an experience. I then found out I could move in front and Hill wasn't responding. I was moving out and I could sense it was going to be my day. You have days like that.

This gave me a significant psychological lift. Six miles into the race, Drayton and Mario Cuevas of Mexico pulled away from the rest of the pack. I love marathoning when this happens. The pace is slow enough for considerable jockeying and re-jockeying for position, and there's nothing I love more than to duel in a race. I moved up and joined them. Cuevas dropped back about nine miles into the race and it was Drayton and I running neck and neck.

I can remember some woman yelling out, "Go, Jerome! Go, Jerome!" It irritated me, hearing a Boston spectator rooting for a Canadian. I was an unknown in my own town. Even though I had Boston and GBTC written across my shirt, nobody knew me. I'd finished third in the International Cross-Country run and nobody knew it. The papers didn't print much about it, if anything. Here I was from the Boston area and Drayton was from Canada. It made me furious to hear this woman yelling for Jerome Drayton. So I just really poured it on.

Finally, he fell back and I never saw him again. As it turned out, he dropped out in Cleveland Circle, not too far from where I now own a running store. I didn't look back right away. I can't remember when I did look back. I think it was when I reached the stretch of hills in Newton and, by then, there was no sign of Drayton.

It had turned into the kind of classic situation that I almost always thrive on. I like to get in duels with other runners and, if I feel fairly decent, it's turned out that I've won most of them. That's when I run my best. If I get into a duel with someone in the middle of the race, I'm usually able to get away from him and hang on until the end.

I may be falling apart as badly as or worse than the other person in the middle of the race, but the closer I get to the finish the less chance there is I'll get caught. I seem to be able to survive. This is because it is psychologically difficult to race someone who's well ahead of you, if you've lost contact with him. Plus, you are becoming more and more fatigued as you enter the final miles of the marathon, and an increased pace is very difficult to handle over those final miles.

That's the way it was with Jerome. I received that tremendous psychological thrill of running along in front of the pack with the press truck and the motorcycles, knowing I was leading the Boston Marathon. It was a staggering experience. I can remember going up the hills and stopping twice to take a drink. A flopping shoelace also caught my eye, so I came to a halt and tied it.

I was calm and composed when I stopped to take a drink. I stopped because I couldn't get a decent swallow while running, and also I remembered my high school track days when I felt great after stopping for a cold drink of water partway through a workout. I was completely in control of the situation. I wasn't worrying about Jerome Drayton or anybody else. I felt I was going to take that drink and if anybody showed up I'd get back into the race and start running again. I felt that strong and that confident at that moment.

I saw the press truck above me at the top of Heartbreak Hill and I thought to myself, "If I really push hard and I run very hard to the top of the hill, it's in the bag." It's a big psychological lift to reach the top of Heartbreak Hill in the lead. It's all downhill from there, a downhill run both literally and figuratively. That's the way it turned out that day.

As I ran the last miles down Beacon Street, I started worrying about Drayton or some other runner moving up on me and my being unable to see him because the crowds were converging into the street right behind me. Jason Kehoe, my friend from Newington, suddenly appeared on a bike. We greeted each other and I calmed down for the rest of the race. I pretended I was completing a training run.

I will never forget rounding the corner and turning onto Boylston Street for the final yards of the race. It's a striking sight. There are thousands of people there, spilling over onto the streets and sidewalks and up on the plaza near the finish line at the Prudential Center. It's all downhill, funneling toward the finish. It still ranks as one of the most thrilling moments of my life.

The only way I can describe it is dreamlike. I thought of my friends and particularly of former college roommate, Amby Burfoot, who had won Boston in 1968. It was just unreal, running to that finish line. I looked at the crowds on the sides and reveled in my victory. But on the victory stand, I suffered something of a reaction. As the wreath was put on my head, my brother, Charlie, jumped up shouting. I waved to him and called, "Never again." I was very tired and psychologically wound down. Marathons are, like any race, a great thrill to win, but unlike shorter races, the price one pays is severe.

On that day, I acquired a sense of what it was like to win the marathon. It was a deeper experience for me than any of my subsequent wins in any of the other marathons. The crowd was so big and so alive. I wanted to go back out there and thank every one of them for helping to make it such a moment. Most of all, I was glad Ellen, my brother, Charlie, my Greater Boston TC teammates, and my friends were there with me.

There are a lot of variables that enable you to excel, to win races and do well. I want to make one thing clear. I have my own feelings about technique and running form. I am not a physiologist. I am not a cardiologist. I am a runner. Yet I still feel my thoughts are just as valid as anybody's in the biomechanics lab, or any cardiologist's from a top hospital. I know few coaches who have raced the marathon well and therefore have the experience to coach the event. I am the one who's out there running and I've learned through doing.

First, running hills. I've tried a couple of different methods and I feel the one Coach Frank O'Rourke taught me a long time ago at Newington High School is still one of the best, particularly for road racing and marathoning, where even-paced running is all important.

He taught me not to push it so hard going up the hill. Save it until you get to the top and then push it hard again. I was so psyched up on that April day in 1975 that I ignored his advice. I flew up Heartbreak Hill. But, I also remembered to try to put good distance between me and the other runners when they couldn't see me on the far side of the hill.

Most of my hill running is geared to the premise that I will pace myself going up the hill and push myself going down. I consider myself a strong downhill runner. I will often let a runner beat me up a hill. I'll catch him on the down side, after he's expended most of his energy going up. I'm relatively fresh and I can catch him from behind when he's unaware of what I'm doing. The key is to catch somebody right away. It gives him some food for thought. Run with him for a short distance, then go by him.

I have had a couple of races that went like this with my Greater Boston TC teammate Randy Thomas. He beat me going up the hill by the State House on Beacon Street in the 1978 Freedom Trail Road Race in Boston. I caught him on the downhill and with about one mile to go, we agreed to come in together. We crossed the finish line together, but foolish AAU rules decreed that a single winner had to be chosen, and Randy was given the nod.

Going uphill, I try to run at a very steady pace. It's similar to the pace I try to run on the flats. I learned this pacing method from Amby Burfoot. I would say my stride probably shortens some. I try to keep my arms moving very symmetrically and very rhythmically. When I run down the hill, I often lift my hands up high for balance and to keep them off my sides. This permits me to expand my chest and take more air into my lungs. I also run with my hands out in front of me for a short distance. If it's a steep downhill, I may do it for a longer stretch. This is primarily for balance.

It's also important to know, psychologically, what your race plan is. Know how you're going to run the hill before you get to it. Have this game plan in mind. Determine whether you want to run up it hard or easy. If you do, you can face up better to the fatigue you are experiencing.

I have tried running very hard up hills during races and I

haven't had as much good luck with it as I've had when I've run up the hill moderately and turned it on going down the other side. I have not been able to run well on short, very steep hills, such as those at the 1978 International Cross-Country Championships in Glasgow, Scotland. One of the toughest hills I've ever run is a short, steep one at the six-mile mark of the seven-mile Litchfield Hills Road Race in Litchfield, Connecticut. That's an anaerobic hill. I had to go into ninth gear two years in a row to get up it.

Short, steep hills are common in cross-country running. It's one reason why I didn't have that much success in college or later in post-collegiate cross-country races. The one exception was in Rabat, when it was a flat course and I could run using rhythm and a long, fluid stride that was not broken up by obstacles and steep hills. These hills often require a lot of upper-body strength and a finely tuned anaerobic capacity; and although I am probably as strong as the average person of my height and weight, I'm not exceptionally strong in the upper body since I haven't done that much weight training in recent years.

In the past, I've rarely done specific hill workouts of any sort. I simply incorporate some hills into my daily runs. I don't change my pace going up hills. I try to run them very steadily. I started doing some repeats in the summer of 1978 with Scott Graham of the Greater Boston TC. We would do three sets up a hill about 400 yards long. We would run repeats of 50 yards, jog down the hill; 75 yards, jog down the hill; 100 yards, jog down the hill and 125 yards. We'd continue our run from there. Such a workout is a hard anaerobic effort and is useful preparing for the shorter road races, from 10,000 meters to 10 miles. I use such workouts before 10,00-meter track races and races such as Falmouth.

Prior to this workout, we would run three miles getting to the hill, and we'd finish up with another six, seven, or eight miles. It was part of a pretty good workout. I think hill training is important to any athlete and any runner. It makes no difference if you are a quarter-miler or a marathoner, but you have to find the type of hill training that is best for you. My favorite types of workouts on hills include doing runs with long, moderately inclined hills. I call them "marathon hills" and feel they are useful in developing myself as a marathoner.

Hill training puts tremendous stress on the heart and lungs. For that reason, it is more applicable as a training device for an advanced runner. But even beginners can incorporate it into their programs. They should do it on a moderate level. I should add that familiarity may breed contempt but, in terms of running on the hills, familiarity is nothing but a plus.

I lived only a few miles from Heartbreak Hill on the Boston Marathon course when I won the race in 1975. I used to train on the hills with Vin Fleming. We had an eighteen-mile course and at the eight-mile mark, we hit the hills. I would do that once each week and by the time of the race, I knew those hills very well.

The same was true in 1978, when I won Boston for the second time. My store is on the course. I would change there, run out to the hills, and run up them almost every day. I trained over the course. I kmew the hills and, once I hit them in the race, psychologically, I was strong. I was relaxed. I knew how to run them and I set the Boston Marathon record of 20:45 for the four hills of Newton, between the firehouse checkpoint and Lake Street.

Weight training is a somewhat controversial tool for improving as a distance runner. I used weights and jumped rope in high school, but only on days when the weather was bad and I was unable to go outside. I would still say it's beneficial to use light weights and high repetitions for upper-body strength. This is recommended on days when your mileage is cut back, and when you feel rested. I wouldn't recommend any kind of weight training if you are fatigued.

I did some light weight training when I was in college and I still do. I use a ten-pound dumbbell and I do twenty presses on each side and twenty curls with each arm. I might do two or three sets, once or twice a week. That is about all I do. I would like to do more, but circumstances, time, and lack of motivation keep me from it. If I were involved in a national team program and I could utilize machines that were available, I might do more. I guess I'm lazy.

Weight training is more beneficial to middle-distance runners and cross-country runners. As a cross-country runner, you require the upper-body strength and the strong back, stomach, and quadricep muscles to carry you over those short, steep hills where you are doing a lot of anaerobic work. This is particularly true on those courses which are muddy or slippery from rain or snow. The marathon is more of a rhythmic run. You ought to be lighter, and you need endurance more than running power. You need the ability to ward off fatigue, which creeps up on you gradually.

For marathons and road runners, it is still useful to resort to some weight training for your arms. Your arms do get tired in a marathon. That's where it helps to have that little extra power. There is also the psychological benefit. You're doing that little bit more than somebody you may be running against. You'll think back about how you did it sometimes during the race. On the other hand, I did only light weight training at Wesleyan, and Amby Burfoot never did any. With the exception of a single-mile race, he always beat me. I used to be amazed anyone so skinny could run so strongly.

The Russians are advocates of weight training and, before I went to Fukuoka in November 1977, I talked to Frank Shorter about it. He said, "Don't worry about the Russians. They run like mechanical men, like toy soldiers." He said, "They use weights so much it makes them too mechanical and less fluid and rhythmic in their movements."

I met Leonid Moiseyev, the 1978 European champion, before

the 1977 Fukuoka race. He smiled, shook my hand, and I
thought I was going to hear crunching sounds. He had a
powerful grip and he did run like a toy soldier. But I won the
race. Moiseyev was a strong second in 2:11:57. He outkicked
me on the track for fifth place in 1978. I'm using a small hand
grip to develop my wrist and my grip. When I meet him again,
I can say, "Moskva, 1980," and see what he says.

After I won the Boston Marathon in 1978, I was being
interviewed in my store and there were questions about Frank
Shorter, who, in his comeback, had run his first Boston and
finished twenty-third. Shorter, whose physical ailments began
at the Falmouth Road Race in August 1977, underwent surgery
shortly after his Boston race for the removal of some chips,
spurs, and cysts from his left foot. He had moved to Boulder,
Colorado, partially because of its altitude. There were questions about altitude training.

"I guess we know where the marathon team of the United
States is," I told one reporter, half-jokingly, half-dead-se-
riously. "It's not in Colorado. It's not in Atlanta. It's right here
in Boston. You don't need high altitude to be good at running
marathons. Randy Thomas finished fifth this year in Boston in
2:11:25. Vinnie Fleming finished fifth last year. All you need is
a good crew, and that's what we have right here." I said this
partly because I was tired of reading about the super marathoners in other cities in certain running magazines, and
partly to dispel the myth that one needs altitude training to be
a world-class runner.

Altitude training is a method some of the best runners in the
world utilize in order to improve. The East Germans have a
working agreement to go to Mexico to train, but they have
never traveled the distance. I personally do not believe you
need altitude training to be a world-class runner as long as the
race is held at sea level. If you are going to compete at high
altitude, you obviously need to train there.

The only time I ever trained at high altitude was in the summer of 1978, when I was in Johannesburg, South Africa, six thousand feet above sea level. I was there for ten days. I was tired from traveling and competing in Europe, but that was not my excuse for feeling dizzy and fatigued. The altitude definitely affected me. I felt it mostly running on hills. I was unable to train any faster than a 6:30 or a 7:00 pace. I was not pleased. Psychologically, altitude had a very negative effect on me.

I don't think that altitude training is a necessary tool for reaching the highest level of fitness. I am only one of several who have proved you can run as fast as anyone else in the world in the marathon without training at altitudes.

Carbohydrate loading refers to a diet used by some of the top marathoners. It was developed by some physiologists who discovered that, by using it, your muscle tissue and your liver could store up extra glycogen, the major fuel for your muscle tissue when you run.

Basically, it is a week-long diet. You go out for one long depletion run and, for the next three days, your diet will consist mostly of protein. Your running during this period will often be very difficult, since you are not getting the blood sugar from carbohydrates and the long depletion run of twenty or more miles will have eliminated your store of glycogen. You don't have as much energy.

For the final three or four days, you switch over to primarily carbohydrates and this enables your muscle tissue and liver to overload an above-average amount of glycogen. This supposedly is going to give you a little more energy throughout the marathon, particularly in the final six miles.

The diet is somewhat risky. You tend to put on a few extra pounds during the last few days before the race. Most top marathoners I know do not use this specific diet. Most of the top runners eat large amounts of carbohydrates in their diets.

The ratio of carbohydrates to protein to fat that I eat is probably four to one to one. I have never used the carbohydrate diet. I simply have a well-balanced diet. I love dairy products, especially milk and cheese, yogurt, ice cream (especially pistachio and butter crunch), and milkshakes. I like seafood—swordfish, tuna, scallops, clams, and abalone. I love to eat cheeseburgers, Fritos, pizza with anchovies, lasagna, spaghetti, hot fudge sundaes, and Heath Bars. Perhaps two days before a marathon I cut back, because I need less food as a result of training less.

There was considerable controversy surrounding the extraordinary double in the five- and ten-thousand-meter races of Lasse Viren of Finland in both the 1972 and 1976 Olympics. After he won the two gold medals in 1976, the question was raised through the press whether, in order to attain that level of excellence, he had employed the concept of blood doping. After all, his superb Olympic performances were contrasted with his less than excellent efforts in the intervening years.

Blood doping is done when an athlete wants to improve his level of fitness, in particular by increasing the amount of hemoglobin (red blood cells) in his system. The athlete will have a specific amount of his blood withdrawn, perhaps one-half pint or more. The blood may be refrigerated, or frozen at a specific temperature which seems to enhance the potency of the process. A period of several weeks is allowed to pass, during which the athlete replenishes his blood supply normally. Then his refrigerated blood is returned to his system, resulting in a surfeit of blood in his system, theoretically enabling the athlete, via his increased red blood cells, to utilize more oxygen.

I have talked with Viren. I have watched him train. I have raced against him several times. From my own experiences and observations, I can say that he doesn't blood dope. I can also say that of all the top athletes I have run against, none of them has utilized this technique.

I have only read about one instance when it was used, and that was when a Finnish steeplechaser in the late 1960s tried it. Apparently, this athlete was not at a very high level of fitness and the blood doping technique helped his performance to a moderate degree. For an athlete as finely tuned as Viren was at the Olympics, blood doping would have a deleterious effect.

If you reach a certain level of fitness and you have a certain amount of hemoglobin, blood doping would cause your blood to thicken. It would inhibit performance. Your blood would not be improved. You may gain some extra blood from it, but there is an inhibiting influence when you reach the highest level of fitness.

I have arrived at the conclusion that the two primary factors in excelling are motivation and heredity. I underwent some extensive tests in October of 1978 at Penn State University on the biomechanical aspects of running. I went on for some stress testing at the Human Performance Laboratory at Ball State University in Muncie, Indiana.

They took chest X rays at Ball State and found my heart was 25 percent larger than that of the average person of the same height and weight. An enlarged heart is a side effect of running. You can pump more blood at a slower rate. Your heart, as a consequence, is doing less work.

Dr. David Costill at Ball State used a cybex machine to test my muscle fiber, and he estimated I have between 75 and 80 percent slow-twitch fibers. A preponderance of slow-twitch muscle fiber indicates you have the potential, physically, to do well in sustained, long-term cardiovascular muscular exercise, such as cross-country skiing and marathoning.

If you have fast-twitch fibers, it indicates an ability for short-term, explosive muscular activity such as sprinting and weight lifting. I considered doing a muscle biopsy as well, but I decided against it. It is done with a needle and can lead to muscle soreness. It would have come shortly before a major competition, the Fukuoka Marathon. Sometime in the future, I may submit to it.

I also underwent a maximum oxygen uptake test on a treadmill. The rate of speed and incline of the treadmill were adjusted by the physiologist to steadily increase, thus forcing me to work even harder. The test lasted about twenty to twenty-five minutes. They measured my heart rate under controlled conditions, and I breathed air into a machine which analyzes how much of the air you expel is oxygen and how much is carbon dioxide. All gases exhaled are analyzed by a computer.

I found that my maximum oxygen uptake was 78.5, a reading that indicates I have a good ability to utilize the oxygen that I take in. It gets to my muscles, and my muscles utilize it very well. I am not expelling as much oxygen as I take in. Dr. Costill indicated that these factors are something you inherit. I was simply able to develop them better through running. This is true of all top runners. It is not something that comes purely through work. All I know is that I was zapped after all the tests. It was harder than any marathon.

What these tests made clear to me was that not everyone can be a top marathoner, just as not everyone can become a top quarterback or tennis player. There are certain limitations. Everybody is always endeavoring to find out what his or her limitations are. You are trying to define your limits. I never really thought I could be a top marathoner, or make an Olympic team, until I ran the 2:09:55 in Boston.

I suppose if I had gone to a physiology lab in 1974, they might have been able to say, "Bill, if you train hard, maybe you can do this." But I never had the opportunity to test myself in a lab until October of 1978. Such an oversight, the lack of physiological testing for athletes showing potential, gives you some insight into the lack of organization of our developmental athletic program.

I always believed that not everyone could be a great natural marathoner, but if you had some ability, motivation might well get you there. I felt in particular that the longer the event became, the more willpower, a lot of mileage, work, and luck became the major factors. I learned, through Dr. Costill, that there is more of an even split between the factors of heredity and motivation. You must have the inherited physiological raw material in order to excel.

Dr. Peter Cavanagh, at the biomechanics lab at Penn State, ran me through some tests to study my technique and my running form. I found I tend to pronate badly with my right foot. I found that a runner will naturally find the stride length which is best for him in terms of utilizing oxygen. You become more efficient as you increase the number of miles you run over a period of years. You self-optimize.

You learn, physiologically, what is best for you. You don't have to be told or be measured on the treadmill to determine what stride length is the most efficient for you. I was tested using seven different stride lengths, running at a 5:00-per-mile pace for six minutes, and it was determined that the most efficient one for me was only two centimeters off what my normal stride was. It was that close.

I have always believed I had basic flaws in my running form because I've been told as much ever since high school, and as recently as Fukuoka, 1977. I was told I tended to bounce too much and spend too much time going up and down in the air between strides. I discovered that it isn't true. I am within the normal limits of vertical oscillation and stride length.

I was also aware that when I ran, I swung my right arm a lot. They were unable to determine what caused this arm swing, but they said I shouldn't try to change it. It was obviously something I did to counter some imbalance. They couldn't pick out exactly what it was.

If you have inconsistencies in your stride or in your running form, don't automatically try to change them before you get a number of different opinions. Perhaps you should even have some scientific expertise behind any opinions before you buy them. Coaches can't give you the kind of scientific, precise film analysis that I received at the lab at Penn State.

6
Failure

THE MARATHON. It is not one of the ultimate challenges, like going to the moon or climbing Mount Everest. The marathon is something that is readily within reach, and when I reached for it, I won Boston. I set the American record. That opened doors. It changed my life. It also set me up for some failures. I learned how the marathon can humble you.

I was invited to race in Enschede, Holland. It is a marathon that is run every other year in late August. The organizers bring in many of the top Europeans and sometimes one or two Americans. It is a quality race, similar in many ways to Fukuoka. The competition and the attention to detail are comparable.

It was a busy time. I received my graduate degree in special education at the end of the summer. I accepted a position teaching emotionally disturbed children at the Edward Everett Hale School in the city of Everett, a few miles outside Boston. Ellen and I were married and we moved to Melrose, a community about ten miles north of Boston.

All of these things came together at the same time. I received the invitation to run at Enschede, and since there was adequate expense money for the race, I decided to go. I was still on a high after Boston. I was in decent shape. I figured I might have a shot at winning Enschede. After all, I had just run one of the fastest marathons ever run. Who could beat me in Holland? I went over there and learned a lesson. You shouldn't run a major marathon when you are doing too many different things that lead to a state of fatigue. The opposite is true. You should be cutting back in your personal activities and getting the right amount of rest.

I went forty hours without sleep. I finally slept the night before the race. I flew across the Atlantic and I felt the jet lag after landing in London. I changed planes, flew to Amsterdam, waited in the airport for two hours for another runner to arrive, and then we took a two-hour train ride, followed by a fifteen-minute car ride to Enschede and my hotel. About four in the afternoon of the day before the race, I tried to rest and evaluate my race for the next day.

I went into it very light-headed and fatigued. Because I felt I could and should win, I went out with the leaders. I developed a side ache after twenty kilometers. At approximately twenty-five kilometers, I saw a runner retching in the center of the road. It was Neil Cusack of Ireland, the 1974 Boston winner. We both knew we'd had it and ran slowly together with the unspoken awareness that we were out of the race.

By the time I hit thirty kilometers, I was experiencing dehydration. It was a warm day, about eighty. So I ended up dropping out, shortly after thirty kilometers. I was suffering from an old malady, cramps. They put me on a stretcher and I just lay there. I was given copious quantities of fluids, which helped a great deal. They later took us to the finish area, where I discovered that Ron Hill, a thirty-six-year-old Englishman whom I had easily defeated at Boston, had won in a course record of 2:15.

What a disappointing way to run a marathon. I set the
American record one time and I was a DNF (Did Not Finish)
the next. I'd been taught a lesson. Before I would attempt a
major marathon again, I would make sure I prepared for it
seriously. It's more than a strike against you if you don't. You
may as well not run the race. There is no sense in it.

I returned in time to start my new job as a teacher of special
education. I had a class of five students between the ages of ten
and twelve. They demanded all my time and energy. I was
looking ahead to running in Fukuoka, and I was trying to gear
my training toward that race. I had set the American record,
but then I had bombed out at Enschede. I also remembered the
words of Ron Hill, in reference to my record race at Boston.
"You may run that fast again," he said, "but then again, you
may not."

From the considerable gossip and feedback I heard and read
in the press, it was clear many runners felt my record race at
Boston was a fluke. I'd had the wind at my back, it was a
downhill course, and it was point-to-point. Put simply, I had
set it on an easy course on an easy day.

We headed into a rigorous New England winter. I would get
up at six o'clock every morning and run the streets of Melrose
and the surrounding towns before school. I went to Fukuoka
for the race on December 7, 1975, and I finished third in
2:11:26. Jerome Drayton won it in 2:10:08, the second fastest
Fukuoka time. Dave Chettle of Australia was second in
2:10:20, the third fastest time on the Fukuoka list.

I was relatively satisfied. I had been training against the
backdrop of a difficult working situation and I was coming off
a poor run at Enschede. After every failure, I always want to
come back hard and do well the next time out. I can remember
telling that to myself over the final miles at Fukuoka. "No
matter what, try to hang on and run a decent race."

I was struggling over the final miles. I was also under the
impression I needed to run a sub 2:20 at Fukuoka to qualify me

for the Olympic trials. Though I knew my pace was 2:11 or so, I was afraid I might not finish because of a torn muscle, severe cramping, or some freak physical factor in those last miles that might slow me to a time over 2:20. As it turned out, my Boston time was sufficient for the trials and I had the fastest time for an American going in.

The Olympic trials became my next objective, and I had to cope with the interrelated aspects of climate and occupation. I had to ask for permission to train on my lunch hour. I was getting up at six o'clock to run, and in the freezing cold of January and February, it was starting to drive me crazy out there alone in the dark. Also, it was dangerous. With the sidewalks covered with snow, I had to run in the road with the cars. Of course, since it was still dark out, automobile drivers often couldn't see me very well, and there was little room on the snow-narrowed streets for runners or cars to maneuver out of the way.

I can remember one day going out, running a half mile and flipping out. I ran back to the house and started to jog in place. It was physically and mentally depressing. I started asking myself, "How am I going to make the American Olympic marathon team by jogging in place?" So, I went to the school committee and asked for permission to run on my lunch hour. If they vetoed my request, I was prepared, like most dedicated amateurs, to quit my job and, as usual, go it alone. But they did grant my request and, on most days, I did six or seven miles. Nine was a good day. Then I'd do ten or twelve miles after school. It made for a long day.

All of the other teachers in the school were women, and most of them were not that athletically inclined. That made me stick out even more. Not only was I the only male in the school with the exception of the janitors, but I was the only one doing a crazy thing like changing into running gear and going out in the cold of winter for a run on my lunch hour. I was fortunate to have the use of a shower in the basement. Each day, as the children lined up in the basement to get their lunches, I'd disappear into that small room, change into my running gear, wave to the kids, and slip out the door to train for the Olympics.

I was given permission to run by the school committee, and that was fine. Unfortunately, my principal was not in favor of it at all. I can still remember her words: "Mr. Rodgers, why don't you concentrate more on your vocation than your avocation?" She used to keep track of me when I went out on my lunch hour to make sure I was back in the classroom on time. She would send kids up to the room to see if I was there.

It was almost a form of harassment. There were many times when it was touch and go. I thought of quitting. There was the considerable burden of making the Olympic team while I was working at a job like this. It's the sort of thing other American athletes have experienced. Tom Fleming had problems with the school committee in Bloomfield, New Jersey. He quit his job. His school committee was too inflexible to allow Tom to coordinate his teaching job with a major world-class training effort. This was a normal situation for an American amateur. What was particularly galling was the fact that I received no pay when I traveled to a race to run for the United States. In fact, United States team members often felt quite fortunate if they received an American team uniform in which to compete for their country.

The job gave me problems right up to the Olympic trials in Eugene, Oregon. I arrived there late on a Thursday night and the race was Saturday. I should have arrived earlier, but I was afraid to take too much time off from work. I always had to ask for time off ahead of time in writing, and then worry about the answer. I had to turn down a few invitations to major races because I felt it was disruptive to my class. A substitute teacher had to come in and the continuity of what I was teaching was upset. Discipline occasionally broke down and the administration wasn't very pleased. All of it wasn't working out very well.

The word "Olympian" has always struck a deep chord

within me. To become an Olympian was everything to me and I thought of different things to make the race loom even larger. I thought of running for my wife Ellen, or for my family. Romantic thoughts? You don't train for the Olympics unless you are a romantic.

The tension in Eugene was incredible. Even though I was the American record holder, was ranked the number-one marathoner in the world for 1975, and had two fast times to my credit, I still did not think of myself as being the superior or even the equal of Frank Shorter. I classified myself with most of the rest of the better of the seventy-odd marathoners there. We were all at least one step behind Frank, one level below him. I found it difficult to sleep in Eugene and frequently felt dizzy and disoriented. I thought it was jet lag from my cross-country trip, but it was mostly tension. I bought junk food from the vending machine outside my hotel room and managed to enjoy it.

About one hour before the race start, I jogged the mile from my hotel to the starting line.

After a short warm-up, I discovered I'd forgotten to pin my competitor's number to my racing singlet, and it was back in my room. I ran back to the room, hastily pinned the number to my vest, and ran back to the starting line, heart thumping.

Eight miles after the race began, Frank made his move and Barry Brown went with him. I stayed with them. I promptly developed a side ache. "This is like a nightmare," I said. "It's like a bad dream. Why is it happening to me?" I stayed two strides behind Barry and Frank, watched them, and tried to relax. I didn't try to race them and the side ache slowly disappeared.

I suddenly started to feel fantastic about 12 miles into the race. Euphoria set in. It became a fun run, in a sense. I was in such a good mood, because I knew I could make the Olympic team. Barry started to fall behind and I almost felt like asking Frank, "Why don't we wait for him?" We were running a 2:10

pace. We ran together, each concentrating on his own race. There is a film of the Olympic trials race which shows us running stride for stride in slow motion. It also reveals one reason why I ran a bit slower than Frank that day.

My legs started to tighten up about twenty-one miles into the race. Once again, I learned you have to make sure you have the option of taking enough fluids during the race. It wasn't extremely hot; however it was in the middle sixties and sunny. I had made no plan to place my own special water bottle at the water stations. I figured the weather had been cool enough in Eugene so far. I was grabbing sponges and cups off the tables.

Frank would run along and pick up his own plastic bottles with a cupped straw. He could pick up the bottles without breaking his running rhythm and without moving his arms too much to take a sip. He would run a little, take a sip, and run some more. The straw on his bottle was large and curved, so he only had to bring the bottle up to his lips, still keeping his arms in a rhythmic, normal running posture. I was bringing my head back, breaking my stride, splashing water on myself, choking and not taking in that much water.

It was a factor in my calves and legs tightening up. I wasn't getting sufficient fluid into my body. I also remember that I drank hardly at all during the major part of the race, having concentrated on just running and slugging fluids early in the event. I also dropped cups and spilled water out of cups. We were moving too fast.

We were about two miles from the finish and we heard that somebody was moving up on us fast. We eventually were told, more correctly, that we had a two-minute to two-and-a-half-minute lead. Frank had said before the race that he was going to slow down if he had control. He didn't seem to slow down very much. I was cramping a little in the calves and I wanted to make sure I finished and qualified. I decided to ease it in. Frank went ahead and won in 2:11:51. I was seven seconds back in 2:11:58.

It was a fantastic feeling, making the Olympic team. I remember watching that finish line get closer and thinking, "Ten steps to the Olympics, nine steps, eight steps, seven steps. . . ." It was a downright emotional moment, crossing that line. Don Kardong came in third and the three of us were heading for Montreal. It was a dream of mine that I had fulfilled. It's the sort of thing you never forget. It made all of the runs on the ice- and snow-clogged streets of Melrose worthwhile.

On the other hand, the cutting finality of the trials hit home. How about those who trained hard for years and were unable to compete due to a recent injury or sickness? How about those who barely missed making the team? It's such a long road to travel and then come up empty.

I went back to Eugene in June for the ten-thousand-meter trials. I had qualified for the trials in my first ten-thousand-meter run in April at the Penn Relays when I ran 28:32.6. I was feeling pretty good and I won my heat in the trials in 28:32 flat. In fact, I was, surprisingly, the fastest American qualifier. Squires and I talked it over before the final and we decided not to go for the Olympic team for ten-thousand meters. Just run a fast time. I told Gary Tuttle, who was a contender in the race, "Don't worry about me as a factor. I'm just running for a fast time."

The ten-thousand-meter final was run on a cool day, and I can still recall how worried I was as we passed two miles in 9:00 flat. My PR at the time, for two miles, was 8:53.6. The race was hotly contested by Frank Shorter, Garry Bjorklund, Craig Virgin, and me until Bjorklund, who had lost a shoe earlier in the race, fell off the pace with a mile or so to go, and I slipped back with a half mile to go.

Bjorklund saw me falter, began sprinting, and passed me with ten yards to go to make the Olympic team. I was pleased with a PR of 28:04.4. My reasoning in not trying to make the team in the ten-thousand was that my chances for a marathon medal would only be hindered by two ten-thousand-meter efforts at Montreal, and that, in any case, I had a very insignificant chance for a medal in the Olympic ten-thousand.

What happened, though, partially as a result of the Olympic trials ten-thousand, was that I aggravated a metatarsal problem in my right foot, and later it would have a telling effect in Montreal. It was something that had bothered me a lot during the previous winter. It was from overuse. The shoes I was wearing were a bit too narrow for my foot. I run on the balls of my feet and I believe the metatarsal bone in the bottom of my foot became irritated and scar tissue built up. It could have been that the nerve between the toes became pinched. Whatever it was, the ball of my foot hurt a lot.

After the ten-thousand-meter trials, I didn't do any more track work before the Olympics. I went over to Boston College one day and tried to run on the track. After I finished, my toes hurt a lot. I said, "Oh, well, I really don't need the track work that much. I'm in pretty good shape." I ran the Peachtree ten-thousand-meter race on the roads in Atlanta and was second to Don Kardong, who edged me by two seconds with his kick in 29:16. It was a hot day and a hilly course. I was confident I was in good shape. Though I'd run hard, I had raced casually, and whether I won didn't seem to matter that much.

The Olympic Marathon was only three weeks away. I didn't think about doing speed work on the track. It didn't seem important to me. I figured the marathon would be run on a hot day and it would be a slow and difficult race. I thought a 2:12, a 2:13, or a 2:14 would win. It never sank into my brain that I needed the speed work to run a 2:12. I never thought it would be run in anything like a 2:09:55, my current American record time.

I was training mostly on my own, sometimes with the guys in the Greater Boston TC. It was hot in New England that summer. I thought it would be adequate heat training. I was training at a 6:30 pace. I now know you simply have to do some form of speed work for the marathon. I didn't, and it turned out to be a critical mistake. I was afraid if I went on the track it might aggravate the foot injury and make it worse. I knew, training this way, I'd at least be able to run. I didn't want to be knocked completely out of the race.

When I arrived at the Olympic Village in Montreal, the foot hurt more. Ellen and I later deduced that my injury was compounded because I was wearing the same model shoe to walk around in as I wore when I was training. Also, most of my training was on the rolling slopes and fairways of a golf course next to the Olympic Village, and the uneven surface must have aggravated the injury. I never took the elevator. I'd run up and down the stairs to and from my room on the fifth floor of the dormitory. I used to have a long walk to the dining room and, if I was going to meet Ellen or some friends at the entrance to the Olympic Village, it meant an additional long distance to go. I ended up limping.

I finally went to see the American medical team and they used ultrasound treatment and iced my foot. That helped. However, no physiologist ever asked me about my training program. No podiatrist asked to check my foot. I never thought to ask. I'd hardly heard of a podiatrist in 1976. No coach came up to see me and ask questions in an attempt to discover the root of my problem. It seems amazing that I, the athlete with the fastest qualifying time for my event, who was now limping around injured in the Olympic Village, was not given more assistance by the staff at Montreal. I wondered if my team-mates felt the same way.

Someone did come by and give us our jerseys and our numbers and offer to fill our bottles for the race. It was as if everyone assumed we knew everything there was to know and all the bases were covered. We were all experienced. Of course, for me it was too late. I should have searched more carefully for the reason for my sore foot. I learned another lesson.

Bill Squires, the Greater Boston track coach, was in Montreal

and he was very concerned about how well I did. We ran and
drove over the course and he helped me plan my training. I ran
sections of the course in an attempt to learn it. We worked out
a strategy. I was going to move hard at thirty kilometers. I
wasn't fit enough to do that, as it turned out, and I think I knew
this before the race. Yet, my thoughts and fears were always
pushed aside by hope. An athlete is always hopeful, and
always should be.

I finally moved out of the Olympic Village about three days
before the race and went to stay with Ellen outside the city of
Montreal. I left because I didn't want to keep walking long
distances on my injured foot for food, to meet Ellen, to walk to
a phone, or to talk to the press. I wasn't alone. There were
athletes such as Shorter, Kardong, Mac Wilkins, and Al
Feuerbach living outside the village.

So, I just went on my own and nobody knew where I was. I
spent a lot of time flat on my back watching the Olympics on
TV and staying off my foot. I went out for easy runs and tried
to get a lot of sleep so I'd be rested for the race. Because of my
foot problem, I cut back on my training earlier than I had
originally planned.

Race day came and it wasn't exceptionally hot. Yet, it was
wet, muggy, and uncomfortable. These conditions were not the
kind I like. The foot never bothered me during the race, but
your concentration usually makes such things subside until
you stop running. It hurts enough then.

I was up with the leaders for about twenty-five kilometers.
From as early as the ten-kilometer mark, I started to feel I
wasn't in shape to be pushing it like that. Still, I knew it was
the only way to run in the Olympics, and I wanted to earn a
medal. Also, I didn't want Lasse Viren to have an easy time of
it. He had decided, after he had won the five-thousand and
ten-thousand-meter gold medals, to try to equal the accomplishment of Emil Zatopek in 1952 and win the triple crown,
adding a gold in the marathon.

I was guessing Viren must not only be a bit sore and fatigued from his five-thousand and ten-thousand heats and final races, but had probably accumulated a few blisters as well on his numerous laps around the track. I thought a hard, early pace might make him think of those blisters a little more.

I felt as early as ten kilometers that I wasn't going to run a good race. It was very, very apparent by twenty kilometers. After that, it became a thing within me just to finish. It was the toughest marathon I'd ever run. I broke down about halfway through it and that left a long distance to go suffering cramps. The cramps were a result of dehydration, combined with the lack of speed work. I finished fortieth in 2:25:14, and later discovered I had still been in the top ten when there was a mere three miles to go.

About thirty kilometers into the race, I can recall Don Kardong passing me and encouraging me. I thanked him for the kind gesture. I've always liked that part of our sport. When another athlete is out of it, there are nothing but good words, offers of help, and pats on the back.

It was a personal struggle, but it was very important to me to get back to the Olympic Stadium, run down that ramp, and circle the track. Running those final miles I was frequently hobbled by cramps and someone from the crowd would yell, "Don't quit, Yankee." I'd yell back, "I haven't quit yet," and start running.

I wasn't even aware of who had won the race when I arrived in the stadium. I looked up at the scoreboard and I saw that Waldemar Cierpinski of East Germany had beaten Shorter for the gold medal. The last I'd seen of the leaders, Frank had made a hard push and Shivnath Singh of India, Cierpinski, Jerome Drayton of Canada, Viren, myself, and a few others had begun to string out behind Frank.

I circled the track, crossed the finish line, and I went into a room underneath the stadium where all the athletes were. I saw Jerome Drayton lying on a cot under a blanket and he was smiling. I saw Kardong, who finished a surprising fourth, sort of wobbling around. I never saw Frank Shorter. All I can remember is all these runners lying around. It was over.

I think one coach came up to me and said I had done my best. That was it. That was the end of the official American involvement with my race. I wanted to know why I had run such a poor race. Was I a genetically poor runner in heat? This is something that has plagued me ever since. I didn't know what it was and there was nobody there to help me find the answer.

I walked out of the stadium and one of the first people I saw was John Powers, a reporter for the *Boston Globe*. He asked me some questions about the race and then he asked me if I had seen Shorter. I said, no, I'd just arrived. It was almost funny. I met Ellen and my brother Charlie. It was dark. We walked back to our car and went home.

I can't remember much about that night. All I recall was feeling that it was somehow a very significant experience. This was the end of it. It was as if your running career had come to an end on a sour note. I didn't go out and get drunk. I had no desire to. I ached too much. I had cramps. I just went home, had something to eat, and went to bed. To be succinct, it was massively depressing. Just crushing. Words cannot convey the utter feeling of losing that one feels over a poor performance at the Olympics.

It hit me the next day at the closing ceremonies. There is much to the Olympic experience. There is the competition, the trading of pins with other athletes, the dining halls with everyone there, the color, the flags, the beauty of the buildings. What I liked more than anything was the pageantry and the emotion of the opening and closing ceremonies. They are two of the most poignant moments of the Olympic Games.

I looked up and saw the satellite images of all those Russian girls dancing and saying, "See you in Moscow in 1980." It was a fantastic feeling. I felt as if I were there already. I would not trade my Olympic experience for anything. The marathon is the final event of the games. It was the end of one Olympics and the beginning of the next.

I have been fortunate in my running career. I haven't had a major injury that has knocked me out for any length of time or has weakened my training significantly on a long-term basis. I have had minor injuries such as quadricep pulls, arch problems, and tendonitis that have shelved me for two weeks. That's been about it, and this has been a key to my continued success.

The only way to cope with situations such as these is to think in terms of the future and how well you want to be. You should think about improving your situation immediately. Do things for yourself. Work at maximizing and strengthening some other areas of your body. Build up the weaker areas when you are unable to train due to an injury or physical setback.

If your legs are strong, work on weights or do isometric exercises for your arms, stomach, or back. Maybe you can use a bicycle or swim. There is always something you can do. Work on an area of your body that is weaker than the injured area.

I always try to take time off from my job. It's important enough for me to get the proper rest and to try to eliminate injuries. I try to find every means I can to eliminate injuries. If I'm injured, I talk to podiatrists, orthopedic surgeons, coaches, athletic trainers and other runners. I contact everybody I can to find out everything I can about possible treatments.

I try each thing out. I had an arch problem one time and I talked to Bob Sevene, a friend from the Greater Boston TC and now the cross-country coach at Boston University. He knows a lot about distance runners and we tried a couple of approaches. One method was to tape my injured arch. That failed to work. I stopped that and tried wearing different shoes, and it turned out that my trouble had to do with the shoes I was wearing. I needed to find a certain shoe for my feet.

You learn through your own experience. I keep stressing that, but it's true. You know your body better than anyone else. You know it better than orthopedic specialists, cardiovascular surgeons, podiatrists. You will learn to know your body better than anyone can know your body. The East Germans call this somatic intelligence. I wouldn't be afraid to try any approach if the injury was serious enough: acupressure, acupuncture, seeing a chiropractor, hypnosis. The important thing is, "Is it going to work?"

I recently read about Alain Mimoun of France. He had a bad case of sciatica before the 1956 Olympics in Melbourne. He tried all types of approaches. He finally went to a holy shrine and bathed in the waters there. It cured the sciatica. He went on to win the gold medal in his first marathon. There is always hope. It's important to think in those terms.

When I am injured, I cut down on my caloric intake. I don't want to put on weight. If the problem is my legs, I stay off my feet as much as possible. I may spend the entire day in bed. If it is more serious, I may use ice or a hydroculator to send heat deep into the muscles. I may use ultrasound treatment. You can buy a hydroculator at your local drugstore for about $7.50. It is a pack or baglike object filled with some mineral or crushed stone, which is soaked in a pot of boiling water. After a towel has been wrapped around the injured area the hydroculator is placed over the towel. It sends moist heat deep into muscle tissue allowing for increased blood circulation in the injured area. Seek out ultrasound at a college or university or at some private medical center. It sends high-frequency sound deep into the muscle tissues and bone and disperses blood throughout the area.

If you have a constant, nagging pain, I recommend not running at all—or, if you have a fever. You will learn on your own what aches you can or can't train through. It's very easy to decide when you should run and when you should not. When it gets to the point where you are altering your stride because of a major ache or pain, then it is time to either lay off or to cut back. Lie down for an hour or two, take a hot bath, get a lot of sleep. Try a massage. Talk to a podiatrist who runs. Investigate what the nature of the injury is. There is a time to run and a time not to run. The times not to run are the times when running today will curtail your running in the weeks, months, and years ahead.

The period of recuperation after an injury is critical. Your mileage, starting out, should be very low and very slow. What I usually do is double my mileage for a while each consecutive day until I am back to normal. If I have had a minor quadricep injury that has sidelined me for a week or more, I may try to go just two or three miles on the first day back. That's it. Just to test it and see how pressure feels on it.

If it feels all right I will go the full two or three miles at a slow pace. If I feel the slightest twinge in the injured area, I'll quit and return. If it is OK, I will double my mileage the next day, maybe do six miles. I will gradually increase it to twelve, fifteen, eighteen miles. The whole point is that you have to take it slowly and give yourself three or four days when you come back from minor injuries.

For major injuries, consult a certified orthopedic specialist, a trainer, or someone who runs and knows a lot about specific injuries. Go to a sports medicine clinic or a hospital where they have qualified personnel who deal with running injuries and who understand the sport.

After a marathon, I usually take some aspirin to ease the recuperation from the muscle-tissue breakdown and the strain. Aspirin helped ease the pain in my left arch after the 1978 New York City Marathon. It also helped eliminate the general aches and fatigue I felt from the race itself. I would recommend taking aspirin every four hours for a few days.

I also take hot baths once or twice a day for two days following a marathon. I drink a lot of fruit juices and I do some easy stretching for a few days after the race. I usually run three or four miles the next day. Sometimes I'll skip it and take a day off if I'm really broken down. The most important thing is to get a lot of sleep and stay off your legs. You are not going to make any athletic progress during the period of recuperation. You have to recover slowly.

Boston, 1977, another dropout. I was really physically whipped. It bothered me that I wasn't able to finish, but it's not the sort of thing that tears me apart. I went into the race tired and without the proper speed work due to two consecutive knee injuries in the two months prior to the race. I became dehydrated and the fatigue was considerable. I decided to quit at the same spot where I had dropped out in my first Boston Marathon four years earlier, at the top of Heartbreak Hill. I felt I'd come full circle as a marathoner. I'd quit my first marathon here, had done some good racing here, and was now back at the beginning again.

When I say the marathon can always humble you, I mean that no matter what level you have reached, what medals you have won, or who you are, no matter how many lessons you think you've learned, you can run into the most difficult situations in a marathon. I mean the ravages of physical fatigue and psychological despair. It happens to beginners. It happens to the best marathoners in the world. It's something we all have in common.

What happened, as I indicated, was that I incurred the two separate knee injuries. I trained for seven weeks at 155 miles per week. I had plenty of distance background, but none of it was speed. I went two months without any speed work and, as a result, I wasn't in the type of shape I thought and hoped I'd be in.

Then finally, I went on the track one week before Boston, and I can remember feeling how hard those 4:55 miles were. I only did about three or four of them. I suppose the choice was mine. Should I have run the race? In retrospect, I suspect I shouldn't have started it. Yet when you are from the area, you have won it before, and the race is suddenly in front of you, the positive reasons to run all coalesce.

I was prone to take a gamble because I thought the field might be weak. Drayton was never a definite starter until he showed up, and he didn't until the night before the race. In fact, I didn't know if he'd run or not until we met an hour before the race. I was also gambling on the weather staying fairly cool, the way I liked it. I ran and lost my two gambles.

I wanted to win that race very badly and, as it turned out, just one person kept me from winning it: Jerome Drayton. We were out there in front of the field by the thirteen-mile mark, but no matter how much I wanted that race and how desperately I tried to win it, there comes a point when, if your preparation has not been sound, your mind and body are not going to carry you through.

You try to be positive and encourage yourself and talk to yourself and use every trick you can. It does nothing for you mentally. Even with one million spectators cheering you on, there comes a point when you totally ignore them and you almost become hostile toward them. All you want to do is get out of there, get a drink of water, go home, and say, "This is ridiculous. What am I doing out here?" I simply wasn't ready. I had hoped for too much and, in the end, deluded myself.

I hit the wall. It's something I try to eliminate when I run a marathon. I don't want to mess around with the wall. I want to be trained well enough so I don't have to experience what is known as the wall. In the fast marathons I've run, I haven't really hit it. It has slowed me down some. But there's never been that dramatic black-and-white difference. There are really two stages in the marathon, unless you are primed for a fast race and you pull it off. Then it becomes one flowing continuity, one continuous run.

When you hit the wall, you suddenly catapult into a whole new world. When I talk about the wall, I mean the psychological and physiological impact you encounter when you start to fall apart. Sometimes it hits you very suddenly. Usually you can feel it building up. There is a tightening in your legs and a dizziness. You are mentally fatigued and your perspectives and your goals change very drastically.

You may have been on a certain target for a certain time. You may have been on schedule to win a race or place in a certain category. Suddenly everything seems to shift. It's as if an earthquake hit you. The whole world changes colors and your objectives become very different. You set different goals and nothing can alter them for you.

That's the thing about the marathon. You are out there alone. It's a hopeless situation if you get hit by the wall because you tend to fall apart physiologically and psychologically. Even with a mile to go, people have been known to collapse. It happened to Drayton in Boston in 1975, when he was only a couple of miles from the finish. It happened to Jim Peters of England as he entered the stadium in the 1954 Commonwealth Games. It happened to Pietri Dorando in the 1908 Olympics. The finish line and victory were within sight. He collapsed. There have been many who buckled and had their dreams go up in smoke in an instant, just a little before the finish line. They hit the wall.

7
Success

NEW YORK CITY. It was my opportunity for redemption, my chance to prove that Montreal was a mistake. Even the best people have their peaks and valleys. It's foolish to say that someone is the best all the time. Credit has to be spread out. Just because Frank Shorter won the gold medal at the 1972 Olympics doesn't make him a better marathoner than, say, Drayton, or Ian Thompson, or Ron Hill. Just because Waldemar Cierpinski won it in Montreal doesn't mean he's the best of our era. He simply was the best on that day.

You are always trying to improve on your won-loss record. Consistency is very important. The Olympics tends to be overrated in terms of evaluating the career of an athlete. It was impossible for me to eliminate feeling rotten about what happened in Montreal, partially because I knew I would be measured by my Olympic race. All I could do was to come back and try to run as well as I could.

There is an element of truth in that with respect to every performance. If you run poorly, you try to come back and do well the next time out. I hadn't aimed at the Olympics for four years. I had only set my sights on Montreal for less than two years. After I won the 1975 Boston Marathon, that was the first time I thought about the Olympics. Thus the crushing finality of fortieth place was not as bad as it would have been if I'd been at a top level for three years or more before the Olympics. Still, the disappointing impact could not be wiped out, only alleviated. For myself.

It's something that every athlete has to deal with and live with as he runs more and more. I'll try for the 1980 Olympics. It may be my last. I may come in fortieth again. It's a depressing, very disheartening thought. You feel bad about losses like the one I had at Montreal, but, good grief, you don't live just for that. I'm not that kind of person. There are too many other races. I'm not going to hang myself if I finish fortieth in the 1980 Olympics. I've never been that way and I never will be.

I didn't run for two days after Montreal. I was too fatigued and too sore. I couldn't run and I had no desire to. My foot also hurt a lot. We drove back to Melrose and two weeks later, I ran a road race in Chelmsford, Massachusetts, which I won. I remember being asked by reporters if I was going to quit running. It was as if the defeat at Montreal was the end of my running career. My parents had asked me the same thing after high school. Was I going to quit running when I went to college?

For me, running no longer comes in breaks such as that and, for a lot of people, it is the same way. It's a life style. For me, competition was still an integral part of it. Maybe just because I bombed out so badly in Montreal, I soor wanted to get back into competition. It wasn't easy running the next week, but I was still very motivated to compete. I wanted to continue running and stay fit, and competition was a natural corollary to it. I also knew fortieth place was not where I rated as a marathoner—Olympics or not!

People asked me after Montreal why I didn't drop out during

the race. "You weren't going to win a medal," was the common argument, "so why didn't you just drop out?" It wasn't that easy. Why didn't I? It was the Olympic Games. People failed to understand the significance of it. If they were in the Olympic Marathon, I'm sure they wouldn't want to drop out. It became important to me to fight my way back into the stadium. Boston, 1977, was a different situation. I thought about finishing, but it would have done me no good to try. Boston is not the ultimate marathon; the Olympic Marathon is.

After Chelmsford, I made a return to Falmouth, a race I won in 1974. It came up three weeks after the Olympic Marathon. Frank Shorter was there and we met at a nightclub on Main Street in Falmouth called The Oar and Anchor. "What have you done since Montreal?" I asked Shorter. "All I've done is lie around a pool, go waterskiing, eat and drink too much, and live the life of laziness. I feel terrible," he said. "That's great," I told him. "That's the way I feel." He beat me.

About this time people started talking about the New York City Marathon, which was to be held in late October. I heard the organizers were inviting all the top runners and hoped to have a field that was comparable to Montreal. I heard Shorter would be there and Viren and Cierpinski might be. This got me going again. I knew 2:25:14 was far from my best. I knew I could do better against most of those guys I lost to in Montreal. New York was going to be my day of atonement.

I knew the weather would be cooler. I knew that I had been in more than fairly decent shape and, if I just rounded my program out a little more and did my speed work, I would be able to run a strong race and see where I really stood against the best in the world. I knew I didn't rank fortieth. I was capable of running with these guys.

Ellen suggested I needed a wider shoe, and this helped eliminate my foot problem. I started to pack in the miles. I had some high-mileage weeks. I had one week when I did about 180 miles. I didn't race very much. I concentrated on my training. I did between 130 and 150 miles per week for the eight weeks before New York. It became a single-minded objective to run well in this race.

Shorter was there, but Viren and Cierpinski were not. However the field did include five of the nine fastest marathoners in history. They were Ron Hill and Ian Thompson of Great Britain, Akio Usami of Japan, Shorter, and me. This was the first year New York went out and brought in the top runners. It used to be a race through Central Park, but it now went through the five boroughs of the city, finishing in the park.

I knew I would be hard to beat. I had prepared properly and I felt well. I have never put in that much mileage. I started training before I went to teach in the morning. I just kept it up. I'd do eight or nine miles on my lunch hour. I'd pack in a few more miles on a weekend. With the cool weather, I felt sure I would run well.

The race was taken out by Pekka Paivarinta of Finland. He raced away from the tollbooths at the start of the race at the Staten Island end of the Verrazano Narrows Bridge as if he were crashing the tollgate. He was something like forty-two seconds in front of the pack at eight miles. I tossed a little shrug to some people in the press bus that was ahead of us and in back of Paivarinta. Who knew?

I pulled even with Paivarinta about ten miles into the race. Chris Stewart of Great Britain went with me and he trailed me over the Queensboro Bridge from Queens to Manhattan. We were to make a little turn into the city, then go up the East River Drive. The course went up along the river in 1976. It now goes up First Avenue. I didn't know Chris Stewart and asked him his name as we dueled at this stage. I did know he'd run a 2:13 before and I would have to be careful with him. Chris seemed to have an awkward running form, and I felt he shouldn't beat me. I ran hard as we pounded over the Queensboro Bridge, and I slipped away.

That's a tough part of the race. There were ten miles to go. I had the lead. I looked back after a bit; I saw no one. It was a little misty and very overcast and gray. I went into the Bronx and, as I came back over the Willis Avenue Bridge into Manhattan, Shorter was just going in the other direction into the Bronx. He smiled and waved and said something like, "Nice going, Billy." I can't remember what I said but I waved back.

I was expecting a big hill in Central Park. A fellow on a bike kept telling me this hill was coming and I kept bracing for it. I never came to it. It was on the old course. I crossed the finish line in 2:10:10, the eighth fastest marathon in history at the time. I beat Shorter by three minutes. Chris Stewart finished third. I had a laurel wreath put on my head by Mayor Beame and he pressed it down on my forehead. All I could say was "Ouch!" The tips of the wire used to hold the wreath together went right into my skull.

It's still the easiest marathon for a fast time that I've ever run. It may have been my best marathon and it certainly gave me a lift. I was close to my Boston time and it was equally gratifying. I had beaten Shorter for the first time in three attempts in a marathon. Even though I had broken his American record in the 1975 Boston Marathon, he had beaten me in the Olympic trials and in the games.

We had gradually developed a pretty competitive rivalry on the roads. Nobody else in the country was able to push Frank that much on the roads or on the track, with the exception of Steve Prefontaine on the track, and perhaps Garry Bjorklund. I had pushed Frank at the trials, but I had been no threat in Montreal.

Now I had beaten him decisively in the New York City Marathon of 1976 and, from then on, I knew that if I had my best day, I could beat him. If he had his day, he could beat me. I think the American running public, in general, always tended to feel that Frank could beat me at will. I believe my

New York City race showed that it was no longer true. To win New York that year was kind of my way of saying it.

Kenny Moore, one of the top American marathoners and a former Olympian who writes about the state of the art for *Sports Illustrated,* has often talked about the ingredients of being successful in a marathon. He said you have to be very rational and cool headed about your marathon. I know what he says is partly true, but I must dispute it. I feel you must empty yourself physically and psychologically as the race progresses. Successful marathoners must lose their cool, and allow their irrational, animal consciousness to take over.

I think Moore's theory is true in the early stages of the race. It's imperative to hold back and save your psychological and physiological energy. It's too tough a race to really blast out at the beginning. You must take it in stride. It's better to let someone else do the early pace work. Stay behind them and let them cut the wind for you.

I did this in New York. I let Paivarinta go crazy in the first eight miles. He was out there at a 4:48 pace or something close to it. I was cool, calm, and collected. I was comfortable. It was almost easy. I knew it was going to be interesting when it toughened up. What was going to happen then? I felt I would do well and this ties in with the concept of keeping your cool early in the race.

If your training has gone well, it gives you that extra lift, that extra strength. That's the difference between winning or losing, doing poorly or doing well. Because of my lack of a well-rounded training program in Montreal, I felt somewhat tense competing there. You feel tension before any race. It usually disappears during the race. If your body is fatigued, it's a different story. You can never relax, and the tension seems to grow until you actually tighten so much you cramp. I felt that was happening to me in Montreal. I fell apart.

But in New York, I had done my anaerobic work, my track work, and the necessary speed work that every marathoner has to do. So, I knew when I broke away from Chris Stewart thirteen miles into the race that I was going to win. It was the first time that I ever had that solid feeling.

Even though I had set the American record previously, I never felt the way I did in New York. I knew, from then on, that in head-to-head competition I could be as good as anybody today who runs the marathon. People had said after my Boston win that the wind was at my back and that was the only reason I had run that fast a time. I would never do it again. I'd run 2:11:26 at Fukuoka, but I hadn't won. I'd finished third. But now I'd beaten some of the top runners in head-to-head confrontation. I knew that if I trained properly and put the knowledge I had acquired about the marathon to work, I could do it again. And again.

I guess you could say I was doing fartlek workouts before I knew the specifics of the concept. This was back in my Wesleyan days when Amby Burfoot and I ran through the countryside outside the city of Middletown. These were the runs I alluded to earlier and, as I prepared for New York in 1976, I was out applying the fartlek method of training.

It was actually spelled out by Gosta Holmer, a Swedish coach at the 1948 Olympics, and what it involves is training over assorted terrains at varying speeds. I went on ten-mile runs before New York. I'd run a hard pickup for about a minute. I varied my training. I'd go into the woods and run cross-country conditions, often zipping up and down the short, steep, rocky trails in the woods that surround the reservoirs for the communities of Stoneham, Winchester, and Melrose, Massachusetts. I call this area my "Finnish training ground." This was good anaerobic work.

I'd go out and run an eight-mile course. I'd run easy for the first three miles. I'd come to a hill and I'd run hard up the hill. I'd get to the top and I'd keep going hard for another one hundred yards or so. I'd slow it down and I'd go easy down the hill. Every time I came to a hill I'd push it pretty hard.

This is the type of training I'd done before the Olympic 10,000-meter trials. It's something I simply carried over to New York. I had the aerobic background. I'd done an average of 150 miles per week for the eight weeks prior to New York. I'd done the speed work as well. I usually try to get in one speed workout every week and usually one race every week. If I don't have a race, I try to do a second speed workout.

I feel it's vitally important to do some speed work that's faster than race pace. You should get on the track where it's hard to cheat on pace, with a watch and teammates prodding you. If I'm aiming for a 2:10 marathon, which is a 4:57 to 4:58 mile pace, I have to get on the track and run faster than that in my speed workouts. I have to simulate the race.

This is why I run a lot of races too. I feel it's a very effective form of preparation for the marathon. It's worked for me in the past. You have to be careful not to overdo it. I've had some close calls. It almost backfired when I ran too many races leading up to the Fukuoka Marathon in 1977. I was very tired from a long fall of hard races, including several marathons. The final straw was a hilly twenty-five-kilometer race in Ohio where I raced in near-blizzard conditions. The stress of the race, the storm, and the other races led to an inner-ear problem which resulted in a loss of hearing in one ear, and my balance was also affected. This condition plagued me throughout the race to some degree.

Given the proper ingredients, I try to gather myself psychologically and physiologically and aim for one particular marathon. Boston is in April. It's hard for me or any runner from a cold climate to do enough speed work at that time of year. There's often too much snow on the ground. New York is in October, at a time when there are a lot of road races and with no snow on the ground, so you can do adequate speed and/or fartlek work. I use these races as preparation for New York. It's the same way with a lot of runners. They use road races as a measuring device.

You have a feeling about racing. You know if you're ready to run well. You also know if you are poorly prepared. There's this nagging little voice inside you telling you something is wrong. All you need is one flaw in your training. It may seem minor, but it turns out not to be.

I'm not the only one who's had the experience. John Vitale, a national-class 2:16 marathoner from Connecticut, did tremendous mileage work before the 1977 Boston Marathon. He didn't do enough speed work. That was the vital flaw in his program. He had a poor race. He learned that there is more to marathoning success than going out and covering massive numbers of miles.

You have to be constantly in touch with everything. Consult your training diary. Determine if it's time for a long run. Do you have a race that week? Can you fit in a speed workout if you have no race? If you have no race, can you fit in a second speed workout? You have to decide, according to your own level of fitness, how much you can handle. You learn through experience.

You are not a complete marathoner until you have gone out there and been nailed a lot of times as well. It's a rare marathoner who has never suffered a devastating defeat. Frank Shorter was one for a long time. He never lost a significant marathon from the end of 1971 until the Olympics of 1976. He found out what it was all about when he started having injuries that developed after Montreal.

I often get letters from people in different parts of the country. They are mostly of high school and college age. Their questions are generally about training programs. Most of them are discouraged about their own running. They feel they are not running well and they are writing to me to find out my thoughts on training.

I received one letter from a sixteen-year-old boy who had run a 4:59 mile and a 10:36 two mile. He was unhappy. I wrote back and said, "That's exactly what I was running when I was sixteen." He said, "I'm a terrible runner." I said, "Just bide your time. People who are beating you now may not be beating you a year from now—or five years from now, or maybe ten years from now. If you enjoy your running and go at it patiently, you'll be around ten years from now and you may be the one who is up there."

You should try for certain goals for the immediate satisfaction of competition. You also have to hang on and look at the future. This is a very significant point. Running is never a waste. Everything you are doing now is all a part of the grand plan. What's going to happen nine years down the road? What's it going to be like in 1989?

Success breeds success. The more you train, the more consistent you become. You cut down wasted motion. You stop swinging your arms too much from side to side. You stop holding your arms up too high or too low. This all evens out. You will never look like someone else. But you can still look at the top runners and pick up certain things—the basics.

If you lean forward too much when you run, you will ultimately develop backaches or some kind of strain in your legs. The perceptive coach can pick this up. It's important to touch bases with knowledgeable people in the sport. Ask them to analyze your running form. Ask questions. Experiment on your own. Do not go at it too hard. Build up slowly. Be patient. There may be a New York like mine in your future. The moment of vindication.

8
Out in Front

The roles were now reversed. I was no longer able to masquerade as the underdog or the marathon runner on the way up. I was now the man to beat. I was out in front. I was expected to perform every time I ran in a major marathon. I found this out when I went back to defend in New York in 1977.

People kept coming up to me saying, "You can set a world record." All of that made me nervous and I was on edge. The field included four of the top six finishers from Montreal. Frank Shorter was present, although he was returning from an injury and he didn't figure to be a contender. Jerome Drayton, Lasse Viren, and Don Kardong were also there. The women's field was also strong, and the total field numbered five thousand.

I gear for the major marathons these days for varying reasons. A primary one is my age. I was nearing thirty when the 1977 New York City Marathon was on the horizon, and now I'm in my early thirties. I feel I have to maximize and utilize the physical abilities I possess right now. I have built up to this: Make the most of it.

Whenever the opportunity to do well is there and you are in decent shape you should seize the opportunity and run that particular race right then and there—hard. You do not get enough opportunities to run quality marathons against the top competition and under suitable weather conditions. If these circumstances are holding true, you must not pass it up. Your career is measured over a short period of time. A top-level marathoner will probably race for a supreme marathon effort only two, perhaps three times a year. Maybe in one of those all the important variables will come together the right way.

The race sponsors, race directors, New York media, treat the runners so well in New York, and the race is so well administered, that it was one I wanted to run. They also hype the race so much that you are under a microscope. They try to build up these duels between the top runners. They seem to be constantly trying to exaggerate the projected winning time, and they are always indicating there might be a world record. I guess this is normal procedure in the Big Apple.

I went to New York two days early, and because of all the activities and the interruptions, I was unable to sleep. I was restless. I never felt very good right from the beginning of the race. There was a little head wind and, combined with our five-minute pace, it felt unduly strong. I heard later that my brother, Charlie, said to some friends, "If Bill wins this, I'm a believer." I guess the odds were against my running a devastating race.

By fifteen miles, the race developed into a duel between Garry Bjorklund and me. Bjorklund, a member of the United States team in the ten-thousand-meter race at Montreal, had run one marathon. He won the Grandma's Marathon in 2:21 back in his home state of Minnesota. I suspected he might be tough and, eventually, he might be one of my main challengers.

There was a big pack for the first half of the race. This was a more competitive race than it had been the year before. The field was stronger. This may have been the best field since

Montreal. That made me apprehensive. That and the fact that I hadn't slept well for two or three nights.

The pack was too large to make any serious moves through the first twelve miles or so. There were too many people still up there, and too many would go with you. The pack slowly started to wear down and thin out, and it finally developed into a head-to-head race between Garry and me. We seemed to race away from the field after fourteen miles and we went at an extremely hard pace for the next six miles. We went over the Queensboro Bridge into Manhattan side by side. I had the feeling Garry didn't know what he was doing, yet I had to go with him.

I finally started to pull away from him with about six miles to go. Ellen was in a press vehicle ahead of me. "You have twenty yards on him," she yelled. I bore down on the pace and broke it open. The weather was cool. I never dehydrated. I was able to relax once I was away by myself.

The wall threatened at twenty-one miles. It was a gamble with my legs. They started to cramp. I tried to run efficiently. I kept telling myself that he's only run one marathon and maybe he's killed himself off after twenty miles. I had been hanging on Garry for a long time. I was pooped. I tended to relax, though, as I pulled away, and this is what is likely to happen when you open up a big gap.

I was headed for home. The closer I came to the finish, the stronger I became psychologically. I knew Garry was going to have a hard time of it catching me. He wound up finishing fifth in 2:15:16. I won in 2:11:28. Jerome Drayton came in second at 2:13:52. It was important to me to see how I'd do against Drayton and Viren in cool weather. Drayton had beaten me in Montreal and in Boston. I hadn't raced Viren since Montreal. He came in seventeenth in 2:19:33, obviously not in top form; though he ran the first half of the race at a five-minute pace.

I wasn't invited to Fukuoka in 1976, even though I'd placed third in 1975 in 2:11:26. I hadn't run well in Montreal so, even though I ran a 2:10:10 in New York, I was uninvited. I went to Japan anyway, two weeks later. I ran a marathon on Sado Island against a team of Japanese relay runners. I came in ahead of the relay team and was timed at 2:08:23, which was ten seconds under the world record of 2:08:33 run by Derek Clayton of Australia on May 30, 1969, in Antwerp.

Of course, it turned out it was about two hundred meters short of the full marathon distance and the time was unacceptable. It translated into a time of just under 2:09 for the full distance. After the race, some of the officials of the Japanese Amateur Athletic Federation sounded me out about staying around and running at Fukuoka. They may have been kidding. But in any case I was still teaching and I had to get back to school.

It was different the following year. I was invited to Fukuoka, and the field was moderately strong. I expected the main challenge to come from Leonid Moiseyev of the Soviet Union. He had placed seventh in Montreal in 2:13:33. Massimo Magnani of Italy was also in Fukuoka and he had finished thirteenth in Montreal in 2:16:56. Here were two more runners whom I was facing for the first time since they had beaten me in the Olympics.

The So brothers headed the Japanese delegation. Shigeru So had finished twentieth in Montreal and he and his twin brother Takeshi So were popular favorites. The Japanese put considerable pressure on them to do well in Fukuoka and their pictures were in all the newspapers. Tom Fleming and Vin Fleming (unrelated), a Greater Boston TC teammate who had finished a surprising fifth in Boston in 1977, were the other Americans.

I went out with Tom Fleming and we took the lead at ten kilometers. I turned to Tom and said, "I'm going to pick it up a little. Do you want to come with me?" He said, "Are you crazy, Rodgers?" I made a surge and, in the best Fukuoka tradition, everybody else seemed to go with me. I was never out of the lead, but for a long time, people were breathing down my neck. I wasn't looking back that much, so I thought I might have shaken some people. No way.

My time was 1:04:20 at the halfway mark and I was running a 2:08:40 pace. All that leading started to wear me down. I finally turned around and saw Moiseyev stalking me. Takeshi So was also right there, together with another Japanese runner. There were four of us. I finally pulled away. So dropped back first, Moiseyev slipped back at about thirty kilometers, and the second Japanese runner wouldn't let go until near the thirty-five-kilometer mark.

The crowd seemed a little more subdued when I broke away from the Japanese runners. Akio Usami won Fukuoka in 1970 and he had been the only runner from Japan to win since the race adopted the international format in 1967. We'd all thrown a party to raise money to send Tommy Leonard, the bartender at the Eliot Lounge in Boston and the guru of New England running, to Fukuoka along with me. He was on the press bus cheering for me and he said it was deadly silent when the Japanese fell back. "I almost fell out of the bus," Leonard said later.

I still heard the applause and the encouragement. They would yell, "Rodgers-san. Go hard, Rodgers-san." There is a tremendous amount of public support and understanding of marathoning in Japan. I think the crowd is as knowledgeable as Boston's crowd. They know who you are. There are only a few top foreigners, and they are looked up to by the Japanese. They know about your past performances and respect runners as superb athletes.

What makes the Fukuoka course unique is that there are no opportunities to build up momentum. There are no hills. It is flat. It's out into the countryside and back again. It's hard to break away in the early stages of the race. There's always the big pack. This is sometimes untrue of Boston and New York. I ran only with Bjorklund for company in New York two years

in a row after thirteen miles. I ran only with Drayton for
company in Boston in 1975 and 1977 after six or eight miles.

You can pass the midway point at Fukuoka and still have
ten runners there, and you are running at a 2:10 pace. It isn't
until the last ten kilometers that the leaders take over. The end
result is a fast time. It's a fast course. The weather is always
cool. You can push hard from the beginning. The competitions
consequently are more intense than Boston or New York.

I'd run so strongly in New York and I'd won by a significant
margin. I knew I was in good shape when I made the surge
eight miles into the race. It was a sudden thing. I knew the
Japanese have a tendency to stay right behind the people they
think are the favorites. They'll dog their footsteps. Moiseyev
was also doing that. This is good strategy up to a point. But
sooner or later you arrive at the moment when you have to
challenge someone, try to pass them, or try to run next to them.

I turned around and I saw Moiseyev shadowing me. It
irritated me. So and the second Japanese runner were there
and I was upset that they were dogging me and watching me in
a position of strength. I also had a feeling they were afraid to
move up. I felt I was controlling the race. I was determining
the pace. If you can do that through the entire race, it is a sign
of physical strength and dominance.

The day turned out to be mine. Moiseyev never really
challenged. The other Japanese runner came up to me at thirty
kilometers and challenged a bit. He quickly fell off. I saw
Moiseyev wearing his little hat. He always wore it. I had seen
pictures of him wearing this hat at Montreal. My fleeting
memory of this changed into a feeling of aggression and
competitiveness. I related it to my experiences in Montreal.
Here we are again. How different the race can be on any given
day.

Since I pushed hard to break away, I'd been telling myself
I'd stop for a drink of water outside Heiwadai Stadium. The
race starts with two laps around the track inside and it finishes

with one and a half laps again in the stadium in front of the crowd. This is the Olympic format. I saw I had a pretty big lead and I could hear the firecrackers going off inside the stadium to let the people know the leader was coming. I stopped, took a drink of water, and ran into the stadium.

This was a great honor. I valued it as much as winning either New York or Boston, and winning it made me the first and only runner to win all three. Fukuoka is a prestige race. It is the annual Holy Grail of marathoning. It is the race the top marathoner wants to win more than any other except the Olympic Marathon. That Frank Shorter could win this race four times consecutively is a testimony to his prowess as a marathoner that is perhaps even more meaningful than his gold medal at Munich. The best are always at Fukuoka. We went to the party at the Nishitetsu Grand Hotel, sang songs, and went out and celebrated that night in the discotheques of the city.

I was the front runner, rated the number-one marathoner in the world for 1977 by *Track and Field News*. I had achieved what I had set out to do at the start of the year. We spent a night in Tokyo, flew to Honolulu, and spent a week relaxing in the warm sunshine of Hawaii. I even tried surfing at Waikiki. It was the end of a wonderful long year in which Boston had been the disappointing start, Fukuoka the climactic end.

After the first few miles in any marathon, I try to observe the top runners. I always try, first of all, to see who's there and go over, in my mind, what they've been doing lately and what they've done in the past. In my mind, I replay races I've had against them and how they've run. Is there anybody new up there? If there is, are they going to drop back after a few miles?

Once I get into the race, I start to press the pace between six and twenty miles. Some of the others are doing the same sort of thing. There are some runners who prefer to run from the back, often forming a second front pack. Late in the race they try to put on a big surge. Don Kardong, Jeff Galloway, Randy Thomas, and Jeff Wells are this way. They put on the push in the last five or six miles. It's a strategy which suits their personalities. I'm the other way around. I push it earlier.

I try to observe how much people are sweating under the given weather conditions. I check their breathing rate, how hard they're breathing. I try to talk to them to see how they respond. In this way, I can determine how fatigued a person is. If someone can say a full sentence to you in the midst of running a sub-5:00 marathon pace at about fifteen miles and it's hot out, you know they're in control of the situation.

Jerome Drayton was that way in Boston, in 1977. I knew I was cooked. I talked to him a couple of times. I asked him if he wanted water. Jerome was dead serious in answering no, and the impression of calm control was enhanced by the dark sunglasses he habitually races in. I could tell he had the situation in hand. I was falling apart. I was trying to pretend I wasn't—I was trying to run efficiently. I talked to him and tried to show no signs of having troubles. He might have picked it up. I started looking for water very seriously. There was no sign of wavering in his voice. He went on to win and I dropped out. When he is wearing these glasses, it is next to impossible to determine his fatigue, since you can't see his eyes.

When I was running in Boston in 1978, the Finnish runner Esa Tikkanen received a bottle of water from one of his handlers and he laughed and said something to him in Finnish. This was fifteen miles into the race and we were all running a sub-5:00 pace. Here he was talking, laughing, and running that fast! He seemed in a great frame of mind. It was down to three of us and I figured he was going to be around at the end, as the other runner and I were utilizing all our energy just racing. We were not in a laughing mood.

I also look at running styles. Do any of them seem to be falling apart a little? Are they running off to the side of the road? Are they looking for shade? Looking for grass or dirt, a softer surface to ease the pain of blisters? Are they looking for water too much? The most important thing is to try to break away. Try to make it as easy on yourself as possible. After putting on this hard push from six to twenty miles, I want to be able to look forward to an easing of the race over the final miles.

If you open up a gap as I did on Bjorklund in New York, you're applying the defeating combination of physical distance and psychological distance. I'm getting closer and closer to the finish line. He's getting more and more worried about that. He's getting more and more tired in the last five or six miles of a marathon. I'm getting tired, too, but I have the psychological advantage of the gap.

This can often carry you over the physical problems. You have the crowds with you. You're the leader. You're winning. You have the motorcycle escort. You're prepared to win. There's tremendous strength that comes from being in the lead. Everything is going your way.

You can also turn around and keep your eye on the guy behind. If he starts to make a move, you increase the pace a little. If he sees you can respond to his move, it's all over. It's getting very tough for him, and once I open up a gap, I try to slow down a trifle. Keep my eye on him and maintain that pace. You don't do anything too exaggerated which would cause you to cramp or result in quick fatigue.

The unusual thing about Boston in 1978 was I was unable to savor my win. I thought I had the race under control. I found out later I ran the final thirteen miles faster than any winner in history. My time was 1:04:39. It turned out Wells ran the final thirteen miles in 1978 in 1:04:22. I kept looking back and I saw him coming on. I thought, at first, it was my Greater Boston TC teammate Randy Thomas and I said, "Oh, my God, he's going to catch me."

Wells had laid back and he came on with an incredibly strong finishing rush. He said he had too much left at the end.

I'm glad he found that out too late. I was tiring. I really had to fight it out over the final mile. I had to pick up my pace drastically. I couldn't cruise in. I couldn't savor the win. I like to be able to look around at the crowd, wave to people, put my hands up indicating I've won and thank them for supporting me. I'm a ham. It's fun. But I couldn't do it this time.

It turned out to be the closest Boston Marathon finish in history. What was a bit ironic was that I had watched the previously closest BAA Marathon finish in 1971 when Alvaro Mejia outsprinted Pat McMahon of Boston by five seconds. I couldn't believe a marathon could come down to such a finish, a virtual one-hundred-yard dash after racing over twenty-six miles.

I was 2:10:13, eighteen seconds off my American record, and the second fastest Boston time. Wells was 2:10:15, the third best Boston time. Tikkanen was third in 2:11:15, a Finnish record, followed by Jack Fultz in 2:11:17, Randy Thomas in 2:11:25 and Kevin Ryan of New Zealand in 2:11:43. Six runners had broken 2:12, making it the fastest field in history. I had run my seventh sub-2:12 time, two more than anyone else.

That completed a sweep of New York, Fukuoka and Boston within six months. One headline said I'd won the Triple Crown. I later found out that officially I hadn't. Amby Burfoot told me I'd have to do it within the same calendar year—not just within a less than twelve-month period. It set up something of a media campaign that focused on Boston, New York, and Fukuoka all in the same year.

That led to New York, 1978. The conditions were somewhat comparable to Boston, 1977. It was an Indian summer day, with the temperature rising to sixty-plus degrees by the time the race started at 10:30 A.M. It was bright and sunny. It would get up into the upper seventies by the time the race was over. Heat worried me. It worried Garry Bjorklund, too.

He had received the big buildup, the cover of the marathon program, and the article inside with the subtitle, "A Man in

Search of a Major Marathon Victory." This was the hype, the
duel the New Yorkers love to create before the race. As it
turned out. Bjorklund set a suicidal pace and I asked, "Is it
going to be like this in the future? Madmen running like this so
early in a race?"

It was a race of pressure in the heat. Whoever survived
would win. I was lucky. I had a more well-rounded training
program going in than I had had going into Boston earlier in
the year. I didn't want to get involved in a suicidal early pace,
but I had to stay in touch. I couldn't lose contact too much. I
ran behind Garry and let him set the pace, at least for part of
the run. The rest of the pack disappeared quickly behind us. •

He'd keep looking back over his shoulder. I sensed he was a
little worried about what was happening and how he was
going to handle the heat. He'd made the commitment. And,
once you do, it's hard to back off, even if it is the smart thing to
do. That's particularly true under bad-risk conditions, like the
heat that day. That's why I test myself to find out how I feel.
Another reason I temporarily pick up the pace is to check the
reaction of the pack.

I was hanging on to Garry. I think he tried to knock me out
early. That's abnormal. It's not the usual way to run a
marathon. I felt we were both going to pay the price and
neither of us would win the race. We were running too hard. I
started to notice the potholes of the course more than in any
previous New York City Marathon. It was my warmest New
York run since my 1974 run in Central Park.

The difference, this time, was I drank a lot of orange juice
about an hour before the race and, about thirty minutes before
the start, some ERG—the "electrolyte replacement with
glucose," a powder mixture which, when mixed with water, is
an excellent replacement fluid for marathoners. All through
the race, I had a lot of help. It was a team effort by Ellen,
Charlie, and a group of friends, relatives, and people who work
at our stores. I had about ten people out there passing me

special bottles of water. Ellen spent the week before the race recruiting volunteers.

There were also thousands of people along the route offering water and there were plenty of official water stands. That all saved me from the heat. I drank more water than I'd ever drunk before in a race. What I didn't drink, I poured on my body. It enabled me to win. Bjorklund slowed considerably going up the Queensboro Bridge and people saw him hunched over. He finally limped home in seventy-sixth place. He destroyed himself in much the same way I had forged a suicidal pace with Jerome Drayton at Boston in 1977.

I moved into the lead starting up over the Queensboro Bridge as we left Queens. When I entered Manhattan, I must have been one hundred yards in front. What went through my mind was, "All right. I'm alone now." If I could hang together, I knew I could win the race. I had a huge lead. The problem was, what was going to happen? Was I done in? The effects of the fast pace in the heat could be insidious. The damage may have been done. I was struggling going up the bridge and I had another twelve miles to go.

I can still remember at one point yelling to the photo truck and asking what mile it was. When they said seventeen miles I groaned and thought, "Oh, boy." Nine miles more in that heat would be tough, but to win the race would be worth it. I was fortunate. I got a lot of water. I also had the psychological lift of being in the lead. That is an incalculable advantage when you're in the latter stages of a marathon.

There is a myth about the loneliness of the long distance runner. Actually it is a half myth, as probably most of my runs are with another runner. There are times when you are out there and it does seem lonely. Even in a "mass" marathon, I have to admit I have felt that way once or twice. You have this feeling of being very much by yourself.

I touched on it once before. This despairing feeling can

sweep over you when you are falling apart in a major marathon as at Boston in 1977. There are millions of people around, but that only seems to accentuate it. "Wow, here I am bombing out and all these people are observing it." In some ways, you simply don't care. In other ways, you do.

After all, why would we be doing all this severe training unless we were aiming for competition? That involves spectators, so we are out there with a relationship to the crowd. It can be a difficult subject to talk about. The crowd, at times, is very much of a motivating factor to run well. But if you fall apart, physically, no crowd motivation in the world is going to bring you back and spur you on to a good performance.

The loneliness visits you more frequently when you are out there training—in particular, at night in the dead of winter. It is no longer any myth. It is very real, a psychological struggle to endure. I don't say, "Why am I out here?" But it's the sort of situation where I feel like just walking back home. I may go by a beautiful pond on a training run and see someone sitting on a bench watching a sailboat go by. I say, "I'd love to just sit down and watch the sailboats go by."

I never do that, though. I'm what they call an "A" class personality, I guess. I'm always moving and I haven't taken that much time off. I'm always racing. I'm always on the go. I'm tending to loosen up more, though. After Fukuoka, 1977, I went to Hawaii, stretched out on the beach, and watched the surfers and the boats go by. That was great, just to relax and unwind.

I am starting to savor my training runs more. I look forward to going out on easy, pleasant runs. For any person who is aiming for that high level of competition, those years of building up your aerobic and anaerobic capacities are tough years. Everybody who has gone through them has to feel the same way. Once you get to the top, it's nowhere nearly as hard to maintain that level, but it's getting there that can be difficult. That's when you feel the loneliness, the discouraging and empty moments. No matter if your goals as a runner are not as high as mine, you will still feel those moments of pushing, forcing yourself, breaking through to new distances, new feelings, and deeper understanding of the sport.

What helped me through these times was being able to run and train with the members of the Greater Boston TC, and, of course, Ellen. She has even started to run with me. She used to bicycle with me on my long runs around Jamaica Pond. The Greater Boston TC has always been very socially oriented. There were always parties. We'd meet at the Eliot Lounge in Boston, where Tommy Leonard bartends. I can remember, in the middle of a track workout, relishing the thought of meeting with Tommy Leonard at the Eliot. We'd all go down there, have some gin and tonics or a Blue Whale (That's an Eliot Lounge special—vodka and curaçao. It looks like Windex.).

I'm at the point in my career now where I've been running hard for six years. I've built up to a pretty high level. More than ever, I want to train with other people. I've won a number of big races, so I'm no longer as hungry. I'm not as intense. I've reached many of my goals, and it's more difficult to get out there and push myself. It helps to be carried along on my runs by someone else.

That's an important thing about dealing with boredom. You run the same course. You see those long stretches spread out in front of you. Sometimes, you can almost flip out from it. It can be difficult, psychologically, to handle it. I'm lucky. In Boston, there are a number of quality runners in the area. I can go out with Greg Meyer, Chuck Riley, Jack Fultz, Randy Thomas, Bob Hodge, Scott Graham, and Vinnie Fleming. It's always been true of the Boston area. Even when I was starting out again in 1973 and I was working at the Fernald School, I'd go over to Bentley College and train with Bob Sevene. Die-hard runners never die. If they do, they die hard.

One of the concomitant aspects of being out in front is the fame and notoriety that goes with it. Because I started winning the major races as the running boom mushroomed, maintaining a certain degree of privacy and trying to lead a personal life has been difficult.

Once again, Ellen has been a significant factor in enabling me to live a somewhat normal life. She acts as a buffer between me and organizations and individuals who want a piece of my time as a competitor, a speaker, a spokesman, or a supporter of some organization or cause. It's enabled me to rest a lot and avoid dealing with many of the distractions. Many are business matters, which is not my forte.

My job is to train well, to run well, to be a public relations man for the stores and the clothing line. I try to answer letters. I go to clinics and speak at YMCAs, running clubs, and before various groups. I travel, do TV and radio shows, and talk to writers. That is what my job has evolved into. When I first opened the store, I tried to work as a shoe salesman. It was possible for a little while, but since then, there are too many attendant matters to handle. And I figured I could always hire someone to sell shoes.

Have I changed? It's impossible to give an objective answer. I've probably become more critical of some of the people I've trained with or I've trained under in the past two or three years. Since money has entered the sport, many runners, coaches, and medical people want their cut of the pie. There have been some conflicts and differences of opinion between me and some of these people.

This is inevitable. That's the business aspect of running, and I've been caught up in it in negative ways. Once, I was involved in a clinic and it became a big mess. I didn't really understand what was going on. I'm learning my lessons. I'm learning that it's best to stay out of that sort of thing. There is only so much you can do. I found I have to concentrate on my running and let other people deal with these situations.

I try to keep my lines of communication very clear. A couple of times I arranged for races or speaking engagements and I didn't have everything clearly defined. What was expected of me? What did I expect from the person who was arranging the race or the speaking engagement? I had some bad experiences and, as in running, I learned from them. It's one more learning process I had to go through.

The most important thing for me is to run well and to keep on running. That's where my priorities lie. That's what comes first.

9
On the Roads

Let's take a backward look to Falmouth, 1974. Noontime on a hot, humid Cape Cod August day. The boy on the rooftop of the Captain Kidd Restaurant in Woods Hole sounded the trumpet, the "Call to the Post." There were 445 of us outside on the street, waiting to take off over the seven miles from Woods Hole and the National Oceanographic Center to a finish line in front of the Brothers 4, a nightclub in Falmouth Heights.

This was the second Falmouth Road Race, known at the time as the Woods Hole to Falmouth Road Race. It was the inspiration and the fantasy of Tommy Leonard, the bartender from the Eliot Lounge in Boston. He had worked at the Brothers 4, and in 1972, he had the TV set turned on when Frank Shorter won the gold medal in the Olympic Marathon.

"I thought at the time," Tommy has said, "that it'd be great to have a road race right here in Falmouth, all the runners going by the Brothers 4." He had helped organize a bicycle race one summer, but running was Tommy Leonard's passion.

"I've never met a runner I didn't like," he has said. So, he started the road race. The first one was run on a Wednesday afternoon in 1973, and about 125 runners showed up to do the course in the rain.

After I recovered from Boston in 1974, I returned to the road, seeking out places to go. I read an article in the *Boston Globe* about Falmouth and Tommy and how he said there would be girls wearing bikinis along the route handing out water. There was talk about a big picnic after the race and a general party atmosphere. It was a different twist to road racing, an event with a lot of pizzazz. It sounded like Tommy. I often think he could promote a road race on the moon.

I was also aware that Marty Liquori was coming and that added to the interest. His brother Steve, who was a student at Boston College, used to go into the Eliot Lounge and Tommy talked him into inviting Marty. He was up at a camp in Poughkeepsie, New York, and he thought it was a drive of three hours or so. It was a lot longer than that. He also thought he would just show up and win.

He was a great miler, but he had no road racing experience. "This is the farthest I've ever run competitively," Liquori said. I was a long-distance runner. I felt, even then, that any long-distance runner worth his salt could put a miler away at anything over ten thousand meters or seven miles. I knew there would be a critical line there and it might be a pretty interesting race. It was.

When the gun went off, Marty and I went out together with a few runners. We broke away pretty early, as the course bends around a lighthouse overlooking Vineyard Sound and heads into two miles of gentle hills through the woods. Liquori suddenly became aware that he was going to have a hard race on his hands. He actually fell back after about a mile and a half.

I ran as hard as I could for about three or four miles and, by then, I was well out in front as we ran by the beaches and headed through a residential area before we went around Falmouth Harbor and up the hill to the Brothers 4. People on the press truck were yelling out, "Who are you?" I yelled back, "Bill Rodgers." I won the race in 34:16 and Liquori finished second in 35:35.

This was my introduction to the media in the Massachusetts area. My name came out Will Rogers and the people wrote how nostalgic it sounded. Will was a nickname given to me by some of my Greater Boston TC teammates. It was short for William, or Willha, which is our GBTC Finnish derivative of William. We all called ourselves by Finnish nicknames out of the respect we had for Finnish distance runners. Most of these Finnish names ended with a "ha" or "ho." So, we had Scotthas, Vin-hos, Todd-hos on our team. We sometimes used Kenyan nicknames for the same reason. Somebody would be Kip. Or, having read of John Ngeno running up a tough hill on his daily training runs and calling it "Ngeno's Hill," we would pick out a hill and name it for someone in the club. There was a "Kirk Pfrangle Hill," for instance.

Some of the writers had asked Tommy Leonard at Falmouth in 1974, "Is it Will Rogers, just like the humorist?" He said, "Yes," which is why it came out that way then. I was still known as "Will" when I won Boston in April 1975, and some people still call me Will, but it usually comes out Bill in the papers, and ever since 1975 they spell Rodgers correctly.

First prize was a Waring blender, something I still mix my banana, milk, and egg milkshakes in. The police also had my car towed from Falmouth Heights. It enraged Tommy Leonard and he started ranting and raving about how an amateur athlete could run a race, win it, and get his car towed in the same town. George Robbat, the owner of the Brothers 4, went down and retrieved it. It took some serious negotiating—he paid the twenty-dollar fine. I received no expense money for the race, and the princely sum of twenty dollars was substantial for me in 1974. I was quite pleased to have won the race and received such a useful piece of merchandise as my first-place prize. I'd already won my share of irons and toasters, but I didn't have a blender.

I never imagined, in the summer of 1974, that road racing would become as big as it has. To me, it was just another race on an August weekend with a few extra touches that set it off from the average race. I never realized there would be what amounts to a road-race circuit. It was a sweet win, a victory over a world-class athlete. I was a giant killer, the unknown who had upstaged the celebrity. It was somewhat unfair to Marty, since he was a better runner on the track. Whatever, in road running I am now in the position he was in then—the guy to beat.

Road racing, in general, has gone through a number of periods of growth and decline in the United States. There are certain areas where it has always been much stronger than in others. Massachusetts has been the keystone state in New England. This is largely due to the influence and the history of the Boston Marathon.

I took to road racing because I never had the leg speed or the fast-twitch fibers in my muscle tissue which would project me as a top middle-distance runner, or anyone who was able to excel at any event up to five thousand meters. I naturally gravitated to the roads, where the distances were from ten thousand meters to the marathon. I also came from Connecticut and, in moving to Massachusetts, found a home.

The tradition preceded me. For fifty years, New England had produced some of the top distance runners in the nation. It was a stagelike situation, where Clarence DeMar came before Johnny Kelley the elder. Johnny Kelley, the younger, came next. Then, Amby Burfoot. I feel, in a way, I am following Amby on the New England scene.

Perhaps it is an outgrowth of our New England climate. We haven't excelled on the tracks, but we run all year on the roads and there are races every month in every conceivable kind of weather. Since there were few track meets available, I took to the roads and it enabled me to learn strategy, technique, and how to race on the roads.

For a long time, when you talked about road racing in America, most people thought in terms of car racing. Unless one of our races was in a particular city where it received decent press attention, the coverage of something such as the Pocono 500 with Al Unser outstripped an important road running race in the morning paper. Now that there are twenty-five million people out there running, this has slowly changed.

I ran my first road race when I was eighteen, in 1966. I placed eighteenth in the Manchester Thanksgiving Day Five-Miler in Connecticut, not too far from my home in Newington. I was the first high school runner to finish. Most of my training in high school had been interval work, and it was very rare for me to go out on the roads for a training run. When I did, it was usually about three miles. I ran one twelve-mile workout during my senior year. That was, for me, as significant as a first marathon is for many people.

As I pointed out before, Amby Burfoot was aware of the importance of a good aerobic base, doing a lot of high-mileage training on the roads. He would try to get me to keep going during the summers. I was too lackadaisical. But my racing in college was all on the track, except for cross-country season. I did well running cross-country, but I seldom tried running on the roads.

I ran one thirteen-mile race in my freshman year in the winter. I bundled on a huge sweater and wore some ordinary pants. It was a terrible experience in the cold. I ran my second road race in college in Meriden, Connecticut, and I placed second behind Pat McMahon of Massachusetts in about fifty-three minutes for ten miles. It was a hard, long race in the heat.

My primary feeling about those races was how brutally hard they were—partly because I ran one of the races in the dead of winter and the second one in the dead of summer. They were

both a little too long for me and they were run under
conditions that were too adverse. Beginning runners should
not get involved in their first races until they have an adequate
background and know that the conditions are favorable. The
fall and early spring in the North are the best times for road
races. The heat of summer and the cold of winter are the worst
times.

Running behind Amby enabled me to build up a base and it
came by running on the roads, particularly out in the country
where there were few cars and distractions. I could concentrate on my running. It was just the open road ahead of us.
There was tremendous diversity of courses, and this was what
appealed to me more than anything. I never became bored
when I was out in the countryside.

I ran my last competitive race on the track at the Coast Guard
Academy in New London, Connecticut, in December 1969. I
ran my next race in Newton, Massachusetts, in February 1973.
It was a twenty-mile race and I placed third. I ran in blue jeans.
That was the real beginning. I ran in a thirty-kilometer race
about one month later and I placed second. I won a twelve-
mile race as a tune-up for Boston, 1973. Because I built up
slowly, I have avoided major injury.

After I won the National Twenty-Kilometer Championship
on the roads of Gloucester in October 1973, the AAU invited
me to compete in the San Blas Road Race in Coamo, Puerto
Rico, a 13.1-mile race. It was my first international road race.
They have always brought in the top runners, Lasse Viren,
Henry Rono; Americans such as Gary Tuttle, John Vitale, Barry
Brown, Chuck Smead, and Amby Burfoot. I was following
Amby again.

I can remember going out through a January blizzard in
Massachusetts to train and prepare for the race. I learned an
interesting lesson. You can't go from cold like that to the
eighty-five-degree heat of Puerto Rico and race two days later.
You can't adapt to the heat in such a short time.

So, I started off slowly, running at a moderate pace for the first two miles. All of a sudden, I saw Lasse Viren ahead of me. I went after him and passed him. We were in the lead and it developed into a duel that also involved Seppo Tuominen of Finland. After about five miles, Tuominen and I lost some of our steam. I led for another mile, until Viren came chugging up beside me and went by me. I hung on and finished seventh, the second American, in 1:08:28. Tom Fleming was the first American finisher.

It's a hard, hilly, hot course, and I came out of the race with blisters. It was an unusual experience, running with the top Europeans and rubbing shoulders with them. I heard how Viren did 150 miles in a week and while I was trying for around 130 to 140, I often didn't get that in. I realized there had to be some of those higher-mileage weeks if I wanted to compete successfully on the international level.

The race is part of a weekend festival, which includes much dancing, singing, amusement rides, and games. Coamo is a small town in the center of Puerto Rico. The festival is named after St. Blaise, the patron saint of the throat. The race is the climax of the weekend. It starts at 4:00 P.M. The area is mountainous. You can see the spires of a church at the finish line for two miles as you come off the mountains. You steadily start coming down, down, down, toward the church, and with one mile to go, you can see a straight line to the church.

You sprint down between a narrow alley of thousands of screaming people. It's an exciting race, but it is a very arduous run. It's a grind in that heat. It seems every time I run it I end up lying in bed with a wet washcloth on my head as I recuperate. After that, we all go out and carouse a little. It is a festive, party atmosphere. I can still see Lasse Viren, Tapio Kantoren, and Seppo Tuominen chugging rum, straight from the bottle, and offering us all a drink. The Finns had taken all three top places that day and they played as hard as they raced.

I went back with Ellen in 1978, partly to escape the New

England weather and partly to get in a hard early-season race. Columbian Domingo Tibaduiza, who had recently won the São Silvestre Midnight Run in São Paulo, Brazil, was there. Chuck Smead, who held the American record for the San Blas course, was running. So were Henry Rono and Washington State–Kenyan teammates Josh Kimento, Joel Cheryiot, and Samson Kimombua. A contingent of Europeans and Latin Americans rounded out the field. This event truly has an international flavor. Unfortunately, they never have a strong field of women, and this is one of the weaknesses of San Blas.

I knew Rono had run 27:47 for ten thousand meters in Australia about a week or two before. I also knew he had not done so well in this half-marathon-distance race the previous year. He had dropped out with stomach troubles. I wondered if his stomach troubles were caused by a man named Miruts Yifter, who was the winner of that race in an incredible course record of 1:02:56. But I knew Rono was running to win this time. I knew I wasn't in 27:47 shape for ten thousand meters, and I didn't know how close I could get to a respectable one hour-plus for this distance. And to make matters worse, I awakened on the morning of the race with diarrhea. I had to take some medication.

I was staying with the Matos family, and their house was at the two-and-a-half-mile mark on the course. I decided to start the race and if I felt really poor, I'd drop out at the house. I started out slowly and as I came past the Mantos house, I saw the four Kenyans up in front running together in the lead. This made me feel very competitive because one or two of the Kenyans had told me they were just going to run easy. I felt I'd go up and try to bust up their group. It took me ten miles to do it, but I passed everybody except Rono.

What happened was that as soon as I started getting close, they'd break away as a group and one of them would fall off. First it was Josh Kimento. I caught up with him. Josh and I talked a bit and after I'd recovered from catching him, I moved on. Next, it was Joel Cheryiot. Finally, it was Kimombua and Rono. When Rono looked back and saw me gaining on him, he took off up the hill. Kimombua fell back and we ran together for a short distance. There's a stretch of three miles between seven and ten miles as you go uphill. When you get to the top, it is downhill to the finish, and this is my strong suit in road running.

I finally caught Rono at perhaps the eleven- or twelve-mile mark. I pulled up to him and said, "You're running a nice race, Henry." He said nothing. When we came to the flat, we ran neck and neck. With about three hundred yards to go, he just outkicked me to the finish and beat me by nine seconds. I was lucky enough to set a new American record of 1:04:55 for the course, and Henry went on to a very big year. He set four world records on the track. I have no illusions. I know he has forty-nine-second quarter speed. I'd still like to race against him on the roads some more in the future. But, that day was a tough one for me. For four or five hours after the race, I had to lie down with a cold washcloth on my head and sip cool drinks.

The road-race circuit has grown out of the current running boom. There are races for everybody. There are often as many as nine or ten on a given Saturday or Sunday in the New England area. Some of them are new. Some are established fixtures. Some have small budgets and low profiles and are run well because of the work of a few individuals who are sufficiently inspired to put on a class race. One of the beauties of road racing is that these races exist. You don't have to go to New York City to run with the twelve thousand.

I ran in thirty-five races in 1978. That includes two cross-country races, three track races, and thirty road races. I had twenty-four wins, three ties, and eight losses. Three of my losses were on the track and two were in cross-country. In my only race ever at that distance, I ran 13:42 for five thousand meters in Oslo, Norway, and I was close to my personal best for ten thousand meters when I ran 28:05 in Stockholm. I ran one ten-thousand-meter race at the Crystal Palace in Great Britain and did 29:09. I was totally destroyed.

Randy Thomas, who emerged as the number-two road racer in America in 1978, tied me in the Freedom Trail Race in Boston and in a half marathon in Cleveland, and Tom Fleming tied me in a Diet Pepsi race in Vernon Gorge, New Jersey. I ran three weekend doubles. I ran a fifteen-kilometer race in Jacksonville, Florida, and the Perrier Cherry Blossom ten-miler in early April. I ran in Mobile, Alabama, in a ten-kilometer race and in a fifteen-kilometer race in Cincinnati on a weekend in March. I also ran in the Lynchburg, Virginia, ten-miler and the Perrier Beverly Hills, California, ten-kilometer in September.

In terms of total accomplishment, 1978 was my best year. I fared poorly in the International Cross-Country Champion-ships in Glasgow, Scotland, but I had experienced flight difficulties, and weather conditions turned the course into a quagmire. It was cold and windy and it kept changing from snow to sleet to rain. It was muddy, with logs and uneven surfaces to run over. I am more of a rhythm runner. I like the flat, wide open roads to run on. I'm better on the roads because of temperament and physiology.

Yet, I had a fine time in Scotland, because we had a great crew of American runners on the team. I got to know Mike Roche, Jeff Wells, and Greg Meyer as a result of the trip and I learned of the big difference between American and European cross-country. The race is regarded with high esteem by European sportsmen. When John Treacy, the runner from Providence College and Villierstown in County Waterford, Ireland, won it for the first time, he became a national hero. It was televised live by the BBC and shown throughout Ireland. Treacy became the first runner in twenty-two years to repeat, when he won the 1979 championship in Limerick, Ireland.

The American team trip to the World Cross-Country Championships has to be one of the finest trips available to an amateur runner. Usually the trip lasts at least one week and is similar to the Olympics, in that a truly international field is represented. That's been true of recent competitions. Originally, the race was run primarily by the English, Scottish, Belgian, and Welsh. The World Cross-Country competition is perhaps the finest quality running competition in the world, the Olympics included.

I believe this to be true because the best runners from a whole variety of distance backgrounds compete against each other at a moderately long distance (twelve kilometers, about seven miles) requiring strength, speed, intelligent pacing, and courage. There may be thirty nations represented by junior, senior, men's, and women's teams. The juniors run first, followed by the senior women and men. Since the course is the same for all participants except for the distance, by the time the senior men get moving, the course is often well worn and chewed up. Often the race is a circuit, perhaps run over the oval of a horsetrack, and is completed two, three or four times.

It is indicative of the male chauvinism of most American sports that few sports fans would recognize the name of Doris Brown, five-time American winner of the International Cross-Country race. To my knowledge, no American senior male has ever won this prestigious race, although several juniors have done so. American teams generally do well at this competition and in 1978, the senior men's team lost to France by only a few points. Usually, the competition is imbued with the ethnic flavor of the host country, and its cultural traditions and displays are featured at these races.

Because of the corporate sponsorship, the top American runners now travel around the country to participate in road races. When I ran at Falmouth in 1974, everything was still pretty local. Tommy Leonard had to go around the community and hustle prizes from merchants. He frequently had more support from his friends in Boston than from people in Falmouth. It's perhaps ironic, as well, that the first American gold medalist in sixty-four years in the Olympic Marathon was brought into a small, recently evolved, local road race, but could not be brought in for the eighty-year-old Boston Marathon.

Some 850 started in 1975, when Frank Shorter was induced to run, and he beat me to the finish, which was now by the ballfield in Falmouth Heights. Another bit of irony is that I wrote to Shorter to ask him to run at the request of Tommy Leonard. There were 2,090 starters in 1976, when Shorter beat me again. By now, sponsorship was forthcoming from a beer company and a store for runners in Boston. Perrier became involved in 1977, when I finally beat Shorter. This was the first involvement of the French mineral water company with the sport it has since become identified with. In 1977, Falmouth was officially closed within two weeks after the supposed fixed limit of 2,500 was surpassed, but the field eventually topped off at 2,850.

The zenith was on August 20, 1978. The field included eleven sub-four-minute milers and sixteen national AAU champions at a variety of distances. There were nine Olympians among the 3,400 official starters. The race had been shut off in May, but acquiring a number had become a status symbol. People were willing to pay for numbers held by people who weren't running. Tommy Leonard dreads picking up the phone at the Eliot Lounge from the day the race is filled until after it is history. He's heard every imaginable complaint, listened to every sob story.

The field has to be limited. It still starts in front of the Captain Kidd just before the little drawbridge that spans the channel into Eel Pond. "I've had nightmares," Leonard has said, "about the drawbridge going up just before the start of the race." The starting area is rather narrow, so it takes runners in the back of the pack a long time to get started. There are spectacular aerial photographs showing the long line of runners filing out of Woods Hole, past the lighthouse and along the ocean.

The timing of the race is perfect. It is in late August, the waning month of a New England summer. You get the top college runners just before they return to school. You get some of the American runners returning from the European circuit. The event does not really have an international flavor, although Hilary Tuiwei of Kenya has run a couple of Falmouths. This is normal for American road races, although I believe more foreigners will be imported to run on the roads and outdoor tracks in the United States in the future. Falmouth is a mixture of competition at all levels—sun and fun and parties. People plan their vacations around it. There is a lot of socializing and that is a very significant and major part of the weekend that is Falmouth.

It's difficult to break away too early in the Falmouth race. One reason, of course, is the field: Craig Virgin, Garry Bjorklund, Greg Fredericks, Hilary Tuiwei, Frank Shorter, Randy Thomas, Greg Meyer, Mike Roche, Alberto Salazar, Marty Liquori, Mike Slack. They have all been there. The women's field has been strong: Joan Benoit, Kim Merritt, Martha White, Gayle Barron, Ellison Goodall, Patti Lyons, Julie Brown, and Marge Rosasco. The second reason it is hard to break away is that the roads are narrow, bending and twisting through the woods and over small hills for the first three miles. When you leave the woods, it flattens out and you start encountering the real crowds that have numbered as many as 25,000.

You go up that final hill, with Vineyard Sound on one side, and over a crest. You have a sprint of 120 yards or so to the finish by the ball field. The crowd at the ball field is huge to begin with and is, of course, swelled even more eventually by all the finishers. There is a giant picnic, with hot dogs and corn on the cob and all kinds of beverages. Fittingly, Perrier mineral water is most abundant. Bill Dougherty, who has been involved with the race since its inception, oversees the food operation. He has since franchised his business and caters to many of the top road races in New England.

Tommy Leonard is the inspiration, the personification of Falmouth. The guys who do the nuts and bolts work are John Carroll, a former runner at Boston College and the coach of the Falmouth Track Club and Rich Sherman, who was formerly the recreation director for the town of Falmouth. They process the entries, paint the numbers in the roads, order and sell the T-shirts, and do much of the organizational work. Tommy deals with the media and recruits the top runners. He even invited the University of Texas Marching Band to come to the 1979 race. He is the dreamer who conceived of this event to raise funds for the Falmouth Track Club, and he is the man who struggles each year to make it better for everyone—every runner and every spectator. This love for the sport has not gone unnoticed by his friends and the spectators at the race. He's actually had "Happy Birthday" sung to him by hundreds of spectators at the awards ceremony.

LYNCHBURG.   This is the top ten-mile race in the country—by far. It is held in a small town up in the mountains of western Virginia, an unlikely setting for such a high-quality event. The course is hilly, out and back like an eccentric ring. The beauty of the countryside enhances the central piece, the race.

It is sponsored by an insurance company, and Rudy Straub, the Director of the Lynchburg race, puts on a tremendously well-run race. The first race was run in 1974, with John Vitale the winner. Lynchburg has attracted fields including Jerome Drayton, Lasse Viren, Frank Shorter, Brendan Foster, Herb Lindsey, Grete Waitz, Jacqueline Hansen, Carol Fridley, Marge Rosasco, the Shea sisters, Miki Gorman, and Ellison Goodall.

The people in the city certainly support the race. The

publicity is excellent and the race sponsor, First Colony Life, spares no expense. Everything is first class. The course is set up so it is impossible to get lost, yet it is hilly and attractive. There are brochures that are put out after the race and results are mailed to the runners. Every time is available for everybody on the day of the race. The awards ceremony, like the timing and complete race administration, is precisely completed. Awards are high quality and unique—such as sets of pewter and rocking chairs. This is a race I look forward to every September.

THE PEACHTREE. Staying in the south, the Atlanta Peachtree Race on July fourth is the largest in that part of the country, a race with consistently top performers. They have had fields in excess of twenty thousand, in spite of the heat. They go out and bring in Viren, Greg Meyer, Don Kardong, Craig Virgin, and Mike Roche. The *Atlanta Journal* is one of the sponsors. Jeff Galloway, with whom I used to run at Wesleyan, and Bill Neace were the race directors until 1979, when Jeff stepped down and Bob Varsha took over.

Until the course was changed in 1978, it was always one of the toughest on the circuit. The first mile was downhill, so everybody went out fast. The last five miles went over rolling hills, with the longest stretches going up. Combined with the terrific heat, it made it a demanding ten-thousand-meter run. Kardong held the record for the old course, when he ran 29:14 before the 1976 Olympics. Craig Virgin established a new course record of 28:30 in 1979.

Peachtree has grown into a people's race. Few races have the facilities, course design, and organization to permit so many people. Falmouth suffers in this regard. The streets are not wide enough. But in Atlanta you run along Peachtree Street, a wide thoroughfare. You do lack the spectators of Falmouth, with the festive, somewhat wild resort atmosphere, and that's probably because people in Atlanta are out of town for the long, hot weekend. But with twenty thousand runners, the interest in the sport is obviously burgeoning in the south. Peachtree also has the most informal of awards ceremonies, in keeping with the spirit of the race.

SPRINGBANK. The scenario for the Springbank Road Race in London, Ontario, is attractive. There are several different races for men and for women, ranging from four and a half miles to the feature, the twelve-miler for men. This race is older than Falmouth, Lynchburg, and Peachtree. The prestige is considerable, nearly matching the Boston in terms of quality of competition. Miruts Yifter of Ethiopia, Neil Cusack of Ireland, Ron Hill, Ian Stewart, Nick Rose, and Tony Simmons of Great Britain, Jerome Drayton and Grant McLaren of Canada, John Anderson, Tom Fleming, Kenny Moore, Frank Shorter, and Duncan McDonald of the United States have all run at Springbank. Francie Larrieu, Brenda Webb, Katy Schilly, and other top women road racers have also raced here.

There is a race here for the leading masters—the over-forty division—and it's one of the best anywhere in the world. It is an opportunity for reunion, which is fairly rare. It is perhaps the best-known road race in Canada, one held in high regard by Americans. The races are all held on the same day in September and they all go a different number of times over the same oval course in Springbank Park. The fields aren't very large, limited somewhat by the narrow asphalt race course through the park. The weather is usually cool. The road winds through a wooded, scenic area. It's a fairly flat course. There is one large hill and in the twelve-mile race, you face it four times. The only weakness has been an occasional inconsistency in management of the race and in the financial support.

FREEDOM TRAIL. The newest of the top road races on the American circuit is the Freedom Trail Road Race in Boston in early Fall. This is also the result of some inspired thinking by Tommy Leonard. "Why not have a road race in the city, starting and finishing by the Waterfront?" he asked. That started the ball rolling and, in 1977, it became a reality. It is put on by the Greater Boston Track Club and, in its first two years, was sponsored by Labatt's, the Canadian beer company. That was somewhat ironic, a Canadian beer company promoting the sport in the United States. Of course, American beer companies are now following suit.

The course takes in many of the stops on the historic Freedom Trail in Boston. It starts and finishes in Waterfront Park, not too far from my second store. It goes over the streets of the North End, into historic Charlestown and past the Bunker Hill Monument, up the Cambridge side of the Charles River and back to Boston through the Back Bay over parts of the Boston Marathon course, along Commonwealth Avenue to Beacon Hill, and into the financial district. It was closed out at three thousand in Year Number 1, was limited to the same number of runners in 1978 and 1979, and the quota was filled in a few weeks.

It is an eight-mile course, with a few small, eighty-yard hills. You hit the final uphill segment about two miles from the finish, when you go up Beacon Street by the State House. There were chaotic overtones the first year, when the traffic control was poor and the press bus was briefly unable to get past a tourist bus by the Bunker Hill Monument. We had to go on the sidewalks, and later on, there were problems with traffic control in the city. Such difficulties are not rare in the inaugural year of a road race.

Problems that were a part of the first year have largely been ironed out. The race does suffer from lack of media exposure in Boston. The newspapers are wrapped up at that time of year with the Red Sox and the end of the baseball season, the Patriots and the pro football teams. The Greater Boston TC and Labatt's held a press conference one year and the press did not show. They were more interested in who the new owners of the Red Sox were. The awards ceremony, which is very informal, is put on at City Hall Plaza. The awards are unique, such as paintings done by Johnny Kelley the elder. There is an outdoor feast, an after the second race, they put on a block party by The Exchange Restaurant, which is race headquarters in the financial district.

The worst thing a runner can possibly do to his or her feet and legs is to run on concrete all the time. Concrete does not give, and the shock is damaging to your joints and muscle tissue. Most of my training is on the side of asphalt-paved roads. You must train over the surface you expect to race over most frequently. I do like to vary the terrain and I try to run on grass or dirt trails. It's easier on your feet.

The number-one enemy of the runner is the automobile, and I'm not referring to the effects of pollution in the air. You should always run facing the traffic. I know of many runners who have been killed or seriously injured by vehicular traffic in the course of a training run. Some of them have been right next to me when they've been struck down. One such driver was an adolescent car thief. Another was a middle-aged woman. After knocking my friend through the air with her car, she confessed, "I have a lot on my mind."

Train your legs for the types of pressures and strains you are going to put them under during a race. If you are preparing for a track race, train more than usual on the track. If you are into cross-country, stick a bit more to the woods and golf courses. For road races, you must get adjusted to road surfaces.

You can adjust without injury if you progress with moderate regularity in both the number of miles you run and how hard you run them. Explore cautiously. I have been running an average of 130 miles per week for several years on the roads and I have never had a serious injury. I do occasionally experience some chronic aggravation to the metatarsal bones on the bottoms of my feet from all the pounding. That's the price you pay. That's only normal.

DOGS.   Even though I've never been bitten by a dog, I have been attacked. What I do is pretend I have a rock in my hands and I make a gesture as if I'm going to throw the rock at the dog. I try to ease my way out of there. I always keep looking behind to make sure the dog isn't sneaking up. Some dogs will do that and try to take a bite out of you. One technique is to cross to the other side of the street if you see a dog ahead of you on your run.

If a dog is persistent, I'll actually look for a rock and try to hit him. I'll throw anything at him. Of course, the usual method of scaring away an attacking dog is to try and kick him. The danger there is that you might injure your leg by wildly lashing out at the animal. Any dog that attacks a person ought to be taught a lesson by being chased away with a stone or stick. I've tried everything. I've even tried climbing trees to elude dogs.

I ran one race in Amherst, Massachusetts. I was leading after three miles of the ten-mile race. All of a sudden, this collie came charging out at me. I froze for an instant, then dashed over to the side of the road. I didn't know if I should sprint and try to run away from the dog or face up to him and fight him. I realized he could run faster than I could. I grabbed a rock, spun around, and nailed the dog right on the snout. It made a loud thunking noise, bounced off the snout, and smashed through the window of the house of the people who owned the dog. I took off and found myself in third place. But I had so much adrenaline flowing, I caught up to the leader and won.

One winter day when I was out with Alberto Salazar, Scott Graham, and Vin Fleming of the Greater Boston TC for a twenty-mile run, we were attacked by this gigantic Great Dane. Salazar was a skinny kid at the time and, for some reason, the Great Dane picked him out as the guy he wanted. I was in the habit of running with my car keys in one hand, and when the dog seemed to be favoring The Rookie, I spun around and threw the keys at the dog as hard as I could. They caught the Great Dane in the side and it shocked him so much, he just turned around and ran. We followed suit, in the opposite direction.

SNOW. It becomes a particularly big problem in the cities. Your normal running areas are eliminated or narrowed down. One incident stands out and it involves cars as well. I was running down a one-way street with Randy Thomas and some others during the winter of 1978 in the Boston area. It was the year of The Blizzard. It was the roughest winter of the century in Boston and even though I escaped from some of it by picking out races in warmer climates, unfortunately, I was there to endure enough of it.

The snow mounds narrowed the width of the roads and, as we ran down this one-way street, I heard a car coming up fast behind me. Randy yelled at the driver as he whizzed by and I reached out and hit the back of the car with my fist. He went on for another fifty yards, stopped, put the car in reverse, and roared back in our direction. He turned the car around, aimed it straight at me, and tried to run me over. I managed to avoid the car and we ran off.

There have been countless instances like this when drivers purposely try to run down runners. Believe it or not, some of them do it just for a lark. They open their car or truck doors and try to hit runners. It happened, on several occasions, to Dave McGillivray, a Greater Boston TC runner who ran from Medford, Oregon, to his hometown of Medford, Mas-sachusetts, in the summer of 1978. He said it was one of the major hazards he encountered on his 3,600 mile run.

You have to be conscious of cars and keep as far as you can to the side of the road. Run on sidewalks, if you can. Do not tempt somebody with a four-thousand-pound weapon under his control. Running in foot-deep snow is preferable to running by the side of the road. I took down the license number of the guy who tried to run me down and reported it to the Registry of Motor Vehicles in Massachusetts with a letter indicating I had witnesses. They never responded. Court action was an alternative, but I let it die.

STRATEGY. Isn't it a geometric axiom that the shortest distance between two points is a straight line? It is an important axiom to remember in road racing. Run the shortest straight line and watch your opposition at sharp corners. I ran in the Lynchburg ten-miler in 1975 and was with Frank Shorter as we came down a hill. We were faced with a ninety-degree right turn. He took a sharp turn. I went wide, because I thought I had too much momentum and I was to the left of Frank. He instantly gained about ten yards on me with a little surge.

It's also wise to be well clear of any runners at corners to avoid bumping and either falling or having your stride and running rhythm altered to your disadvantage. Well before the turn be sure you're in good position. You won't be caught on the inside and be squeezed to the curb. This is especially important early in a road race when the field is crowded and maneuverability is limited.

Strategy is important on the roads. Perhaps not as important as it is on the track, but it is a significant factor. It gives you the edge. What it all comes down to, once again, is experience. You learn to specialize and key your training for the type of racing you are into. You learn to adapt your strides to road racing. There is more to it than simply being a good runner and keeping in the best physical condition.

10
On the Track

SARATOGA, CALIFORNIA, 1979. Cloudy, overcast, a light rain. There was a slight trace of a breeze cutting through the early February air. Back home in Boston, they were living through the deep freeze, something quite close to The Blizzard of 1978, minus the deep snow. In the winter of 1979, records were set for consecutive days when the thermometer failed to rise above freezing. I was happy to miss at least part of the long New England winter.

I was about to go for a world record, my first. When I started to plan the venture, I was thinking of two world records and, as it turned out, they were within reach. What I was aiming at was the world record of 1:14:17 for twenty-five kilometers owned by Pekka Paivarinta of Finland and run at Oulu on May 15, 1975, and the thirty-kilometer standard of 1:31:31 run by Jim Alder of Great Britain in London on September 5, 1970.

This was all an outgrowth of the hour run I did on the track at Boston University on August 9, 1977. That was the idea of Billy Squires, the Greater Boston TC coach, who thought I could set a number of American records on the track. I went over about 7:00 P.M. and ran most of the race by myself, dodging frisbees and running amid the distractions of soccer games going on in the infield.

I was fortunate to have a good day and I bettered three American records, all previously held by Gary Tuttle. I set the fifteen-kilometer record of 43:39.8, the twenty-kilometer record of 58:15, and the one-hour run record of 12 miles, 1,351 yards, and two feet. The pace was about 4:42 per mile. The world record for the hour run is 13 miles, 24 yards. For twenty kilometers, the mark is 57:25, by Jos Hermens of Holland. I wasn't too far off these world records in my first attempt and I left the track in a good frame of mind with Ellen, Billy Squires, and some other friends for the Eliot Lounge and a few gin and tonics.

We continued talking about the concept of going for the world record for the hour run. I started leafing through the pages of *Track & Field News* and noted that the world records for twenty-five and thirty kilometers were within reach. I felt the thirty-kilometer-record was a bit soft. I knew I was going out West to train for a few weeks in the winter of 1979 and, with the favorable weather, I'd have a shot at it. It was an ideal time. It wasn't close to the Olympic Trials or any major marathon or road race. I figured I'd be in good shape, since with dry ground and moderate temperatures I'd be able to do both intensive mileage and some speed work. So, why not go for it?

There were a few obstructions. I talked to some different companies about sponsoring the event and maybe helping to bring in some top runners to be a part of it. Television coverage was a hoped-for possibility. They all backed down. Everything seemed to be falling through at the last minute. I had the track, then I lost it.

Brian Maxwell, an assistant coach at Berkeley, and Ron Wayne, a marathoner and former resident of Massachusetts who is now living in Berkeley, were trying to help me set the race up. Brian had originally made plans for me to race just before a track meet between California, UCLA, and a third school. That weekend date suddenly was not available to me anymore, and when I asked Brian about the use of the track during the week to go for the world record, he indicated it would be very difficult. Joggers used the track and the school would be upset if they were to complain about their time on the track being taken over.

About five days before I had to leave for the West Coast, I ran into Dave Prokop, the organizer of the Springbank race in London, Ontario. He and Ellen finally started the wheels in motion. Prokop called up the AAU officials, contacted the starter and the timers, called track officials, and had the track measured and remeasured for all the distances. He made up the required program for the race, filled out all the necessary forms, and received an AAU sanction. We set a date. *Track & Field News* was contacted and, since their offices were close to the track that we finally secured in Saratoga, Tom Jordan, one of their top writers showed up.

I invited Gary Tuttle to participate. I was going to pay him out of my own pocket to come up from Ventura. Nobody else was willing to help out with the expenses. He bowed out due to some work involvement. I invited Duncan McDonald and he changed his mind at the last minute. So did a couple of other top runners. This is understandable because of the unusual circumstances surrounding the run—and they had been contacted at the eleventh hour. Few runners could be either ready or interested in running a hard twenty-five or thirty kilometers on a track on such short notice.

Thus, I went it alone, pretty much as I had done eighteen months earlier at Boston University. When Gary Tuttle and Duncan McDonald didn't appear for the race and when I noticed the wind, rain, and cloudy skies, I felt depressed before the start and several people suggested perhaps putting the race off to a better time. But I knew I had to try for it then. There had been too much preparation, not only by myself but by many people.

I felt sluggish, physically, as I fell into the required pace necessary to break the record. Jim Van Dine and Mike Porter, two long-distance runners from the San Francisco Bay area, were pushing the early pace. Ellen would tell me whether I was faster or slower than the record pace on each lap, and the timers read the splits. Small groups of spectators yelled encouragement and told me my split times.

After three or four miles, I forged ahead of Jim and began the push for the record. I never enjoyed the race, seldom felt relaxed or rhythmic and comfortable. I had always felt dubious about whether I could break the twenty-five-kilometer record, which was far superior to the thirty-kilometer mark. I consoled myself by remembering that even if I missed the twenty-five, I could get the thirty easily. With two laps to go, I was one second better than the old twenty-five record and now I suddenly felt confident.

When I crossed the line, I was exhausted and gasping for air. I was not positive I had the record and I literally stopped in my tracks upon crossing the line to ask if I had beaten it. No one knew. Dave Prokop ran up and shouted for me to continue running all the way to the thirty-kilometer mark, as I had to do if I was going to set a record for that distance, or even for the twenty-five kilometer world mark. This was because the race was an official thirty-kilometer race, and the twenty-five-kilometer world mark simply would be done en route.

I jogged slowly forward, furious that no one could tell me if I had achieved that hard-fought-for twenty-five goal. As I jogged down the far straight, several people told me I'd made it—my time was 1:14:12—and suddenly I felt no fatigue. It was a delayed satisfaction, but the pleasure was overwhelming when it came. It obliterated the huge blisters on my right foot and the dense fatigue I felt.

For the fun of it, I picked up the pace. People were also yelling for me to go for the thirty-kilometer mark as well. But, I had now already resolved that if I got the twenty-five record, I would jog home to thirty to fulfill the requirement, but would put off attempting to break that record for another occasion. Jim Van Dine, who also suffered from blistered feet, and I jogged several laps together and, with about a mile to go, I picked up the pace to the thirty-kilometer finish line and finished in 1:31:50.

I had not tried to set a new world record for thirty kilometers, but even so I did set the American record for the distance. At this point I should tell you that there are no official world records at all for any distance on runs made on the road. Thus, though I have run the fastest clocking in the world for thirty kilometers, on the road or on the track—in 1976 at the National Thirty-Kilometer Championship in Albany-Schenectady—my 1:29:04 is not an official world record because it was not run on the track. Instead, Jim Alder's 1:31:31 is the figure. In distance running, world records leap from ten thousand meters (Henry Rono of Kenya's 27:22 made in 1978) to the aforementioned twenty-five kilometers and thirty kilometers. I hope to break the thirty kilometers world record one of these days and I also feel that there is one other world record distinctly within my grasp on the right day, the one-hour run.

Somehow, there was a touch of incongruity to my Saratoga run. Here I was, a road runner and marathoner setting a current world record—on the track. I was especially pleased as no American holds any world record at any distance over one thousand meters. It was my way of saying, first, Americans can be good and set world records in long distances if they wish and, second, a good road racer can switch and race quite well on the track.

In my fifteen years of running up to that point, I hadn't really raced a tremendous amount on the track. I'd divide my career into three stages on the track: schoolboy, college, and postgraduate.

Schoolboy improvement was a 10:00 two-miler as a sophomore, a 9:48 as a junior, and a 9:36 as a senior. As I mentioned, I did a 4:28.8 mile as a senior. I never had much of a kick at the end of a race, attributable to an absence of fast-twitch muscle tissue and a lack of intensified training. Training was 220s, 440s, 880s with not much in terms of hill repeats and long runs to build strength for a sprint.

I ran my first two-miler in 10:45, on a dirt indoor track at the University of Connecticut in Storrs. I remember the smell of the dirt, the closeness of the crowds, and the aroma of atomic bomb liniment. I was sixteen.

Everything was so casual, so nonpressured. We only ran two or three meets indoors every year and they were usually on basketball courts. We'd run around cones stuck out there in the gym. We'd set up chairs and run around them. It was all at a very simple, basic level and the experience was hardly translatable to outdoor achievement. Even though we trained hard, it was not sophisticated work. Not many American coaches were utilizing the concepts of Arthur Lydiard, who stressed the need to build up an aerobic base, and following it up with anaerobic conditioning.

Wesleyan had an even more limited indoor track program. The meets were more like fun meets. Outdoor track was somewhat more expansive. My two-mile times went from 9:33 as a freshman, to 9:23 as a sophomore to 8:58.8 as a senior. Most of my training was on the roads. I really wasn't training for track when I was at Wesleyan. Perhaps I would have made a better road racer even in that era, but track was the college sport.

I seldom employed strategy on the track, or even in my cross-country races. I'd simply go out and, because I thought I had the necessary endurance, my strategy was to try to hang on to the lead runner or force the pace myself. Because I never

Winning first place in the Connecticut High School Class-A Cross-Country Championships for Newington High School, 1966.

With Amby Burfoot (*left*) and my coach, Billy Squires (*center*), after my first Boston Marathon victory, in April 1975. I ran 2:09:55.

NEW BRITAIN HERALD

The start of the Falmouth, August 1976.

Frank Shorter and I leading the field in the 1976 Falmouth.

Talking to eighty-year-old marathoner, Marty Cavanagh, at Falmouth.

I was still up there at this stage of the 1976 Olympics at Montreal. Left to right: Shivnath Singh, India; Lasse Viren, Finland; Waldemar Cierpinski, East Germany (behind Viren); Frank Shorter, U.S.A.; Jerome Drayton, Canada; and me.

KENT SMITH

Eight thousand runners competed in the Ohme thirty-kilometer
run in Japan, in 1976.

HOCHI-SHIMBUN, JAPAN

HOCHI-SHIMBUN, JAPAN

Along with Tom Fleming, I had made the turn and was on the way back at this point in the Ohme.

The view from the other side.

HOCHI-SHIMBUN, JAPAN

I won in the end.

Tom, a Japanese
runner and I
received the Ohme
awards.

I won the New York City Marathon in 1976 in 2:10:10. This photo shows me near the finish line in Central Park.

Amby Burfoot at Falmouth, 1977.

Joe Concannon (*right*). and Fred Lebow (*left*)

Randy Thomas and I led after eight miles in the 1977 Labatt's Freedom Trail run in Boston.

The crowds at the finish of the Labatt's Freedom Trail run, 1977.

Jerome Drayton with me, after he won the Springbank twelve-mile event.

Breaking the tape in 2:10:55 to win the Fukuoka Marathon, 1977.

Even though I can't sign my name in Japanese, I do have my fans.

Ellen and I, ready for business at the opening of our store, November 1977.

Crossing the finish line of the 1977 New York City Marathon, the winner in 2:11:28.

In March 1978 I competed in the World Cross-Country Championships in Glasgow, Scotland. "Competed" was about it—I finished forty-fourth.

Bob Hall, wheelchair athlete, is behind me and Al Salazar in the 1978 Falmouth Road Race.

CHARLIE RODGERS

I led Al Salazar at this stage of the 1978 Falmouth. He suffered heat prostration but hung on to take tenth place. I was the winner.

This is the way we all started at Falmouth that year.

Tommy Leonard (in white shirt and cap) at Falmouth.

Joan Benoit was the winner of the women's division, Falmouth, 1978.

Ellen seems happier than I after I won the 1978 Boston Marathon.

The remarkable Grete Waitz of Norway more than shared honors with me after our respective victories in the 1978 New York City Marathon. Her time of 2:32:30 set a new women's world record, which she bettered in the 1979 race, winning in 2:27:33.

Garry Bjorklund and
Toshiko Seko, of Japan,
were crowding me closely
at twenty miles during the
Boston Marathon, 1979.

DICK RAPHAEL

Seko dogged me just
about all the way.

But I won.

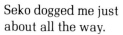

The state dinner, held for Prime Minister Ohira of Japan, was a memorable event for the Rodgers family. Left to right: the prime minister's wife, Rosalyn Carter, the prime minister, President Jimmy Carter, Ellen, and me.

had a big kick, even my winning times were relatively slow. In one of my better competitions, I ran a triple against the University of Connecticut as a freshman and I won the two-mile in 9:47 and placed second in both the 880 in 2:01 and in the mile in 4:22.

I left the track after that indoor meet at the Coast Guard Academy in December 1969, and I never set foot on one again until sometime in 1974, when I started to experiment at some indoor meets in the New England area. I ran a 28:34 six-mile in the summer of 1974, one month after my first six-mile ever, a 30:19 at the New England AAU Championships in Quincy, Massachusetts. I'd always try to go out hard, to utilize the endurance I had and to compensate for my lack of sprint speed. I'd try to wear the other runners down. Sometimes it worked, sometimes it didn't.

If there was a runner who excelled at distances up to five thousand meters, he could stay next to me until about a quarter of a mile to go and simply outkick me. It was a frustrating experience. I would win most road races. I was a 2:19 marathoner. Yet when I went on the track, I might run an 8:52 two-mile (a PR) and still come in eighth. It is an experience that has always dogged me.

I went to Europe in the summer of 1978, for races in London, Oslo, and Stockholm. My racing in Europe on the track was a combination vacation for Ellen and me and a semi-serious attempt at some track racing. Following Boston in 1978, I raced frequently on the roads and did more track training than usual. Randy Thomas, Bob Hodge, and some other Greater Boston TC teammates were also training for track races, pointing for the National AAU ten-thousand-meter race.

One workout Randy and I did was twelve quarter-miles in 0:62 or 0:63 with a two-hundred-meter jog interval. We ran all out on our last quarter, Randy doing 0:57 and I 0:58, close to my PR. I gabbed to my teammates about getting "Henrickens" or "Henry" as we respectfully termed the superb Kenyan distance runner, Henry Rono, who was in the midst of slaughtering four of the most prestigious world records in track and field: the five thousand meters, three-thousand-meter steeplechase, and the ten-thousand- and three-thousand-meter-runs.

So I was in good shape, but not in superb track shape as measured by European standards and, even though I was pleased with my two good races in Europe in the summer of 1978, I was irked and irritated that so many people would beat me in any race. After doing some track training with Greg Meyer and Alberto Salazar upon my return, I've come to the conclusion I need twice-a-week speed workouts in order to race well on the track against the best.

During my stay in Europe, I ran a 13:42 five-thousand and finished fifth. Considering that this was my first five-thousand ever, I was quite pleased. I really felt like a track runner. I ran a 28:04.9 ten-thousand, a time that is close to my PR, in a race in Stockholm and finished eighth. It demonstrated, in essence, where the United States stands in the five- and ten-thousand, races that are run worldwide so frequently.

The United States has won a grand total of two gold medals in those two important events at the Olympics, and both were in 1964 at Tokyo. Bob Schul won the gold in the five-thousand and Billy Mills won it in the ten-thousand. Since then, slim pickings. The late Steve Prefontaine came in fourth in the five-thousand meters in 1972. The prospects for 1980 are not much brighter.

Part of it is because we simply do not put on the track meets. Why? I'd lay the blame squarely at the feet of the AAU and the United States Olympic committee. Since they are the two organizations that purport to develop the sport of track and field, they should be the ones to assume the blame for our failures. There are many quality indoor meets, very few when the outdoor season begins. Why this is so, I'm not sure. In order to compete, the top athletes must go to Europe.

I do believe there is too much emphasis in the United States on indoor track to the detriment of outdoor track. This is particularly true in New England, where coaches seem to be hell-bent on gearing their athletes for indoor track. I think that smacks of small-time thinking, particularly as it applies to distance runners. When their mileage is cut back for two to three months in the winter, in order to train for what is usually the longest indoor event, the two-mile run, they lose some strengthening background work that would help them when it counts—outdoors in the five-thousand and the ten-thousand. I do believe outdoor track is going to grow in the United States and, in fact, there are a number of new high-quality meets popping up all over the United States. The Tom Black Meet in Knoxville, Tennessee, and the New Jersey Track Classic at Rutgers are two of these. When corporations, the AAU, and the US Olympic Committee start to think a little more clearly'and act a little more coherently, we'll see Americans competing with both quality and quantity at the long-distance track events.

Our system is adequate for the high school and college athlete. After that where do you turn? The only decent ten-thousand-meter race for runners out of college in the entire Northeast is at the Penn Relays, and it follows the Boston Marathon by only two weeks. This, of course, eliminates many top distance runners, because it's not likely that one will race one's best ten-thousand meters only two weeks after a hard marathon. You have to travel to Tennessee or California to find another quality ten-thousand-meter race.

Of the Americans who have fared well on the track in recent years, the two who stand out most prominently are Marty Liquori and Frank Shorter. They continued their track training after college, went to Europe immediately after graduating, and discovered what running on the tracks was all about. European weather in the summer is cool, the public is appreciative and knowledgeable, and the runners are accorded respect, treated well by the media, and given adequate expense money. There are better meets, and better competition. Track directors are looking for people with potential and, with all the competition over there, Americans do well to go to Europe. I might have concentrated on track more had I gone to Europe to run before I was thirty. When I did go over and saw how much fun it was, how inspirational, I planned to go back, and only wished I had been a youngster of twenty-two or twenty-three so I could have competed on the track against the best more often at the right age.

Part of the breakdown in the United States can be traced to the colleges and high schools, where the people with the power don't want to change to "new sports." They might be out of a job. They have little interest or desire to work with track clubs, corporate sponsors, or organizations who want to put on track meets or road races. They'd rather promote football and the traditional sports they're more familiar with. I think Americans would be sufficiently interested in track-and-field meets to make them economically feasible. They brought the pro-track circuit to Boston University one summer and sold it out. Pro track lasted for a couple of years, throughout the country, and that was the largest crowd to see it. Of course, pro track died because amateur-track people did better financially than the pros. With a renewed interest in running in the United States, perhaps a pro-track circuit would really go now.

The best track runners maintain the continuity from high school to college and beyond. But it is possible, as I did, to take time off, run on the roads and return. You develop a great amount of strength in road racing, which enables you to run well on the track. I ran the Olympic trials ten-thousand in 1976 with very little track background that year, and had a time of 28:04.4. I missed the Olympic team by half a second.

Is running on the roads detrimental to performing well in track and cross-country? I don't think so. I am saddened by the young junior and senior high school students who would love to road race throughout the year, many of them without the necessary fast-twitch muscle fiber necessary to excel at the only distances available to them in their regular school track programs. Unfortunately, their coaches and other misinformed individuals feel it is detrimental to them to compete in road races during their competitive seasons. Many coaches think road training and racing "deadens the legs" and slows their athletes down. This is only true if training and racing are too excessive. In fact, the endurance and strength gained from road racing would help most of these younger runners and perhaps even some of those middle-distance runners. After all, Peter Snell did road work and he did fairly well at track. All he did was win a gold medal in the eight-hundred meter and a gold in the fifteen-hundred meter in the 1964 Olympics. Strength comes from running on the roads.

Track-and-field fans and coaches should be pleased with the growth of road racing in the United States. It is inevitably going to lead to better coverage of the sports of cross-country and track and field. It's the height of absurdity to say that the positive growth of road racing can hurt track and field in any way.

To be a strategic runner, though, you have to go out there on the track and learn what it's all about. Especially indoors. This is a different experience. In my few distressing appearances on indoor tracks, I found myself boxed on the inside and everybody suddenly passing me on the outside. I'd end up being almost the last person in a field of runners with about one or two laps to go, and everybody would be kicking. I had to learn to pass on a straightaway, with a quick burst of speed. If you try to pass on a turn, you spend too much time running out of the lane and it lengthens the distance.

I went to the 1976 Millrose Games for the two-mile and it had been two years between indoor track races for me. Suleiman Nyambui of Tanzania, an experienced indoor track racer, was there. So was another younger Tanzanian runner, a newcomer to indoor track. I think he felt equally uncomfortable as we collided at the start of the race, and we were both falling off the track throughout the race. After a half mile, I was in oxygen debt. Oxygen debt occurs when the body's muscle tissue and cardiovascular system are not functioning as well as they should, either through inadequate pre-race training or poor race pacing. I never developed a sense of rhythm. I never had a feeling I was racing, and there was no possibility for strategy. It just seemed to be an all-out sprint.

Part of this was because I had no track to train on, another problem common to Americans in the North. Once you get out of college, access to an indoor track is limited. I can remember going to Tufts University in Medford, Massachusetts, and getting kicked out because they had to turn out the lights at a certain time. I'd be outside in the dark and freezing cold of February wondering what the hell was going on.

Harvard University opened a gorgeous new indoor facility in the winter of 1977, yet it is damned hard to get into. Bob Sevene, a respected and well-known coach and runner in New England, and I were hoping to do a track workout on the track in January of 1979. Bob had bought a membership in order to train there and, for a dollar, I could get in too. Bad planning. There was a women's track meet there that evening, so we ran out into the fifteen-degree night air over to the old Harvard facility where there was a dirt, playground-sized track. We ran about half a mile and the lights were turned out on us. Remember the commercial, "Don't fence them out"? It happens constantly with track athletes.

Why aren't there more tracks open to the public—not just to the world-class competitors, but to people with potential? Why isn't there a sense of feeling for the public? In 1976 I was preparing for the Millrose Games for fun, but many former collegians in our area wanted to train hard for indoor track. But they were resurfacing the indoor track at Tufts that winter. In the dead of winter. Why not do it in the summer?

I wound up going to a high school track to do my speed work, and if you've ever been through the experience you know what I mean when I say, "It's the pits." There is tennis, basketball, field hockey, wrestling, lacrosse, and everything else going on. Schoolboy track facilities are limited. The state legislature appropriated money for an indoor facility for the schoolboys and schoolgirls of Massachusetts in 1960. They never turned the first shovelful of earth because of petty politics.

Training on a track is one useful form of preparation for the marathon. I find it enables me to sharpen up and develop a sense of rhythm and feeling for a race pace. It's essential for the world-class marathoner. You can also wear your racing shoes when you do these workouts, thereby breaking in the shoes under noncompetitive conditions. It simulates racing conditions. Squires always had us do long intervals at race pace or slightly faster than race pace. We'd do repeat miles at 4:40, 4:45 and 4:50 pace. A 4:57 pace is about a 2:10 marathon. In between, we'd do a quarter-mile jog at an easy seven-minute-mile pace.

Our basic approach has always been toward moderation. This is what Squires and Bob Sevene believe in. It is a long-term approach, one that aims at eliminating injuries, which often result from excessively intense track workouts. We usually do halves, quarters, and three-quarter repeats with a 220 or 330 jog in between. The pace is anywhere from sixty-six to sixty-eight seconds.

Sometimes you have to do more intense repetitions at a faster pace, in particular if you wish to excel at track distances from fifteen hundred to ten thousand meters. When Alberto Salazar came back from the University of Oregon to prepare for the Falmouth Road Race in August 1978, he was doing repeat 4:30 miles on the track, perhaps four of them, with a three-minute jog interval. This was foreign to our club. We rarely did more than a three-quarter mile at a sixty-five- to sixty-eight-second pace. The Rookie was doing 4:30 repeat miles so Randy Thomas and myself went with him. All it ever takes is someone to lead the way and, of course, Randy and I would be racing Al shortly at Falmouth and felt we'd better do faster workouts too.

Greg Meyer, who won the 1978 National AAU Cross-Country Championship and has run a sub-four-minute mile indoors, moved to the Boston area from Michigan in the fall of 1978. He did a workout that included an 8:59 two-mile, followed by a six-minute rest. Then, with five-minute jog-rests between, he did a 4:20 mile, a 9:11 two-mile and a 3:12 three quarter, and finished with a mile and three-quarter run. Nobody had done anything like that around New England. This intense approach to running was foreign to the Boston area. Most top-level New Englanders and runners in the Greater Boston TC haven't trained that hard and intensely, but many of us are now aware that such concentrated efforts are crucially necessary to race well on the track. Particularly at five-thousand- and ten-thousand-meter distances.

There are three reasons why I never ran much indoor track. The first is the danger. It is easy to become injured running the intense, fast pace and rounding the sharp corners on varying surfaces. Naturally, the lack of quality indoor meets in New England is a second reason. The third was that I found out a long time ago that I was a better road runner than a track runner. You have to do what you are best at, and it's a waste of your time and energy to delude yourself continually trying to be good in events you have little or no aptitude for.

You have to specialize your training for a specific distance. The most successful runners are those who know exactly what they want and how to go about getting there. If you want to run the mile, the five-thousand, and the marathon, you are flirting with disaster. You may step up from the ten-thousand to the marathon and drop down again, but you must space out your training so you can specialize temporarily for a month or two at one or the other event.

Training on the track can be boring, particularly if you try to do most of your running on one. It's both boring and difficult, psychologically, to do track work alone. But there is a sense of a challenge. You try to overcome boredom by "pushing through" it in your training. There is a "testing," a daring to force yourself around a track over many laps. This may sound masochistic, but forcing yourself is a part of competitive running and you either are good at it and become better at it, or you never take up the challenge. I've run as many as 80 laps on an outdoor track preparing for a marathon. I ran 125 laps on the old indoor track at the Huntington Avenue YMCA in Boston when I returned to running. It makes you dizzy, but in a crazy way it tests your willpower, your motivation, and your desire. You can become caught up in the centrifugal pull, the swirl and rhythm of roller-coasting on the track, particularly on the banked, indoor tracks.

Interval training, by nature, can be difficult. It was the most popular form of training worldwide from the 1950s through the early and middle 1960s. Since the advent of aerobic training, it has diminished somewhat. To alleviate the boredom of track work, you can train with other people. Try different tricks, different forms of track workouts. Vary the intensity of running effort, "rest" intervals, and the duration of individual running attempts and total workout time.

There are different techniques you can use. If I ran eight or ten miles in a morning workout, I might be a bit tired for my second workout. I'd drop behind some other runner and follow him. If I were doing twenty quarters or eight half miles, I might take the lead in only one or two. My teammates would break the wind for me, minimizing wind resistance. We all help each other. It's much easier, in training, to follow another runner.

It's also a social occasion. We talk and fool around and joke and play different games on the track. One is to try and see how close we can get to hitting the exact time split we're aiming for in the workout. We're not too competitive, as a rule. This is the mark of maturity; saving the racing for the race is only common sense, yet I've seen many fine runners get caught up in intense competitions with each other in track workouts. When I see this happening, I say to myself, "whoa" and think how I'll race hard in an upcoming race, but not now. A competitive runner will be a successful racer only when he learns when to be competitive.

It's more to your benefit to run these splits according to how you feel, as opposed to how someone else feels, such as a coach or another runner. You run according to your aches and your legs. If you have a feeling of fatigue, you can't do the same workout. If you ran twenty-five miles the day before, you can't do what someone who only ran ten miles can do. He's fresh. You aren't. The same holds true if the miles were five for a beginner, compared with two miles for another beginner.

Before you train on the track your coach should ask you how you feel, whether you feel recovered from the previous day's workout. Talk to the other runners you plan to train with and find out what they have in mind, what they want to get out of the workout. Coaches and runners should all be aware of where they stand in terms of their training. It is simple communication. Do not get caught up in competitive racing when you are, in fact, training. An alert coach will stifle this kind of activity. There is a time for racing and there is a time for training.

There are classic examples of top competitors' "leaving it on the track" in training. This often occurs prior to a major competition, probably a result of the nervous tension that slowly builds up in you. It can be high school, college, or international. When I get to within a few weeks before a major competition, I remind myself that there's little improvement I can make through training harder in that short period of time left—that it's more important to coast a bit in the final week or so and avoid injury or overwork. Sometimes, a runner can get so carried away in workouts that he's tired when the serious competition arrives. He may be nervous, the adrenaline starts flowing, and the workout quickly becomes too intense before he's aware of it. He loses sight of the competition ahead and the workout becomes his race.

I know of one runner in our club who did three repeat miles in spectacular times, each of them near his personal best for the mile. If he could have saved any one of them for the race, he would have turned in a fantastic performance. He was so carried away and he was running so well on that training day that he ran all three of them extremely hard. It took so much out of him that he wasn't able to race or train well for several months.

You should walk off the track feeling you've finished a very good workout. You should have the feeling that you've built yourself up, not torn yourself down. It's OK to walk away tired, fatigued, and really slightly pooped. What you have to keep in mind is that tomorrow you're going to go out and run some more. Ask yourself, "Will I still have the same motivation, desire, and strength that I had today? How much more than my usual effort am I putting forth in this workout? Will my calves or hamstrings be sore, inhibiting my normal run?"

Save something. Moderation is the password, even on the track. It takes time to get used to the track, just as it does the roads. It's a gradual building process. Even for the experienced track runner, going back on the track after a short layoff of a few weeks or a month or two requires time to become familiar with the sharp turns and different surfaces and to settle into a comfortable rhythm and a faster-than-normal training pace. Your first workouts on the track should be moderate, with a slow increase in intensity of effort, duration of effort for an individual run, and total workout time as you feel stronger.

The change from training on the roads to the track can be difficult. There's an unusual stress on your knees, your Achilles tendons, your hamstrings, your calf muscles, and your feet. It's particularly true that there's more stress on the balls of your feet and your knees. You are utilizing a different training pace and your running form must adapt to the size and shape of each individual track. These changes mean different muscle and tendon strain.

It's even more important to note when it comes to indoor track training. Such tracks are generally smaller, the track is often banked, and the stresses are different. John Walker, a New Zealander and current world-record holder for the mile and two-thousand-meter run, has said Americans place too much emphasis on indoor track and, to a degree, he's correct. American coaches often seem to goad athletes to run indoors, playing it up as the ultimate in running. I suppose an indoor track victory means as many "points" for some coaches as an outdoor victory. But the real truth is that the world records that really count and the most important performances are those run on four-hundred-meter outdoor tracks.

Approach whatever track workout you are doing according to how you feel. I often contact one or two people in my club and try to set up a date for a track workout based on how my training has been progressing. If I'm doing thirty miles of running on a Sunday, I'll try to ease up Monday and Tuesday and aim for a track workout on Wednesday. On Friday, I might do a light hill workout or I'll race on the weekend.

It's important to make sure you haven't done too much intensive training or put in too many miles the day before a track workout. You want your legs to be fairly "fresh," to feel "light." Your whole body should be feeling "light." You might rest—cut back on your mileage slightly—a day or two before a track workout. Nothing can make you feel worse than a hard track effort when you're worn out—except, possibly, if you've eaten too much or too poorly just before the workout.

If you have sore spots in your legs, you may aggravate them on the track. Just as in racing, it's wise not to do situps or pushups prior to a track workout. They tighten up your stomach muscles, arms and shoulders too much and you don't want that to happen. You ought to be relaxed going into a track workout, both physically and psychologically. An easy run and ten minutes of stretching prior to the workout will be beneficial. You want a light film of perspiration on your body prior to the workout.

11
Boston

BOSTON. It is the oldest and the best known of our continuing marathons, organized and put on every year, except one, since its inception in 1897. It can also be the messiest and the most loosely organized of our major marathons, inviting criticism from everyone from Frank Shorter to the unofficial entrant who asks, "Why?"

It is organized by the Boston Athletic Association, presided over by a kindly man named Will Cloney and the irascible Jock Semple. For a long time, they toiled in anonymity, cloaked in the intimacy of an event that attracted only a few hundred runners. They stepped off the press bus and into notoriety on that April day in 1967 when they spotted Kathy Switzer running. Jock tried to rip off her number and throw her out of the race. The picture went all over the world and they were anonymous no more.

That was before women were permitted in, before the running boom and the liberation movement and Title IX, and all that. That was a light-year ago, one year before my college roommate at Wesleyan became the first American to win Boston in eleven years. That was before the marathon, its significance, and its allure became a part of me. Even when Amby Burfoot won it that year, what it really meant hadn't yet sunk in for me, and several years would pass before it would.

Because Boston is the first of the major American marathons in the calendar year, it is the race I now point for throughout the cold of a New England winter. It also is held in middle April when, with the melting of the snow and warmer temperatures, road racing is just becoming possible in New England. You can feel the running world coming alive as it approaches. Ellen and I opened the first Bill Rodgers Running Center on Chestnut Hill Avenue near Cleveland Circle on the course, and as the race approaches all the conversations in the store inevitably turn to Boston.

The race Amby won was my first real exposure to it. Young Johnny Kelley, a schoolteacher and a recent graduate of Boston University who ran for the BAA, had been the last American to win it in 1957. He and Amby were both from the New London area and, as it turned out, Kelley coached Amby when he was growing up in Connecticut. Of the five Americans to win Boston since the elder Johnny Kelley won his second in 1945, through 1978, three of us have been from the Nutmeg State.

This was a major dream for Amby, the driving force, as I mentioned earlier, behind all of his work and training. It was the paramount thing in his life. I had been training with him all that winter in 1968. He ran twice daily, while I used to go out just once. I had no desire, in those days, to run road races and I had no taste at all for the marathon. I'd run two road races in college. Amby persuaded me to try both of them. One was a thirteen-miler in winter, and I suffered through it in the cold. I hadn't dressed properly, and it was too difficult a race for me. It just seemed to take forever!

I congratulated Amby heartily when he returned to campus that April day in 1968, and that was pretty much all there was to it. It didn't have any substantial impact on my life. I stood in awe of Amby, as it was, simply because he was such a phenomenal runner. Marathoning was something that was foreign to me. I realized it was a significant achievement, but in 1968 there were more myths and apprehensions about the distance than there are today. Now people take the marathon seriously but they take it in stride. Then it was all viewed through a glass darkly.

After that, I never came in contact with Boston again until I moved here. I saw my first Boston in 1971 as a spectator. I lived fairly near Symphony Hall in the Back Bay section of the city, and the Boston Marathon finishes at the Prudential Center, one-quarter of a mile or so from my former apartment. I walked over there and saw the finish of it two years in a row and, together with everything else, this stoked the old fires. I became motivated to run the marathon, and Boston, 1973, was my first.

The race is held on Patriot's Day in April, starting in the sleepy little town of Hopkinton which is crowded and filled with runners, writers, photographers, and officials until the race begins at noon. When I won it the first time in 1975, it started at Hayden Rowe by the Village Green. Some criticism was leveled by Jerome Drayton after his 1977 Boston win about the starting-line problems, so everything was moved to Main Street, which eliminated one sharp corner you used to have to take heading out of town toward Ashland. Before this course change the runners sprinted like hell for a good position so they could negotiate that corner successfully. That's not the way to start a marathon!

The course is a part of marathoning lore. Through the countryside of Ashland, over the city streets of Framingham, by a lake in Natick, past the students of Wellesley College, into the Newtons and up Heartbreak Hill to Boston College, over the streets of Brookline, through Kenmore Square and the crowds of Red Sox fans likely to be heading in or out of

Fenway Park, to the finish line at The Pru. Actually, less than two miles of the race are in the city.

Boston turns me on, Boston turns me off. Obviously, it is among the elite of marathons in the world. It can also be too elitist, with its archaic rules of amateurism and its refusal to step into the modern world of marathoning. Even with its history of poor administration, it has ranked as one of the Big Three in the world outside of the Olympics.

I have spoken out about the amateur outlook on the part of the organizers and the city in the past. I don't believe some of the people involved appreciate or understand the significance of the Boston Marathon on a worldwide basis. It has always been run this way. It has survived. It seems it will continue to be run this way, although I must give credit to the many volunteers who persevere under difficult, occasionally chaotic, conditions. In the past two years, many significant improvements have lifted the level of race administration. The level of competition is moderately high, although generally somewhat below the European Championships, which are held every four years. It is generally below Fukuoka. Its field of ten sub-2:10 marathoners in 1979 indicated that even with its indifference, the shoe companies would ensure a quality field by bringing in the top runners.

The first to criticize Boston was Shorter, who went on ABC television after the Montreal Olympics and said, "The good people of Boston expect you to hitchhike down the Mass Pike" to be able to run in it. He said Boston makes no attempt to "assemble the best field. You go somewhere else and you're treated so well, you want to run well. If it's so attractive somewhere else, why not go there?"

He was quoted as saying, "I did ask them not to use what I said. I said, 'This is illustrative. It isn't fair to use it. I'm using one race as an example.' I also used it as a counterpoint to the way amateur sports are in East Germany. What we do in the next few years depends on whether or not we want to win gold medals." He said all this in 1976. Not much has changed in the intervening years.

The fact that none of the top runners in the United States, not to mention the world, have their expenses, their airfare, and their hotels taken care of is the essence of what Shorter referred to. The conventional wisdom is, "This is one of the greatest athletic events in the world. You're lucky to run in this race." Shorter essentially said, "I can go to another race in Europe and receive very good expense money. If I go to Boston, they won't even pay my plane fare."

This is somewhat ironic. He was the first American to win a gold medal for the United States in the Olympic Marathon in sixty-four years. To be treated that way is, I think, insulting to a great American athlete. I would have said the same thing if I had won the gold. I spoke out about it in Phoenix and my quotes were taken somewhat out of context. Frank lives in Boulder, Colorado. I live in the Boston area. It's convenient for me to run Boston.

Drayton leveled the next barrage of criticism at Boston in 1977. This was the year he won and I dropped out at the top of Heartbreak Hill. Drayton has been somewhat outspoken in the past. He has not endeared himself to some of the people who have been at the target of his criticism. He finished Boston, was steered into the interview area in a barber shop in the Prudential Center basement, and stropped the razor.

"At the start," he said, "I got really jostled and kicked and booted around. I twisted my ankle and I was kicked in the calf. I was a goner in the first mile. Fortunately, I was able to recover. I'm a little disappointed with this marathon. For one thing, it takes on the prestige of Fukuoka, supposedly, but you figure that after eighty-one tries here, they'd set out official watering tables.

"It may be fine for people who run for the sake of running a marathon here. But if you want high-quality performance, you've got to take care of these people. If you're not going to have tables where you can put your own drinks, at least put some water there. Rodgers was set up. This is his hometown. He had his wife at different points giving him his own special drink. It irritates me. It's just unfair. It doesn't appeal to me. What's the point of training for this, when you can get beat by circumstances beyond your control.

"I knew I was going to have to take a chance on getting water from people and I didn't know what was in those cups. I can't take ERG. I can't take Gatorade. The only thing I can take is water. So, my strategy changed. I decided to hang onto Rodgers. I figured I'd let him lead until maybe Heartbreak Hill. If he hadn't dropped by then, I would make one last effort. As it turned out, I didn't have to put one in.

"The start is another reason I may not come back. I got really jostled around. We never got a notice when the gun was going to go off. Nobody said, 'A minute to go.' Next thing I knew, there were fifty guys pushing. One guy was grabbing my shirt and pulling me down. It was too scary. You train hard for ten weeks or so and then you come down here and it's all over in the first ten yards. It's not worth it. You don't even have to wear a number. Who's going to check on you?

"The organizers have to make up their mind if they want quantity or quality. Out of the three thousand people, it was said there were only ten good runners. I would have cut it down to two. If you want to make money out of it, why charge only two dollars? There is no way this marathon compares with Fukuoka in organization. This is a good marathon, but it can turn into a disaster. Seed the first fifty, put a rope behind them, and start the rest ten minutes later."

Drayton, of course, came back in 1978. Shorter ran Boston for the first time the same year. Boston officials reacted to the criticism and made some changes. I agreed with Drayton. The start was indeed too crowded and chaotic. He was pushed, shoved, and tripped at the start. I was there. There was no control at the starting line. They needed more marshals controlling the crowd and moving the people back. They needed a better selection process for the front runners. They needed a rope between the top fifty competitors and the rest of the crowd to make sure they had an even break and an even start.

He also complained about the absence of official water stops. If there were some, he indicated, they were not well marked. He said he couldn't see them at all. He was partially correct on this. But he was inaccurate in the sense that this was his fifth Boston and he knew what was what. He should have come prepared and had people out there ready to give him water along the route. I do this in Boston and I also do it in New York, just as many marathoners do. Perhaps his dark sunglasses, which he always wears when racing, obscured his vision enough so he couldn't tell the difference between ERG, water, or Gatorade.

Derek Clayton of Australia, the world-record holder in the marathon (2:08:34, 1969) told me he never ran Boston because it was absurd that the race directors wouldn't cover his expenses. In short, what's done at Boston flies in the face of normal major-race procedures.

Jack Fultz won Boston in the heat of 1976. He returned the following year and his car was towed away. He presumed that he would be treated decently by the city as the defending champion in the Boston Marathon. He went to marathon officials to see if he could get any help in getting his car back. No help was forthcoming. Something finally appeared in the papers and one city official, Peter Meade, paid the fine out of his own pocket. When I had my car towed after winning the 1976 New York City Marathon, the officials of the New York Road Runners Club paid the ninety-dollar fine.

The same thing occurred, strangely enough, when I won the Falmouth Road Race back in 1974. Tommy Leonard, the race director, went to great lengths to ensure that I got my car back and did not have to pay the fine. You're probably wondering why runners get their cars towed so frequently. That's a good question. Whatever the answer, I now take a plane to New York and a boat driven by my weekend host Bill Crowley to the starting line at Falmouth.

Crowd control has always been a major problem at Boston. Fultz told me after the 1978 race that he felt he might have finished third instead of fourth if there had been better crowd control. There was a big bus wedged into the crowd lining the street on Commonwealth Avenue as he ran down the hill by Boston College. He was caught between the bus and the crowd and it was tough to get past the bus. The crowd was pressing in. He had no room to run.

The problem was accentuated when you got to Wellesley, about ten to twelve miles from the finish. The crowd always squeezes into the centers of these little towns we run through. When you go up the hills of Newton and past Boston College into the city, it becomes critical. It was obvious that there had to be some kind of coordinated effort by the BAA and the people at the Prudential. They take credit for the marathon so they had to take the criticism too. I'm glad to say they realized it, and improvements have now been implemented for future races.

Boston is unique in that it passes through several communities. The New York Marathon is within New York, and just one police force is involved. But, Boston race officials have to face up to more complex problems. They have to organize a group and train them in terms of crowd control. Either put up sawhorses along the way at the parts of the course where the crowds are the largest, or get the National Guard and the various community police forces to do their jobs. I am at a loss to understand why the communities that the marathon passes through do not respect the Boston Marathon as an athletic institution and cooperate better. I'd think they would regard it as a wonderful annual Happening.

Kevin White, the mayor of Boston, has been quoted in the

Boston Globe about the indifference of the city. "Ballyhoo has never been a part of Boston. We don't have a tourism bureau that functions very well. Our attitude is, 'Come if you want. This is what we do. We're not soliciting. We view a lot of things that way.' I don't think you can artificially induce something. I think there was a tradition here. The marathon is an international event. Maybe we ought to do more to make it more pleasant. The fact that we do nothing and it's the way it is says something. A million people showed up to see it."

I think that is an absurd way to view this thing. It's a very simplistic viewpoint. It's looking only at the size of the crowd. It's not looking at the marathoners. The point is that there are thousands of marathoners out there who have trained and have qualified and are in very good shape. They are in better shape than many of the better so-called professional athletes in our country. They're treated disrespectfully. They don't get adequately marked split times along the course. They don't get enough water from official race water stations. These are the two most important things. The third is having better crowd control and that is why I agreed with Drayton when he croaked about the administration of the race.

It's true that the tradition is there. You don't have to induce that artificially. The point is that if a runner from Japan, Finland, or Ethiopia shows up for the race, you should treat him well. I go to Japan and all the runners bring gifts from their countries and exchange them with other runners. Our AAU gives me nothing, not even pins, to trade with other foreign athletes. I return from Japan with a positive feeling about the way I have been treated.

When foreign runners leave Boston and return to their countries, they talk to the press and other athletes and officials there and they tell them: "Not much was done for us there. They didn't take us out to dinner. They didn't pay for my air fare. They didn't do anything for me. On top of that, the race wasn't administered very well." I think that is a bad taste to leave in the mouth of a foreign competitor. Not to mention the average American competitor, who has gone through much to come to this race in April.

I think the race owes it to all these people to do a better job. I think it owes it to its tradition. The administrators owe it to the runners who have qualified to put on a little more well-managed race. They are resting on their laurels. They can do a better job. If all these people have worked so hard to earn the opportunity to run Boston, the city of Boston, the BAA, and the Prudential people should work a little harder as well.

It is true that in 1979, race officials did an excellent job of finish-line control. And after that race, the city and Mayor White honored the Greater Boston TC for its outstanding team performance with a civic reception at historic Faneuil Hall. Maybe Boston is getting the message!

At international marathons, foreign athletes are usually given the opportunity by the race director, their Sports federation, and government officials to take trips or cultural tours where they visit historical points of interest and museums and meet some of the people of that country. We were taken to the home of a famous Japanese pot maker in Fukuoka in 1978. He showed us his home, his collection of pottery, and the kiln where the pots are baked. His wife served us tea as the ancient tea ceremony was discussed, and when it came time to leave, we were presented with gifts of his work. A comparable visit to Boston by a foreign athlete might include a tour of venerable Harvard University or attending a performance of the Boston Pops at Symphony Hall.

I don't think Boston will ever match the Olympics or the European Championships. But, it could be run as well as New York is. I don't believe, logistically, the course is as difficult to follow. It's basically a straight point to point course. If they continue to improve the crowd control, I don't see why they should have any logistic problems. They don't run the race through a tremendous number of intersections. The roads are not as poorly paved as those in New York generally are.

In terms of upgrading the quality of competition, the major change that should be made is that the organizers should bring in some of the top competitors from around the world as well as the top runners in the United States. They should take care of their expense money, pay their hotel and food bills, and pay their air fare. This is normal procedure at races all over the world and is perfectly in compliance with AAU rules. In fact, the AAU have indicated they believe our amateurs ought to be helped whenever possible. Yet at Boston, amateur long-distance runners receive no help. The people who qualify for the race should be given accurate time splits, water at regular, clearly marked intervals, a T-shirt or medal, and a meal at the finish. They should, in general, be treated with more forethought and appreciation.

The absence of commercialism has hurt the Boston Marathon. This is why New York has surpassed Boston in many ways. One reason they do a better job is because they have the funds. They don't have to rely on the Prudential, or any one company for everything. The Prudential Insurance Company and Honeywell do offer a lot to the Boston Marathon. I simply believe more still needs to be done to make it the best race possible and that requires more funds, either from Prudential, Honeywell or some other corporation(s). A poll of American marathoners by *The Runner* or *Runner's World* would be effective in determining what the runners want at Boston.

There are a lot of potential sponsors who might like to kick in some money, and this could make Boston a better race. Just because they want to give some money to the race and advertise that they are a race sponsor does not hurt the race. I think most runners would agree with me about that. Falmouth is evidence of the success of having a major sponsor. With Perrier as the sponsor in 1978, the most competitive, successful race ever was held. Another example is the Lynchburg, Virginia, ten-miler, which is backed by a local insurance company. The best-run races usually are the races with adequate financial backing.

Tiger shoe pays for the official Boston numbers. Tiger is displayed on the number. Isn't that commercialization? To say that it isn't is ridiculous. Gatorade was the so-called official drink for years, and Gatorade is the athletic drink you can take during the race. I was pleased to see ERG replace Gatorade as the official drink of the BAA race in 1979. I believe ERG is more effective than Gatorade as a replacement fluid for marathoners. That's simply my opinion—actually I find drinking water is probably the best thing of all. In any event, commercialization certainly does exist to some extent, so why not expand it to the point where it can actually help the race and the runners more?

Boston is basically a downhill course. Surveys with geodetic instruments have shown that Hopkinton is 490 feet above sea level. The finish line altitude is 65 feet above sea level. There are some significant uphill sections to the course. The toughest ones lie between the 18-mile to 21-mile points. You go up a series of three hills. The last one is the fabled Heartbreak Hill, which is approximately 600 yards long.

The difficult part of Boston, traditionally, can turn out to be the time of year. I understand that it snowed on the morning of the 1967 race. If it is cool, Boston is not a bad course, but it can also be very hot. It was ninety degrees on the day of the 1976 race. I didn't run, because of the upcoming Olympic trials. Somebody asked me at the starting line what he should do. My comment was simply, "Don't run." I just wouldn't on that day. If it is hot, there is no shade along the course. You have to be very careful, particularly in the early stages of the race. This is through the countryside, where there are few people. There is not that much water available as you run through Ashland and this is the most important time, early in the race on a hot day, to get water.

The most important thing to remember about Boston, perhaps more so than with most marathons, is to start out carefully. Hold back. It's a downhill start, and if you can hold back, pace yourself well, and save your energy, you will be better off when you hit the hills leading up to Heartbreak Hill. Holding back is wise strategy in any marathon. It is more so at Boston, because of the downhill start and the fact that you are running low on glucose (energy) at about the eighteen-mile mark, just where the hills begin. Many people have been burned out in Boston because it seems so easy at the beginning. When you hit that eighteen-mile mark and the hills, you may be out of gas.

The hills are not that tough, though, if they are taken in stride and you have paced yourself well. If you haven't, and it is hot, you can be in real trouble by the time you get there. They come at a critical point in the race. I've dropped out twice on the hills. Each time it was hot and I wasn't well trained for the race.

Once you can get over those hills, it's not a tough race to the finish. To begin with, there's the psychological advantage of knowing it's all downhill from then on. I train on the hills almost every day when I'm in the Boston area. When you get over the hills, you also have the crowd going for you. And the crowd can carry you from there. It gets bigger and more enthusiastic as you approach the finish, particularly over the final eight miles. The roar of the crowd can be deafening, but it's mighty encouraging.

If you run Boston, I suggest you have friends along the course to give you water. Either that or lobby the race administration to have official water stops that are clearly marked so you can see them amid the crowds. Officials should wear brightly colored jackets and hats. There should be several officials near the water stations. The water stops should be at regular intervals. In most professionally run marathons, they are spaced every five thousand meters. Because of the crowds at Boston, which obscure the vision of the runner, banners on poles, indicating that a water stop is ahead, should be readily visible to the runners well before they reach that point. In fact, in 1979 these basic but important steps were finally initiated.

I think, overall, it's an easier course than New York. It's not a tough course over the final four miles. You have the downhill sections and you have the crowds. It's similar to Fukuoka, in some ways, and it may be a little easier. Shorter said, with better crowd control, a world record might have been run in 1978, with the favorable conditions of cool weather and a tail wind. On a recent ten-mile run with Derek Clayton, he told me if anyone sets a world record at Boston he would send them a telegram informing the runner the new record wouldn't count since it was set on a point-to-point course.

Fukuoka has nineteen sub-2:12 times through the end of 1978. Boston has twelve through 1979. New York has three. Of course New York is much, much younger than either Boston or Fukuoka. Only six of the Boston times were turned in at the time when I beat Jeff Wells in 1978, the year the race had one of the finest fields in history. It's very rare to get most of the best marathoners in the world on the same course, especially at Boston. Usually when it has happened, in the Peace Race Marathon in Czechoslovakia, or in the Karl Marx Memorial Race in East Germany, or in Enschede, Holland, the winning times and the times of the top finishers have not been that fast. This can be explained because of unfavorable weather and the toughness of the courses. Boston is not that tough, unless it is hot. If it is hot, the course is brutal.

There are two aspects that are very positive about Boston. One is the general excitement that permeates the race. New York is more spectacular and better run. There you have major television coverage. The corporations are involved. As a front runner, though, Boston has generated more excitement for me.

There are the motorcycle cops and even they seem to be involved in the race. For some reason, there is something very unique about Boston. Some of it has to be that runners always return there. It is Mecca-like. With the high school bands, balloon sellers, antique cars, and a healthy smattering of clowns in the race, it's all very small-town, circuslike.

It's an old, historic event and so many of the people along the course have been watching it with their families for years. It's also a college area. You run past Wellesley College, Boston College, and past apartments filled with students. It's a holiday in Massachusetts, and a great many of the spectators are knowledgeable and intense about the race. I am constantly running into people who say, "Well, my father used to take me out as a child to see the Boston Marathon." There are some enthusiastic marathon afficianados running in the Boston area. The last ten miles of Boston are unrepeated and unmatched anywhere in the world in terms of spectator response and excitement. That's one very positive thing about the race.

Boston also loves a winner. It's a very sports-oriented city, to begin with. The two major newspapers give saturation coverage to sports. The crowds at the finish line reflect it. They don't hold back. When you finish in New York, there's a decent crowd, but they are relatively new to marathoning and are often in bleachers. It's not like Boston. The New York Central Park crowd isn't as big, as enthusiastic, or as swept up by the event. It's good, but it's more controlled. They don't completely understand the marathon yet, and the finish is not in as dramatic a setting as at Boston. All hell breaks loose when you turn the corner to the finish in Boston. The people are what make Boston an enduring experience.

QUALIFYING TIMES. Boston used to let everyone in, at least every male over the age of eighteen who sent in an entry blank. They finally elected to impose qualifying times. By 1974 you had to have broken three hours on a certified marathon course within the preceding calendar year if you were a male under the age of forty. You had to have broken 3:30 if you were a male over forty or a female. After the 1979 Boston Marathon, officials lowered the qualifying times from 3:00 to 2:50 for men under forty; from 3:30 to 3:10 for men over forty; and from 3:30 to 3:20 for women. Isn't that somewhat discriminatory?

Once again, I can only reiterate that with adequate support I think an open Boston Marathon would be possible. Bigger is often not best, however, and after participating in some overcrowded races I see Will Cloney's points more realistically. I think we'll have to see how Boston 1980 turns out. Whether men over forty and women competitors have been unfairly treated with the new standards is another question. Both groups are segments of our society to whom we should give more encouragement and reachable incentives regarding health and fitness. Both groups have been losers in the past.

I believe in open races. It's a controversial subject. But what happens is you get everyone who wants to run, and for some reason, has not qualified, showing up at Hopkinton anyway. All that does is complicate the traffic problem. Qualified runners are held up in traffic and fail to make the start. It also complicates recording the finishers.

If it is logistically feasible, in terms of space at the start and the finish—and this could be done with adequate crowd control—there should be no qualifying times required. Boston is viewed as an American championship. It is the goal of all marathoners in America. They all want to come and run Boston. This is where all the great marathoners have run in the past. The great ones have been here at least once.

I think the qualifying standard should be eliminated, not continually lowered. With corporate, regional, and city support, this could be done. I have received all kinds of proposals from people in the mail about the qualifying times and how to run the race for everybody. Some of them are weighted with mathematical equations relating to the size of the road and the number of runners, and spelling out how it could be done.

The roads the marathoners run on in Boston are just as wide as the roads that you run over in New York. That should be no problem. It's all a matter of, where there's a will, there's a way. If you have the willpower, the interest, and the motivation, you do it. This is why they have to decide whether or not to commercialize the Boston Marathon.

Will Cloney and Jock Semple have long played major roles at Boston. Cloney has been the catalyst, Semple displays the temperament. They deserve all the respect and acknowledgement that is directed their way. They make and shape the personality of the race. They are the reason it is what it is. I am critical of several aspects of the race, but I have a deep respect for the two men.

I met Will in 1975, when I won Boston. I went to Japan with him to run in the thirty-kilometer race in Ohme in February 1976. The first two Americans to finish in Boston are invited to run in Ohme. The first two Japanese to finish Ohme are invited to run in Boston. I have gone to concerts at Symphony Hall with Will and, when I won the Will Cloney Trophy as the 1978 and 1979 Boston champion, I was touched by the significance of it. This trophy was designed specifically to honor Will Cloney for the work he has done to make Boston the great race it is. Of any medal, trophy, or prize I have ever won, this is one of the most meaningful. I have photographs and drawings of the trophy on my office wall in Boston.

Even though I have differences of opinion with Will on the matter of amateurism and how Boston should be run, this is my individual view as a runner. Will runs the race. He is a major factor in how it is to be run. He has had a lot of experience. He's smart. I have a lot of respect for him. I know him as a kind, friendly man. He works tremendously hard. Jock is the same way. They have pushed themselves right to the edge. They do tremendous amounts of work for the race.

They need more help. At least they are finally starting to get it
from the people at the Prudential, and this is a step in the right
direction.

The Multiple Sclerosis Society of America contacted Will, in
1977, to see if they could approach the marathon runners and
ask them to have friends and relatives fill out pledge forms to
raise money to fight multiple sclerosis. Will said, "Sure." They
contacted me and asked if I'd be honorary chairman. I went
out to meet Will at his house for pictures to illustrate the
campaign. Few people knew that Will was very ill at the time.
Yet, he did the work. Thousands of dollars have been raised
for multiple sclerosis, partly because Will recognized that the
Boston Marathon is more than just a race.

I first met Jock in 1973 when I placed third in a thirty-
kilometer race in Newton, Massachusetts. I joined the BAA. He
gave me the application. He's given me rubdowns and advice
on training. He's talked to me about travel expenses for races.
He's seen me race. He's given me encouragement along the
course. He's given me water. He's driven me to races in his car.
He picked me to win Boston in 1975, when nobody else did.
He has been, in general, a very positive force in my running
career, to say nothing of the careers of many other runners.

He has had his clashes with the women runners in the past.
He did jump off the bus and try to rip the number from Kathy
Switzer's shirt. The mark of a well-rounded person is the
ability to recognize a hasty mistake, to rebound, to come back
and account for some misunderstandings. He has done it so
well that he was the guy who fired the starting gun at the 1978
Bonne Bell ten-thousand-meter race for women in Boston.
Avon invited him to New York recently to promote their new
series of races for women only.

I have the greatest respect for Will and for Jock. They are the
personification of the Boston Marathon. They represent all of
the volunteers who work at Boston and at any of the many
marathons. They are the least-talked-about people in the sport

of running. It is one of the inadequacies of the sport that the volunteers who turn out on race day get no coverage or recognition. I thank them all here by thanking people such as Will Cloney and Jock Semple for their roles in the sport of running.

12
New York

New York is the new kid on the block. Brash, cocky, and out to establish an instant reputation, it moved into the neighborhood on October 24, 1976. This marathon is a production that feeds on the media hype and the infusion of corporate funds, the absolute antithesis of Boston. If Boston defends its amateuristic approach to the marathon, New York flaunts its relationship with big business. Still, it is all carried out very inoffensively, very tastefully.

This race has done a lot for the image of the city, providing a warm welcome to outsiders who had previously been fed negative thoughts about New York. There is the start at the tollbooths at the Staten Island end of the Verrazano Narrows Bridge, the run over the vast span of the bridge itself, the neighborhoods of the city, the crowds, and the finish near the Tavern on the Green in Central Park.

The New York City Marathon began modestly, as a run in Central Park on September 13, 1970. Then there were fewer than 150 runners who circled about Central Park four times and finished near Columbus Circle. Of course, New York ran the first marathon ever staged in the United States in 1896. As I mentioned, I first heard about it in 1974, when I went to New York and finished fifth in 2:35:59. Nina Kuscsik ran in 1970, and when women were permitted to run officially in AAU-sanctioned events, she won the women's New York City Marathon title in 1972.

Women have since been an integral part of New York. In 1975, the race served as the second AAU Women's Marathon Championship. In 1978, also an AAU championship for women, there were 1,134 women in a total field of 11,218 and Grete Waitz, a Norwegian schoolteacher from Oslo, turned her first marathon effort into a world record of 2:32:30. It was not an extremely fast course, and it was hot, in the middle to upper seventies, so that was indeed a remarkable performance.

New York is geared for bigness, and the New York City Marathon went big in 1976, when the sponsoring New York Road Runners Club invited top runners from around the world. The list of corporate sponsorship has included Manufacturer's Hanover, Perrier, the Rudin Family, New York Telephone, Finnair, New Times magazine, Etonic, and the Allen Carpet Company. This last laid down one mile of DuPont carpet over the grating on the Queensboro Bridge.

You follow the long blue line, pass the people outside the churches in Brooklyn, cross the bridge to Manhattan, run up through a funnel of humanity on First Avenue, and finally work your way down again to finish your run through the quiet stretches of Central Park. The finish area is transformed into one giant medical center, picnic area, and all over the place people are looking for friends and family who ran. That the marathon finishes in Central Park, where there's plenty of room for expansion, should the need arise, bodes well for the future of the race, although it contrasts with the frantic excitement generated in the tiny area available at the finish line at Boston.

What is important about New York is the professional manner in which it is put on. It has become, almost overnight, one of the major marathons in the world. In 1977, sponsors and race directors of the New York City Marathon created a better-quality race with better competition than Boston had ever achieved. New York was a small, run-of-the-mill race that was no different from hundreds of other marathons in the United States when I ran it in 1974. There are few marathons that rise above the rest in the United States. For a while it was Boston alone. Now there are Boston and New York. After that, there are Maryland, Honolulu, Culver City, the Skylon Marathon in upstate New York, Nike-OTC, and Newport, Rhode Island. Chicago is another question. It is debatable whether the large numbers of runners who began the race in 1978 helped elevate that race to a position of prestige among American marathons.

New York was an intimate race in 1974, with little press coverage and a minimal effort by the people involved in the New York Road Runners Club. They had practically no assistance, virtually no money, and not enough volunteers. There was nothing spectacular about it, nothing to arouse the imagination and interest of the general public. First prize was a trip to Athens, Greece, to run in the marathon there, on the course where it all began. I don't even know what the rest of the prizes were. People didn't turn out to watch the race. I remember running while bicycles and frisbees were zipping by. It was hardly more than what we would consider a fun run today.

That changed in 1976 when the New York Road Runners went to a number of banks, potential sponsors, and certain politicians in the city and said, "What about running a five-borough marathon?" The people who organized the effort were led by Fred Lebow, the indefatigable president of the club who has been involved with the race since its inception and serves as race director.

George Spitz, a writer and runner, had gone to Ted Corbitt, a former Olympic marathoner, and suggested such a race. Corbitt had already thought about it and had a course in mind. It all ended up in the lap of Percy Sutton, the borough president of Manhattan, who carried it to Mayor Abraham Beame. The family of the late Samuel Rudin, who was a runner, put their support behind it, and the trophy that goes to the winner is named in his memory. It is a silver tray from Tiffany's engraved with the marathon route.

The city backed it. One group after another came in. One borough, then another. Lebow kept being the catalyst. They came up with a lot of volunteers, but they also had the funds to do the job properly. They turned it into a great race. They became the first marathon to attract major network television coverage in 1978. It went all over the world via satellite. This should have happened in Boston. It didn't. It all happened in New York.

The quality of the field enhances the New York race. They consciously make an effort to bring in the best runners. They had the strongest women's field assembled anywhere in 1978, even stronger than the Avon Women's International Race held earlier in the year. They ended up with coverage in the news weeklies and they had the cover of *Sports Illustrated*. The entire spectacle was something that appealed to the mass media.

The runners were treated well. I have heard few criticisms of New York from runners, with the possible exception of New Zealand marathoner Jack Foster, who was ripped off for sixty dollars by a cabbie on his way from the airport to the city. There was ample water along the course, and the water stations were well marked. You could spot them easily as you approached, and you could also get ERG.

There were clocks around the course to give you your times. These might have been better marked, but they were still adequate. They had excellent crowd control. You ran through a cordon of sawhorses going up First Avenue. The people of the city were really happily wrapped up in it. I know of one runner who runs up First Avenue every year yelling, "Big Apple, you're delicious" to the people lining the route. It made a headline in the *Boston Globe* and was read into the record at a City Council meeting in New York.

You all come together at the finish line even though you may lose something: You lack the individual attention you may receive elsewhere because there are so many runners spread out over the grassy fields of Central Park. You might be on the ground with cramps and nobody is there to assist you. Your friends and relatives may not be able to find you because there are so many people. But these are situations you have to cope with in any mass marathon, and you should accept the inevitability of them before you enter. You should make plans to meet somebody special in a particular spot near the finish line.

There was ample medical support. They were able to take care of the difficulties that developed once they became aware of them. They had silver blankets to wrap around the runners at the finish, which were uniquely designed to insulate and warm the exhausted runner. There was a meal available. There were free T-shirts, hats, a tray showing the course, and souvenir posters. They offered a variety of things to the runner. They did a superb job for an event of this magnitude.

One of the drawbacks of New York was the presence of so many vehicles on the course and so many helicopters overhead. The helicopters dipped too low and blew up gigantic whirlwinds and dust and grit into my eyes. This hit a lot of the leaders. It happened three or four times. There were too many vehicles on the course. They were all filled with sponsors, officials, photographers, and writers, and perhaps too many people who had no good reason to be there. On this ground, I must plead guilty myself, at least in terms of intentions. I asked race officials if my wife could have a position on a vehicle where she could easily view the race. My request was rejected. I noticed fumes from the motorcycle policemen much more than I ever have in Boston, and surprisingly it was worse when I ran into Central Park. Maybe it was because traffic was closed off and you were away from cars in an isolated atmosphere.

The lack of an adequate interview area for the winner is one flaw of New York. I was taken to a place where I was unable to sit down. I was dragged several hundred yards in one direction and then one hundred yards in another direction. I was lugged two hundred yards into the middle of a field, and there was no seat to sit down on when I arrived there. When you finish a race, what you want to do first is take a drink and stretch a little. After that, you want to sit down. Once you've done that, there should be an opportunity for the press to interview you in an adequate area. Instead you have all these microphones shoved into your face the moment you cross the finish line. All they need is a cordoned-off area with a loudspeaker system that would enable the runner, a few minutes later, to answer all the questions for everyone at the same time. For a marathon that thrives on media attention, it's a question whether the media or the runner is treated more shabbily.

There is one thing that alienated me about New York and makes me feel more positive about Boston. That is the mistreatment of the wheelchair athlete. The New York organizers have been hostile toward the participation of people in wheelchairs who want to compete. Boston has opened its race to the wheelchair athlete and, in fact, has conducted a National Wheelchair Marathon Championship as an adjunct to the Boston Marathon. This has had the blessing of Will Cloney and the BAA.

I have always felt the wheelchair athlete should be permitted to compete in circumstances where, logistically, it does not create a safety hazard, I see no reason why the wheelchair athlete is any more of a hazard than the runner is. The competitors in Boston are experienced and they handle their chairs very well. They are trained athletes, like the able-bodied runners, and there is no reason to keep them off the course.

If you want to talk about safety hazards in New York, what about all the helicopters hovering over the 11,218 runners at the start and then stirring up dust all along the course? Or all the Subarus constantly zipping around the leading competitors? I think these were more of a safety hazard than one or two wheelchair athletes on the course. I have been in races all around the country with wheelchair athletes and I've never encountered any problem, and I know of no other athletes who have.

Public response to the wheelchair athlete is overwhelmingly positive. It's positive from the runners in the race and from the spectators watching the race. They love seeing these athletes in wheelchairs participating in the race. There is, however, some criticism that it takes away from the publicity of the top runners. There may be some justification in this, but it's overdone.

Wheelchair marathoning is something new. I view it much as I view women running marathons, which is also relatively new. They too get tremendous amounts of publicity, because it is an emerging phenomenon. More and more women are running marathons, and the press is proper in recognizing it. I think the woman marathoner and the wheelchair athlete both deserve tremendous credit for breaking ground. The Kathy Switzers, Nina Kuscsiks, and Jacqueline Hansens deserve recognition along with the Bob Halls and Mark Murrays. They were the pioneers.

All of the attention simply gets more participants of all kinds out there competing, and that's good. You have to look at any kind of running as a tool in the goal of national fitness. That's part of the concept of these mass marathons. People watch them and then later take part. I think it takes great courage to be a wheelchair competitor and a pioneer, to be an initiator and to try events that are neither popular nor easy to do.

For the New York officials to veto the wheelchair athletes is narrow-minded. It is also a question of ethics. It is discriminatory. The ultimate goal of many wheelchair athletes is to compete in races with other wheelchair athletes. The point must be made that disabled people can be real athletes and within their framework they can accomplish as much as an able-bodied person. I foresee major competitions with large numbers of wheelchair athletes at all distances. This kind of racing will grow, much as women's competition has. There are now lots of major events for women, and corporate support for them is continuing to grow.

But the sector of the population that has captured my* feelings and support the most is the forty-, fifty-, and sixty-year-olds. They are a group that up to now has never received, and still doesn't sufficiently receive, much support or encouragement to involve themselves in sports as a part of their life style. And that is completely wrong. Some of them are really quite good, and all of them are inspiring.

Fred Lebow is the heart and soul of the New York City Marathon, a tireless worker and worrier who serves as president of the New York Road Runners Club and director of the race. He has put the imprint of his personality, character, and feelings on the marathon. All of these are integrated into the fiber of the five-borough run.

He works incredibly hard, as hard as Will Cloney and Jock Semple do in Boston. He does the work of two men. He looks after the details personally, even making sure the blue line is put down a day or two before the race. In a bad attempt at a practical joke, three people put a bogus blue line down in the early morning hours before the 1978 race, but they were arrested in the act.

Lebow oversees the administration of the race, contacting runners, sponsors, and the media. He traveled to East Germany to try to convince the federation there to permit Waldemar

Cierpinski to run in New York. He was at Fukuoka in 1977, taking notes on how the Japanese run the marathon there and riding the press bus to observe the logistics of the race and how it is policed. In fact, Lebow has attempted to contact the top runners from Europe, Asia, South America—the world—in an effort to make New York the world's best marathon.

I think, at times, Lebow does overrate certain runners on past performance, rather than recognize who is running well at the moment. Overall, this does not diminish his talents as a race administrator. He is a runner himself and he has an understanding and appreciation of what goes into a race. "The most important goal," he has said, "is to put on a good race for the runners." He does.

He weeds out the sponsors, selecting the best. They have an effective scheduling system in New York. They put on an entire series of races throughout the year, and the marathon is their gem. The difference in the treatment of the runners in New York and Boston is marked. I've told you about how Jack Fultz had his car towed in Boston and nobody came to his assistance for some time, while I had my car towed in New York and the New York Road Runners Club paid to get it back.

They bring in many of the top runners to New York for clinics. They had a medical symposium on the marathon and it was one of the biggest ever held. The United Nations has had programs and receptions tied in with the international competitors, and they also gave out an award. The Tavern on the Green gave me a magnum of champagne when I won in 1976, and they hosted a dinner for two.

The top women competitors are also better recognized in New York. I understand that the people at Bonne Bell wanted to present a gold medal with a diamond chip to the first woman finisher at Boston, but it was vetoed by BAA officials. There never was an award to the first master to finish at Boston until 1977.

One major difference between Boston and New York is that

New York is a wholly urban marathon. It starts in Staten Island, progresses through Brooklyn, Queens, Manhattan Island, and the Bronx, and finishes back in Central Park in Manhattan. It is run between large buildings, old and deserted warehouses, past skyscrapers and over manholes and potholes of the city streets. You run into all the ethnic groups, cheering in their own languages. It adds a real flavor to the course.

Boston is strictly point-to-point. The ethnic flavor is not there. It's not an urban marathon, in that sense. It's run through the countryside and the smaller towns. You spend maybe one or two minutes passing through the centers of the towns. You never acquire the feeling that you are running in the city until you come close to the finish at the Prudential.

I like the Boston course a little better, though. I like the point-to-point concept. I have a better understanding and feeling of where I'm going. When I run in New York, I'm never sure where I'm heading. I'm just following this blue line and these race trucks. I can't remember where I was or where I'm aiming next, I can't pick out the landmarks the way I can in Boston. Maybe it's simply because I know the city of Boston better, but there's less confusion and more clarity in my mind during the race in Boston, with the exception that Boston does not have official, clearly marked mileage markers for the runners at regular intervals, and New York does.

The start at New York is preferable, though. It's wide out there at the tollbooth plaza at the end of the Verrazano Narrows Bridge. You don't have any problems with jostling or pushing. There's plenty of time to spread out and ample room to do so. It's an impressive start, running over the bridge. That stays with you, even after running it three or four times. Chris Stewart, the British runner who has run well in New York on several occasions, has said, "There is no finer place in the world to start a race." It is spectacular. It is that way, as well, when you cross the Queensboro Bridge, heading into Manhattan with the backdrop of the skyscrapers of the city.

Conversely, as I've said before, Boston has a more spectacular finish. The New York finish is less awe-inspiring for the runner, partly because the last fifty to one hundred yards of Boston are downhill whereas New York finishes on a slight upgrade which tends to take the zing out of a glorious finish. There is a decent crowd there, but the amphitheater effect of Boston is lacking, where all the people are waiting in anticipation for the winner. The crowd noise never diminishes. You get the feeling that the crowd is crazy about the runners in Boston.

Things are more subdued in New York, with the exception of the route along First Avenue, but interest in the New York Marathon keeps growing, and that may change in the years to come. I like Boston because the crowds get bigger as you approach the Pru. You have a clear view of it. In New York you ignore the scenery after a while. It becomes confusing. Of course, to be fair, I don't know the city well enough, but it seems to me there are so many turns and intersections and strange areas to pass through.

13
Fukuoka

This is the Holy Grail, the Super Bowl of marathoning. I first heard of it when Amby Burfoot ran Fukuoka in 1968. I myself first ran it in 1975. If you are a runner conscious of your position on the world lists, this is where you want to be on the first Sunday in December every year. Fukuoka, simply put, is where it is at.

The city of one million is on the island of Kyushu, the southernmost in the Japanese archipelago. It was a gateway of culture, the cradle of Japanese civilization. It is not only a cultural but also a commercial center, noted for silk textiles and the Hakata doll, a figurine made of clay dating from the 1600s. It is less than two hours by air from Tokyo, eight hours by high-speed train.

Fukuoka was the site of a marathon as early as 1947, when Japan was recovering from the ravages of the war. From its inception, it has been sponsored by the *Asahi* newspaper, with its daily circulation of seven million. Spectators wave red and white paper flags handed out by the newspaper, and the lead runners pass through a sea of flags on the course.

There is an esoteric character to the race, largely because of its remoteness from the world at large and because it is an elitist field. It was elevated to the status of unofficial world championship in 1966, when Japanese amateur athletic officials invited a select group of top marathoners to compete with as many as eighty Japanese runners.

The race starts and finishes in Heiwadai Stadium, near the site of the ancient Fukuoka Castle. You head out through the city streets and along a course that winds around Hakata Bay, before retreating over the same route and finishing up on the track in Heiwadai. You face a headwind going out, a tailwind on the return, and the course is noted for its fast times. It is so flat that on some of the streets it seems you can see for miles ahead and behind you. The course design leads to an unrelenting pace throughout the entire race.

Through the end of 1978, there have been nineteen sub-2:12 times at Fukuoka. I ran a 2:10:55 in 1977 and a 2:11:26 in 1975. There have been twelve sub-2:12 times in Boston through 1979, six of them in the fast 1978 race. The Fukuoka course, under the prevailing cool conditions, invites fast times, and the Japanese see to it that a classic field is there to run them.

Only at Fukuoka, the Olympics, and perhaps the European Championships every four years is there such a large group of runners still fighting strongly for the race at the halfway mark.

When Amby ran it in 1968, his time was 2:14:28, just .08 off the then American record of Buddy Edelen. I can remember him telling me that his sixth-place time was the fastest that he was capable of at the time. I knew he had trained very hard for the race, logging up to thirty-five miles on some training runs. That all boggled my mind in those days, and still does to some extent.

My feeling for Fukuoka grew out of what Amby did, even though my participation would be some seven years in the future. My interest returned when I started to read about Frank Shorter going to Fukuoka and winning every year. Most Americans never ventured very far in terms of marathon competitions. He was the exception. He went to Fukuoka and won in 1971 prior to his gold medal Olympic performance, and repeated in 1972, 1973, and 1974. He was the first American to win (I am the only other) and he is the only runner to win it four times. Jerome Drayton of Canada has won it three times.

You had to break 2:30 to get into the race. Press coverage, outside Japan, was minimal. Because it was run at noon on Sunday in Japan, that meant it finished after midnight on Saturday on the East Coast of the United States. By the time wire copy reached America, most papers had gone to bed for the night. All of which meant no report at all in the Sunday papers and no more than a tiny paragraph or two that might make it into the Monday papers.

This added to the mystique of Fukuoka, the fact that only a knowledgeable clique of American runners knew about it, and only a few Americans had run in it. Kenny Moore, who ran a 2:11:35, then an American record, in the 1970 Fukuoka International Marathon, wrote an article about it for *Sports Illustrated*. Buddy Edelen, Burfoot, Shorter, 1973 Boston winner Jon Anderson, and Moore were the only Americans invited to run until I went in 1975. Six Americans ran in 1978, double the previous high. American shoe companies have started sending their representative marathoners, and so the field has been bulked up. New Balance has sent Tom Fleming, Vin Fleming and Randy Thomas. Nike has sent Tony Sandoval and Lionel Ortega. Garry Bjorklund raced Fukuoka well in 1978, with a PR of 2:13:15. He had won a trip to Fukuoka by winning another road race.

In terms of fast times, everything is in order. If you can hang on, you are guaranteed a fast time. I believe Fukuoka is so flat and easy that it's possible to run less than a good race and still get a pretty fast time. Witness my own 2:12:51 in 1978. If you look at the winning times, they are pretty consistent over the years. Derek Clayton, in fact, ran the fastest winning time

(2:09:36) in the second race in 1967. If you go quite deep into the finishers, the same is true. In the 1978 race, won by Toshihiko Seko of Japan, Fukuoka produced the fastest seventh-, eighth-, ninth-, and tenth-place marathon times in history. Chris Wardlaw of Australia was seventh in 2:13:03; Randy Thomas was eighth in 2:13:11, Garry Bjorklund was ninth in 2:13:15, and Rich Hughson of Canada was tenth in 2:13:21.

Even though there are more people running marathons and more people moving up from the steeplechase, à la Cierpinski and other track distance runners, Clayton remains the only one to break the 2:10 barrier at Fukuoka. I think it only fair to add that Japanese athletic officials have told me the course was two hundred meters short when Derek set the course record. Yet, Derek told me he had the Japanese ascertain the length of the course to be sure of the record.

Officially, Jerome Drayton ran the second fastest time (2:10:08) in 1975, when I was third. Dave Chettle of Australia has the third best time (2:10:20), and Seko has the fourth fastest (2:10:21) after his surprise win in 1978. If the course actually was two hundred meters short when Clayton set the record, it would be equated to a 2:10-plus time, meaning Drayton may really own the best Fukuoka time.

The exceptions to the course's flatness consist of a slight upgrade at ten kilometers, and a short steep hill just before you enter the stadium. At the halfway point, you make a turn around a cone in the road out in the countryside on the peninsula. The crowd thins out when you leave the city, but it thickens and the people wave flags madly when you return. When you approach the stadium as the winner, firecrackers go off. I could hear them in 1978, as I was about three-quarters of a mile from the finish line and I thought, "Last year, they were for me."

No marathon is run any better. Mistakes are rarely made. Everything is checked and rechecked. The race is run according to international rules, which means runners cannot receive any assistance from anybody else in the race or on the course. If you develop a leg cramp and someone should run out and try to massage your leg, you are disqualified. If you are handed water, the same is true. Runners are not to share their water bottles with one another.

What you do is place your preferred drink in a little plastic bottle with your name on a tag. Race officials give it to you in the lobby of the Nishitetsu Grand Hotel, probably the finest hotel in Fukuoka. All of this is done one or two days before the race, according to International Amateur Athletic Federation regulations. They check the contents, making sure it is acceptable. They place your bottles at five-kilometer intervals on the course. You must recognize the tag, pick up the bottle as you run by, and take it from there. In Boston and New York, you can take water from people on the course.

Each foreign runner has an interpreter who aids him with the language barriers and assists him in his preparations for the race. A thorough physical examination, including blood pressure, urine sample, and pulse is done the day before the race by a crew of doctors and nurses. Should a runner need medical treatment for injury or illness, his needs are quickly taken care of. For example, in 1977, I had a sinus problem, which affected my balance and hearing. I was taken for medical treatment twice before the race. Unfortunately, neither treatment helped, and I ran the race half-deaf. Trevor Wright of Great Britain, who received acupuncture treatment for a leg injury before the 1978 race, said it helped considerably and he ran his fastest marathon, a 2:12:31 for fourth place.

Fukuoka is televised as a live event in Japan by a major network. That adds the television crews to the vehicles on the course. The press truck is forced to stay behind the lead runner or runners. Crowds are enthusiastic, but nothing like Boston or New York. There are no helicopters, no dogs to jump out and annoy you. The crowd stays back on the curbs, with the police and army personnel blending in. There is a general discipline that is lacking in American crowds. It is a Japanese trademark that the crowds are knowledgeable, aware of who you are and respectful.

If a runner starts falling back after a certain point, he is pulled off the course. If you are more than twenty minutes behind the leader midway into the race, they pick you up and put you on a bus. Two runners from Saudi Arabia traveled to Fukuoka in 1977 and, as their coach said, "We came all this way and they never were allowed to finish." Since the road is never completely closed to traffic out on the peninsula, they want to get the runners off the course early and attend to the ceremonies inside the stadium.

Japanese officials all wear official jackets and hats easily recognizable on the course. At each water station they read off your splits. Everything is very clear cut. There is little of the confusion that you often find at Boston and New York. Marathoning is an honored tradition in Japan, and the people appreciate those who run in Fukuoka. The appreciation is evident from the time you arrive until you leave. The treatment is white glove.

You may be a relative unknown, but you are met at the airport and made to feel at home. A half dozen or more photographers are also waiting there. The top marathoners treasure an invitation to Fukuoka, an opportunity to participate in a world-championship event. Some runners have paid their own way to get there. Chettle did when he ran the 2:10:20 in 1975. Drayton has done it. Because of the prestige attached to Fukuoka, runners will go to those lengths.

I have been taken to a factory where Hakata dolls are made, to City Hall, and to famous Japanese temples. The opening ceremony is held on Saturday afternoon, and Japanese women do a traditional folk dance. There was even a top spinner, a sort of magician, performing this year. The foreign runners are introduced on stage at the City Hall, given bouquets of flowers by the schoolchildren of Fukuoka, and presented gifts by the citizenry.

Because the race is on live national television, the winner is recognized all over the country. I was asked for autographs in department stores, on the street, in the hotel lobby, and at a restaurant where a group of us went for a late night snack the night after I won in 1977. Live television has been a part of the Fukuoka Marathon for several years, but it only came to the United States for the first time for a few minutes during the New York City Marathon in 1978. Have we been out of step? Yes, but we're getting there.

Everybody wants to give you something at Fukuoka. The winner, in particular, is showered with awards, trophies, and gifts. I've had babies held up for me to kiss, and a schoolgirl who came up to me as I left the stadium offered me a doughnut! High school girls came to the Nishitetsu Grand Hotel seeking my autograph, schoolboys wanted my number in the lobby. I was made to feel as if I were Elvis Presley in concert.

Press coverage is intense. You are met by popping flashbulbs from the first minute at the airport, interviewed on television every day. Since I had the fastest time of any competitor entering the 1975 race, my first, I was installed as the favorite and, consequently, I was introduced to the media very early. I went through the airplane terminal, sat down in a suite, and found my picture in the papers the next day. Since I was the defending champion in 1978, every time I stopped to talk to someone on the track, I was surrounded by cameras.

The finishing ceremony is brief, simple, but unforgettable. The top ten finishers are seated facing the crowd in Heiwadai Stadium. Schoolgirls in uniforms carry prizes on trays and the top amateur athletic official, Hanji Aoki, presents the awards personally. This is the Olympic treatment, minus the playing of national anthems. A band is present and appropriately stirring music is a part of the ceremony. The race is treated in a

serious vein, no clowning or circuslike atmosphere at
Fukuoka. Every award is made in Japanese and English. When
the Japanese swept the first three spots in 1978, the ceremony
was a particularly moving experience for the crowd.

Even with all the pomp and ceremony, there is an underly-
ing practicality to the finish. When you finish, they throw a
blanket around you to keep you warm. That's done in New
York, too, except there you are crushed by the media if you
win. But in Fukuoka, you are taken over to a tent, asked how
you feel, and given a drink, whatever you like, hot or cold.
Fruit is available if you're hungry. If you want to stretch or lie
down, there are cots, blankets and ample room. You take your
drinks and blanket to the award ceremonies, sit down, and are
left alone to recover.

When you win, you are put on a large platform and you feel
like a king on a throne, answering questions and having your
picture taken. When I was up there in 1977, I felt a little chill
and Tommy Leonard, who made the trip to Japan that year,
gave me his Falmouth Track Club jacket to wear. Incongruous
as it was, it served the purpose.

There is a party back at the Nishitetsu Grand Hotel that
evening, with officials, the American consul, Princess Nic-
hitibi, media, all the runners and coaches enjoying a lavish
buffet, and all you want to drink. Tommy Leonard went up on
the stage when he was there in 1977, started singing "You Are
My Sunshine," and we all wound up joining in. After that,
runners from all the different countries sang songs of their
homeland. Leonard started a new Fukuoka tradition and it was
picked up again in 1978. I can still remember Lasse Viren
laughing, hooting, and mimicking the Russians, Leonid
Moiseyev and his coach, as they sang a dour folk song in 1977.

You usually end up in Tokyo, where editors of the *Hochi
Shimbun* pick you up, transport you, take you to the Ginza
section for dinner and some nightclubbing, and then wish you
well as you leave the country. The *Hochi* newspaper sponsors

the Ohme race in February, a sister race of the Boston Marathon. Two Americans are invited to Ohme every year after Boston, and two Japanese are invited to run in Boston.

FUKUOKA, 1978. It had Olympic overtones. Jerome Drayton was there, bidding to match Frank Shorter as the only four-time winner. "I would never come here," he said, "unless I felt I was physically ready to win it. It's too far to go and too important to me to come here and fool around."

Waldemar Cierpinski, the 1976 Marathon gold medalist, came from East Germany. He had been a recent fourth-place finisher in the European Championships in early September in Prague. Leonid Moiseyev, the European champion (2:11:58), who finished second to me in 1977, was there. Shigeru So, who ran the second best marathon time ever (2:09:06) in Beppu, Japan, earlier in the year, was one of an emerging group of Japanese runners.

The largest American field in history included Randy Thomas, my Greater Boston TC teammate who had finished fifth (2:11:25) in Boston and by-passed New York; Garry Bjorklund, the guy who had piled it on in the heat at New York; and Tom Fleming, who had been fourth at Fukuoka in 1977 and has two seconds in Boston to his credit. It was, overall, a deadly marathon field, with more depth than any field since Montreal.

So and Fleming took it out, with So simply moving away by himself by the time we were heading out into the countryside. We watched Tom fall back after about five kilometers, but unfortunately, So never seemed likely to slow down. He led at five kilometers (15:19), ten (30:26), fifteen (45:36), twenty (1:00:50), midway (1:04:12) into the race, twenty-five kilometers (1:16:15), thirty (1:31:48) and thirty-five kilometers (1:47:30) before he faded.

It was depressing, as early as fifteen kilometers, to see So with such a lead. Moiseyev, Cierpinski, and the rest of us were back in a pack and we stayed somewhat together. So was

1:04:12 at the halfway point, about ten seconds faster than what I had run to that point one year earlier, when I finished in 2:10:55. He had the television truck up in front, focusing on him.

I felt detached, not able to compete against a runner so far away from me. I had lost that relationship between two runners I feel when I run my best. It was also difficult because nobody in the pack would pass me to try to chase So. Everyone stayed either right next to me, or right behind me. They thought, as I did, that So would ultimately slow down and one of us would make his move.

Before I left for Japan, I had come down with the flu. It was just before Thanksgiving and I was unable to visit my parents in Newington, Connecticut. Before I contracted the flu, I thought I was capable of a 2:11. After picking up the flu, I cut my mileage down to 60 a week. My normal mileage would have been about 130. This threw everything out of kilter. I had to come back from that low mileage and try to build up to 20 miles a day. It hurt. I thought I might not have much chance to win the race, but I thought I had a decent shot at second or third. However, I always say, "That's running." There are no "ifs" in this sport. I like it that way.

I stayed in second place through the first thirteen miles, then two Japanese runners named Toshihiko Seko and Hideki Kita, plus Chris Wardlaw of Australia went by me. I felt considerably fatigued, a way I never feel if I'm having a decent race, at least not at the twenty-kilometer point of a race. I knew I was in trouble. As a matter of fact, I wasn't thinking of 2:12. I was thinking of quitting.

I developed a side ache. Perhaps it was because of the flu. But, I also had made a classic mistake, which I only make about once or twice each year. I had breakfast the morning of the race. I had an omelet, bacon, toast, coffee, and orange juice. It was about three or four hours before the race. I never should have done it and I cursed myself at the halfway point.

I think I did it because I was a little worried about the race.

There was a lot of pressure on me as defending champion and as a person who had a good shot at winning the Triple Crown—Boston, New York, and Fukuoka in one year. I still knew I had a shot to win. People conceive of me as fanatical and obsessed with winning and at times I am. Some other times, I'm actually casual about racing and competing. I try to be casual and, therefore, I sometimes do something crazy like that. It was a critical mistake which I intend never to make again.

Why so much food? I ate breakfast at 8:30 or 9:00 and since the race would start at noon, I figured I could get away with eating a fairly small breakfast. I felt I wasn't going to finish the race until 2:10 or 2:15 and I should have a little food in me. The myth still exists that you need food for strength, and I occasionally succumb to it, but it is pretty clear that an athlete performs best on an empty stomach.

Tom Fleming is always strict about his pre-race diet. He will never eat anything at all on the morning of a race. We sat down together that morning in Japan over breakfast with our wives, and he was kidding me about all the food I was eating. I had a big breakfast on the morning of the Ohme, Japan, race one year and I won it. That was cheating, but I got away with it that time. I recall how freaked out Tom was that I'd do such a crazy thing. But this time the field was too tough and I'd pay for my folly.

Even though you are not having a top day at Fukuoka, as I have said, it is the type of course where you can still run a pretty fast time if you keep moving. You have to die pretty badly to run slowly at Fukuoka. As I came up the hill into the stadium, I looked behind me and I saw a runner in red gaining on me. As he came closer, I realized it wasn't Randy Thomas, but Moiseyev.

He ran behind me for a few strides on the track. I tried to respond, but I was exhausted. He passed me very steadily as we did the final four hundred meters. There was no way I could successfully battle him. He beat me by seven seconds, finishing fifth. I was sixth, and after I crossed the finish line and went over to a cot, Ellen told me the Japanese had taken one, two, and three.

Seko won it in 2:10:21, a great time and one that I probably couldn't have equaled in this race even without the flu and breakfast. Kita was second in 2:11:05. So was third in 2:11:41, followed by Trevor Wright of Great Britain (2:12:31), Moiseyev (2:12:44), and me (2:12:51). All I could think of was, "The Japanese have returned."

This was the way it had been in Boston in the late 1960s, when the Japanese runners dominated. They had swept the top three spots. That had also been a total domination of the race by one country, which I've seen happen in only a very few road races where many foreign countries are involved. It happened at San Blas in 1974, when the Finns went one, two, three.

Such domination shows up when a small group of top distance runners of one country have become really intense about an event and have focused on it. The Japanese made such an effort for the 1978 Fukuoka race. The Japan amateur athletic federation had been hard on the Japanese runners, because of their track record at Fukuoka. They played up their failures. Now they could play up their successes.

The Triple Crown. It is a concept more familiar to other sports, particularly horseracing. Tennis and golf have their grand slams. But the concept has never been a part of the marathon scene. It became a phrase after a headline in a Boston paper was picked up in the *Racer's Record Book*, put together by the BAA after the 1978 Boston Marathon. I had won New York, Fukuoka, and Boston in less than six months, and the headline said I had donned the Triple Crown.

Amby Burfoot, who was the East Coast editor of *Runner's World*, made a correction. "You have to do it in a calendar year," he told me. "You have to win Boston, New York, and Fukuoka in the same year to win the Triple Crown." Very few runners had ever run in all three in their careers, never mind in the same year. In fact, Tom Fleming and I were the only ones to do it in 1978. Of course, I had won the first two races in the latter months of 1977 and Boston in early 1978, so the wires and the media played up the Triple Crown theme.

For some reason, I felt more pressure to win New York in 1978, I think, than I did to win Fukuoka. Maybe I lost my intensity after I had the flu. I'm not sure how to describe it. It was all sort of confusing. I was strong for New York, weaker for Fukuoka. There was so much media hype in New York, in addition to the challenge of Bjorklund. If I were to win at Fukuoka, yes, it would be a significant achievement. If I didn't, I'd be upset. That was my attitude going in. Yet, I felt I could run a pretty fast marathon even without winning. I would be satisfied with a sub-2:12.

Originally, there had been a kind of Triple Crown concept based on the São Paulo, Brazil, Midnight Run on January first, the San Blas half marathon in Coamo, Puerto Rico, on the first Sunday in February, and Boston. Some meet directors in recent years had been trying to promote that as the Triple Crown of road racing.

The present Triple Crown concept is very American. Two of the races are in the United States. Even though they are two of the best and the biggest in the world, it is difficult to conceive of an Australian, a South American, a Russian, or an East German often becoming involved in them. Because of that, it is hardly fair to view these races in an international sense.

If foreign athletes and officials are unaware of the concept, they are very aware of an individual who could win all three in the same year. They'd have their eyes on him. I can attest to that. I still like the idea of a Triple Crown, and sometime in the future, I'll shoot for it again.

Actually, the primary thing on my mind as I went to

Fukuoka was to earn the number-one ranking in the world for the second straight year and the third time in four years. *Track & Field News* compiles the rankings for its annual issue every January. I felt if I won there was no doubt I would be number one. If Moiseyev won, he would be ranked number one because of his European Championship, followed by a Fukuoka win. If So won, I felt he would be the number-one man.

As it turned out, *Track & Field News* picked Moiseyev "in an upset" as the number-one marathoner for 1978. The reasoning was that he beat me in Fukuoka, in our only head-to-head confrontation. He had beaten a teammate, Nikolay Penzin, by one second in Prague. To say the least, I was not too happy with the rankings, feeling I should have been ranked number one in the world. It is important to me, to my career, to my feelings. I care about my ranking as a marathoner.

The *Track & Field News* rankings are done by an Englishman, who probably saw the European Championships, but who did not see Boston or New York or even Fukuoka. I can run a lot of races, and can have ten sub-2:12 marathons or even fifteen or twenty. But all I can do is run and let others evaluate. It irritates me that the recognized "authority" is so limited in his sphere and bases his judgment on a really insular experience and viewpoint.

14
Women, Health, and Fitness

The scene in Central Park, in the immediate aftermath of the 1978 New York City Marathon, was somewhat akin to a major airport on a long holiday weekend. Can order be created out of chaos? As the first-place finisher, I was herded across a meadow to a tiny bandstand and led up to a cramped area, where I patiently tried to answer the questions that were hurled at me from every direction.

I was unaware, at the time, that a woman named Grete Waitz was on the opposite side of the same bandstand, answering questions like, "Who are you?" She was a Norwegian school-teacher from Oslo, an unpublicized entry in the race, and on this hot day out there in the five boroughs of the city, she had made history, a world record in her first marathon.

She had been invited to run New York about one week before the race. "I wanted to try a marathon," she casually told the press. She went out and ran 2:32:30, lowering the world record for women by more than two minutes. Christia Vahlen-sieck of France had set the previous standard of 2:34:47 one year earlier in a marathon in West Berlin.

What was particularly significant about the time was that it was set on a hot day, in weather hardly conducive to such a performance. If it had been cooler, she would have had a decent shot at breaking 2:30, making her the first woman to run in the 2:20s. Nearly as important was the fact that this marathon was her first. In addition, she seldom had run farther than twelve miles in any training runs. Track buffs were familiar with the name Grete Waitz, and her marathon record is not so surprising, taken within the context that she is a two-time world cross-country champion and one of the top women fifteen-hundred-meter and three-thousand-meter runners in the world, and has been for several years. In short, she had been a big name in track and field and now she had become a big name in marathoning.

If there was a dramatic lowering of marathon times by women in the 1970s, it is surely a portent for the 1980s. For so long, there were only a few women marathoners in the United States. Roberta Gibbs slipped from some bushes into the Boston Marathon field in 1966, and later in several other years. That a woman would run the marathon was half a joke and half mind-boggling to many people. Kathy Switzer ran as K. Switzer, Number 261, in 1967, when her entry had been officially accepted. When she was spotted, as I said, Jock Semple of the BAA tried to throw her off the course, saying she was not an "official entry."

Women could not run officially in an AAU marathon until 1972, and the United States Olympic Committee has done little, if anything, to push for the marathon as an Olympic event for women. Women are just beginning to scratch the surface of distance running in the world, to put the same effort into it that men have for decades. South America, Africa, and most parts of Asia are still very minimally involved.

When and if the top long-distance performers (1,500m. to

10,000m.) in the track world start running the marathon, times are going to dip even more dramatically. So far, most of the women who have moved into the marathon are primarily road runners, and they have lacked the background of a high school and college track program. For a long time, women were simply shoved into the background in sports programs, and, to a great extent, they still have a ways to go before their opportunities to excel are equal to those of men.

The women's liberation movement and the advent of Title IX on the collegiate level has changed all of this, to some degree. Equal amounts of scholarship aid and equal locker space for women are the result, at least on paper. The corporations are taking proper note of the changes taking place in regard to women in running, with L'Eggs, Colgate-Palmolive, Avon, and Bonne Bell stepping to the forefront. Cultural myths that women aren't competitive and aggressive are being knocked down. Have you ever seen Jan Merrill and Francie Larrieu lock up in an indoor fifteen-hundred-meter race? Or have you heard of Marty Cooksey virtually pulling herself over the finish line of the 1978 New York City Marathon on her hands and knees?

The marketing people at L'Eggs Corporation lured the ten-thousand-meter mini-marathon for women in Central Park away from Bonne Bell in 1978. Out of this race came a more positive image for the company. They used to spend $100,000 to put on a tennis tournament for a few women. They discovered that for about $90,000 they could put on the mini-marathon for more than four thousand women. They received page-one coverage in the *New York Times* and a positive identification with an event that improved the health and spirits of the community.

Women are out running in increasingly larger numbers, a fact I notice daily when I head out from our Running Center in Cleveland Circle and pass by the reservoir near Boston College. Even in the really cold days of winter, it seemed there were more women out there than men. It is a sign of the times, the carry-over from the liberation movement, and a reflection of the feeling of independence women now relish as a part of their daily lives.

When the times in the marathon start to plunge, the inevitable question both for men and women is, "Where is the limit?" Whereas the world record of Derek Clayton of Australia has remained frozen at 2:08:33.6 since 1969, the world record for women has been lowered from 3:07:26 in 1967 to 2:27:31. It is not physiologically possible for a woman to run as fast as a man in an event as "short" as the marathon, although there's a theory that women seem to handle their race fatigue better than men at this distance. I keep recalling how fresh Gayle Barron looked the morning after her win in PR time at Boston in 1978.

I think women are capable, in the next decade, of running in the middle 2:20s. I'd predict a 2:24, a 2:25 or a 2:26 by the middle 1980s. There were seven women who had broken 2:40 through the end of 1978, and 2:40 became even less of a barrier in 1979.

There is a marvelous American of Japanese descent named Miki Gorman, who ran a 2:39:11 in her 1976 New York win when she was over forty. She is a gutsy, determined performer who is respected all over the world. She has won in Japan and Europe in major competitions. She's not extremely fast on the tracks or over shorter distances, but she has logged hundred-mile weeks, hundred-mile races, and has won New York and Boston twice. With this kind of desire, anything is possible.

The main reason, I feel, that women are not going to run as fast as men in a marathon is because women do not have the muscles to enable them to reach as high a performance level. There is a point where the body starts to utilize fat more than the carbohydrates stored in muscle tissue and, at that point, it is possible a woman might produce a clocking as fast or faster than a man. In terms of physiology, it might be at fifty miles, perhaps after six to eight hours of running.

I don't believe there is adequate data to pinpoint the

distance where such a change might occur. Women can handle fatigue and stress better than men, but the overall powering factor in a marathon race is the speed-strength combination. There are some people who say that, at least theoretically, a woman can run as fast as a man in a marathon. I believe they are wrong. On the other hand, I admit to feeling a bit uncomfortable when discussing what women or men cannot do. I like to think of what women and men can do.

There are statements in the literature of the sport that are downright ludicrous. Some coaches said a young runner named Wesley Paul, who was nine years old at the time, was likely to break two hours in a marathon one day. He holds the world record for his age group in the marathon and has done 2:55, but it will be about fifteen years before he will reach his peak as a long-distance runner or marathoner. Physiologically, the present understanding is that a human is capable of a 2:06 or 2:05 marathon. Maybe Wesley will beat two hours in fifteen years, if man's evolution proceeds that rapidly, but I don't know of any coaches, doctors, or anybody else who is qualified to predict that someone is going to break two hours in a marathon fifteen years or so down the road, based on what he's done at the age of nine.

HEALTH. I received a phone call from a writer at *The Washington Post* on the day following the death of Representative Goodloe E. Byron of Maryland of a heart attack while running in Washington, D.C. Here was a classic case of newspaper overreaction. A journalist went out for some flashy newspaper material just because the man who died was a runner.

The automatic Pavlovian response was to call me. Even though the writer said he called me to get a balanced approach to the story, I'm sure he found a lot of people who reacted, "Oh, my God, yes. Jogging is terrible!" There are many doctors who would come out and say the same thing. Take a look at them. See how fat and overweight some of them are. Ask them what their pulse is. Ask them about their own physical history. Don't take anything for granted, just because they have M.D. after their names. They're not gods.

I like to think of the doctor who told Clarence DeMar, who later came to be known as "Mr. Marathon" after he won Boston seven times, not to run because his heart couldn't take it. Clarence took the advice for several years, until the doctor died of a heart attack. I believe American medical men do a fine job of putting plastic veins and pacemakers into people, but when any of them spout off about not being sure "jogging" is healthy for you, I feel sick to my stomach.

The truth was that Goodloe Byron had been told by doctors not to run. There was a family history of heart trouble, and he had experienced some himself. Actually, his wife said she felt he lived longer than he would have if he hadn't been a runner. It is true that a few people have suffered heart attacks during races, but they almost always have had some genetic biological weaknesses in their background. They might well have suc-cumbed during any strenuous exercise—or playing poker, for that matter. These heart-attack victims were probably unaware of their genetic flaws because they weren't stress-tested or given a thorough physical examination. Basically, doctors who make blanket recommendations not to get involved in physical exercise are ignorant practitioners who are doing a disservice to the public.

It seems that more and more people are flocking to hospitals. Aren't our medical bills high enough? Don't enough people die at age forty or fifty from heart attacks here in America? What's wrong with practicing some form of preventive medicine? This can be mostly defined in terms of aerobic exercise. There are various forms. I just happen to think running is one of the best ways to maintain a sound level of cardiovascular fitness, the most important kind of fitness.

Currently, there is an overwhelming amount of data ac-

cumulated by cardiovascular researchers pointing to the physiologically positive effects of running. Yet, many doctors and
researchers are reluctant to make statements that regular
aerobic exercise is good for you. In fact, let me tell you this: It
is vitally *necessary* for you and will improve your life and
make you relatively immune from heart attacks or diseases
related to your arterial system.

From my own experiences, from reading literature on
running, heart disease, and related health problems, and from
talking to thousands of runners, my feeling is that you not only
improve your health by running, but you feel psychologically
better as a result of it. Movement is a positive action for your
mind and your body. I mentioned the eighty-year-old man I
ran with in a hilly marathon one December in Maryland who
had so much energy left after the race he went to a party and
demonstrated the extent of his vitality by doing calisthenics,
standing on his head, dancing, and raising hell for several
hours.

I often see people thirty or forty years younger who are far
below the same level of fitness enjoyed by that man of eighty.
What is important is that fitness is within the reach of most
people. That's one reason why there are so many people
running. We're finding out what our boundaries are. General
medical opinion tends to be too conservative. Staying out of
the hospital is what should be stressed, not fear of too much
exercise.

When I was in Washington for the dedication of the Perrier
Parcours in the spring of 1978, I met one of the directors of the
American Medical Association. I indicated how in this country there was little effort on the part of the government to
educate the public about the positive aspects of exercise. It
was like talking to a wall.

Sure, there are messages on cigarette packages warning you
that if you smoke you might get cancer. How about something
positive? How about Frank Shorter or Marty Liquori, two of

America's most widely known runners, being shown on TV running and saying, "Hey, I'm in good shape. How about you?" I asked the AMA man why we support negative health policies, such as subsidies to the tobacco industry. He said, in effect, that people have their jobs tied up in the industry. A true politician. It was the most incredible rationale I'd ever heard in my life, coming from a guy who was supposed to be a spokesman for the American Medical Association.

He said he ran a mile or two daily and his sons were athletic. *Yet, when I suggested we ought to export tobacco to our enemies, he just sloughed it off.* To me, his response epitomizes to a great extent why there is a problem with heart disease in this country—why there are so many occupied hospital beds in the United States, and why we have a staggering problem with health bills. Many doctors simply have no interest in promoting fitness as preventive medicine. The fact is that we have to take it upon ourselves to go out there and maintain a minimal level of fitness to keep us away from the hospitals.

There are, however, other doctors, nurses, and medical personnel who work in clinics and practice and preach the positive aspects of exercise. The American Medical Joggers Association is one such group. You are better off going to a doctor who is aware of what running is all about, and who does not continually harp on the need for doing more research before he can recommend that you begin aerobic exercise.

Research is one way for doctors to get more federal money to continue never-ending research. Many of these medical people will never make a decision, either positive or negative, in regard to the benefits derived from aerobic exercise. They'll just make money. There are many opinions on running expressed in newspapers and magazines by medical people who do not run and therefore cannot know much about it. They may be enlightened doctors with Ph.D.'s from Harvard, but they are still very ignorant about the subject of running.

There was a *Playboy* magazine article a few years ago that warned about the dangers to your "health" if you ran. The doctor who wrote the article had no qualified data to back up his claim. Ignorant people occasionally come up with the intelligent remark that "running can kill you." They've heard of some individual with a previous heart problem who died while running. These are people who write for the splash effect of it. They want to shock people to attention and they don't care if what they write is severely distorted or completely false. Some of them are doctors. There is even a book entitled *The Non-Runner's Book.* It's humorous, and humor is healthy—but not at the expense of people who are dying from heart attacks. And we in the United States have experienced a virtual epidemic of heart disease for several years.

It's unfortunate so many people take such writing *seriously* and argue against exercise. Who was the guy who said, "When I feel I have the urge to exercise, I just wait until it passes?" That guy probably died when he was about fifty-three from lack of exercise or a related illness. He's probably not moving, or rolling over at all anymore. He's probably pushing up daisies.

FITNESS.   There is a contrast between the benefits you get from exercise that is casual and positive and "play oriented" and the exercise you may get out of your job. Somebody who is digging a ditch, or a housewife cleaning up all day, is not benefiting in terms of cardiovascular fitness. You need sustained, aerobic exercise of twenty minutes, a half hour, or more to derive the maximum benefits from your effort.

Your heart rate has to rise to a certain level, to one-half or two-thirds of its maximum in order for your cardiovascular system to realize some benefits. Some individuals in sports who are categorized by our media as great athletes actually have poor cardiovascular systems. Where the effort is short, sporadic, and intermittent, the benefit is minimal. Football is an example of such a sport. Baseball is another sport where cardiovascular fitness is not much of a factor.

I'd also include sprinters in this category. You can run one hundred yards holding your breath and you are not really using your heart. You are not developing your cardiovascular system when all you run are the short sprints. What is important is the development of the heart and lung systems.

Work can be a form of stress, and most people's jobs don't enable them to develop their cardiovascular systems. The woman or man who mops the floor, stops and rests, then thirty minutes later does the laundry and rests for an hour before polishing the furniture may get tired, but such efforts are probably too intermittent, boring, and too short term to aid cardiovascular fitness. If you lug furniture around and lift pianos, it's hurting you. It's tearing you down, not building you up; whereas continued aerobic exercise, which raises your heartbeat to two-thirds of its maximum level for about twenty minutes to a half hour four times a week, is good for you. It's as simple as that.

STRETCHING. Flexibility exercises are an important part of maintaining a running program. A running program should incorporate flexibility exercises for two reasons. They enable you to continue your normal exercises and your running with less difficulty and less tightness before, during, and after the run. By stretching, you will also help eliminate problems as you get older, when your tendons tighten, your ligaments become less flexible, and your muscle tissue takes a bit longer to recover from the wear and tear of training and, perhaps, racing.

After exercise, when the blood is flowing through the tissues, you are more supple. You're more loose. It's easy to do stretching exercises. It's an easy thing to lie down on the floor and do them. You want the opportunity to relax and rest anyhow. Since you're headed toward the shower from your run, it's a convenient time to raise a little more perspiration from your stretching. Also, you're not as impatient as you were before the run. That's one of the major reasons that many runners pass up the stretching exercises before they go out to run.

Stretching is imperative after a run, and is even more important following a race. I don't mean calisthenics. I mean the type of stretch where you hold it. You don't bounce. Sustain each stretch for from five to twenty seconds. Do several sets of different types of stretches, such as toe touches, bent-knee situps, leaning against the wall. There are any number of stretches, but perhaps a half dozen basic ones are all that are necessary. Dr. Sheehan has illustrated the basic stretches a runner needs to stay semi-supple.

Most people can get by with a minimal amount of stretching, maybe as little as ten to twenty minutes a day. If you can do more, work it into your schedule and make it a part of your running life style. You will be the person who very seldom has an injury from the tightness that is the result of daily training, a lack of stretching, and poor rest.

One of the exercises I do is to lie on my back and pull my legs back over my head. Or, I just lie on my back and push my legs up toward the ceiling and let the blood flow down through my legs. Or I put my leg up on a chair and put my head down toward my knee and do a gradual stretch. Yoga is healthy exercise for runners. It's fun to try, and you'll find three or four exercises you can concentrate on.

The whole point is that flexibility is very important for a runner. It allows you to be more comfortable in your training, therefore enabling you to enjoy your training more. It helps eliminate injuries. If you can go out every day and the aches are no longer there as much, it means you won't have to change your stride to adapt to the aches you feel.

By stretching after a race, you are doing nearly the same thing for yourself as having a massage. A massage is good for you, psychologically, and it also gets the blood flowing through your arteries and veins and helps eliminate lactic acid. When you run, you tighten up the posterior muscles you use the most. You need the opposing effect, so you stretch them out. If you do stretch regularly in moderation, you'll be active longer and have less chance of injury than that runner who skips stretching.

Apart from stretching regularly after exercise, I always do some stretching before a major race. It's as important for me as the half mile or mile I do to warm up prior to a race. I always do an exercise in which I lie down on my back and stretch my hamstring muscles. I do wall leaners, to stretch my calf muscles and Achilles tendons. I try to stretch my legs as much as I can so they feel flexible and full of spring.

I want full movement in every area, and therefore I stretch at every angle. If I am in a situation where I have to suddenly sprint or pick up the pace, I want my legs to feel comfortable and flexible. I want the muscle tissues warmed up before the gun goes off, especially because so many races begin with a hard sprint for position—or, just to avoid being trampled. This goes hand in hand with my mile or half mile warm-up. This is what I do and, as history shows, it's worked out well for me.

Beginners, in particular, are going to feel tightness and sore, aching spots in their legs as a result of running. They'll also feel an overall body fatigue. Stretching will help alleviate these problems. It is imperative in the critical first few months of running. It's also wise to stretch a bit more when you increase your regular daily runs in either duration or intensity. Your body has to adapt to running over a period of years, and stretching makes these new demands on your system less annoying.

You never totally eliminate the need for stretching, because of the concomitant tightness that results from every run. I've been running for over fifteen years and I still need to stretch after a workout and sometimes, as I've said, before. Bob Sevene, who coaches at Boston University and was a trainer and clinician at the Bill Rodgers Running Center in Cleveland Circle in Boston, says many of the runners who come in incurred their injuries because of a lack of stretching. Their legs were too tight or their feet lost their flexibility, and the result was an injury to the knee, calf, the Achilles, or some spot in the feet where they may have been weak.

Still, there are some runners, such as ultramarathoner Park Barner, who have said they feel stretching isn't worth the time involved. You have to remember that he's a superb athlete with an unusual metabolism who runs tremendous distances at a slow pace—a pace he's become accustomed to. From my experience, the shorter the distance you run and the higher the speed you run at, the more you must be warmed up. If not, the risk of tearing or straining a muscle is maximized. This is even more valid under competitive conditions. Tom Osler, a well-known runner, writer of running literature, and college professor, also professes little interest or belief in stretching as a useful form of preventive therapy for a runner. Tom is also an ultramarathoner, however, and he admits the possibility that running at a much slower pace of 9:00 to 10:00 per mile, at a very regular pace, may cut down on the aching muscles and tender tendons.

INJURIES. As you run, you learn to pick out the warning signs of injuries. First, there is a certain amount of stoicism you must have, because, to a degree, you must "pay your dues." You often don't know what some possible injury feels like, even though someone else may have described it to you. If you do feel something coming on, talk to a few experienced trainers, runners, or coaches.

If there is a minor sharp pain in a very localized area, I find it usually appears after a period of relatively heavy training and/or a lack of sleep. That's the worst combination there is. Amby Burfoot, the 1968 Boston Marathon champion, kept telling me back in the 1960s that to be successful as a marathoner, you must get the proper rest and sleep. Through years of experience, I've learned he was right. Injuries are going to blossom if you're tired. I can remember talking to a fellow in Cleveland who was working ten hours a day at a Ford plant on the night shift. He was breaking down from trying to run twice a day. My advice to him was to take his lunch hour off to run, and only work out one other time in his off-hours.

Without enough sleep, you're going to feel every ache and pain and many of these can be serious. When you're tired, your body defenses are down. The weaker parts of your body start to suffer from the strain inflicted on them from this fatigue. It's often better to skip a workout and get a good night or morning or afternoon of rest.

I occasionally pass up second workouts when I feel that way. If I do thirteen miles in the morning and feel extremely tired at night, to go out again is foolish. It's more important to get some sleep. When you sleep, your body recovers and builds up. You make progress. If you run a lot, you need to sleep a lot. You go through the building process when you sleep. When you're running, you're tearing down the muscle tissue. That's what sleep is for and, if you want to be successful, don't skip it. I realize different people require different amounts of sleep. You have to be sure you don't delude yourself into thinking you need less than you really do. I need between eight and ten hours sleep each night or I'm not at my best the next day, and I want to be at my best as many days as I can be.

I can remember going out for a hard ten-mile run on a very wet, cold, and windy day in March 1973. I went out the next day and I was still extremely fatigued. I suddenly felt a sharp twinge in my right quadriceps. I tried to go on. I was still trying to accumulate more miles, as I figured that would make me stronger. Although I could feel this small, half-dollar–sized tight spot above my knee get tighter and tighter, I kept saying to myself, "But I've got to get in seven more miles this run to get my twenty miles for the day." Runners can be downright pigheaded.

I soon realized I couldn't go on, it was causing me so much

pain. I couldn't lift my leg any longer! My quadriceps had a slight tear in it. I took about three days off, went out, and tried to run ten miles. I was all right for the first five, but I walked in after that. I had tried to come back too quickly and I paid the price. My next comeback was much more gradual and was successful.

When you have sharp twinges of pain in your Achilles, hamstrings, or your calves, rest them. Try icing the affected area and mild massage. My advice is to cut back on your training and get sufficient sleep. Don't do speed workouts, hill workouts, or long runs. Try to run on flat surfaces like dirt or asphalt, as grass is too uneven and fields or golf courses too bumpy. Try to avoid concrete because it's too hard. If you can find a smooth dirt trail, that's the best place to run. Keep your pace even and monitor how that weak spot feels every step of your run. If there are indications the soreness is returning *stop* running, and walk back. I make my "comeback runs" from minor injuries very short, and slow.

ORTHOTICS. The running boom has liberated the podiatrists and thrust them into the vanguard of the sport. They are the foot specialists, the people who have made metatarsal bones and dorsiflexion a part of sports vocabulary. Product lines have followed, all kinds of panaceas for the ailing foot.

These devices, made of various materials, to place within the shoe, are known by the term "orthotics." There are all types of inserts: heel cups, metatarsal pads, arch supports. Some of them are useful and can help alleviate many problems. They can keep the foot in the proper position in the shoe, a steady, neutral position. Since many running shoes do not provide this support, orthotics stabilize the foot.

But there can be an overemphasis on orthotics. As I pointed out earlier, many injuries can be avoided by incorporating the proper stretching exercises into your program. Don't just go and put orthotics in your shoes. Experiment first with different shoes and try stretching and various weight exercises to correct imbalance in your stride, your foot plant, your running technique.

Sometimes orthotics are necessary but, before you rush out to buy anything that might have been recommended by a specialist or a friend, talk with runners who have suffered injuries to their feet, have tried orthotics, and find out what they have to say. Do they feel everybody needs a pair of orthotics? Some podiatrists will say you do. It's their business. They're making money. Seek out somebody with an unbiased approach who will also advise you on some alternative or supplementary methods of eliminating the injuries, and try to find the best specialist you can, one whom many runners recommend.

ELECTROLYTE REPLACEMENT.   Whenever a runner finds himself caught up in intense environmental conditions of high heat and humidity or extreme cold, extra fluid replacement is essential. Often runners are dehydrated before a race and are unaware of it. They have not consumed enough fluids. It is difficult for a long-distance runner to drink too much fluid, especially when training regularly under hot, humid conditions.

Water, of course, can never hurt you—or, at least, rarely. After I contracted dysentery from drinking the regular tap water in Rabat, Morocco, in 1975, I learned to drink bottled water whenever the quality of the local water was in doubt. There are no calories, and water works quickly in your body. Natural fruit juices are also recommended. They're both high in vitamin C and natural sugar and are a good source of vitamins. Something such as Kool-Aid is ineffective. You will not benefit that much from such empty calories. Most importantly, just as with the food you eat, a varied source of liquids with plenty of water is most desirable.

Electrolyte replacements are a somewhat controversial subject, like many other subjects among runners. I have used ERG for several years. I do not receive any compensation from the company to use it. I use it because I think, from personal experience, it is a good drink to take and is superior to others. It's always seemed helpful in terms of my long training runs. My legs seem to ache less when I drink ERG the day before. I drink ERG most heavily in the summer months when I want to be extra certain that I'm replenishing the potassium and magnesium I have lost.

You do need a sufficient amount of potassium, magnesium, vitamin C, and sugar in your muscle cells and in the fluid level of your body. These are known as electrolytes. An athlete must be even more careful than the ordinary person to ensure that these entities are present in sufficient amounts in his body. When you dehydrate, there is a water and probably an electrolyte imbalance in your muscle tissue and you start to cramp. This problem can be alleviated by drinking adequate fluids prior to and during the run or race, pacing yourself well, and being as well trained as possible. When it is extremely hot or (even if it seems paradoxical) extremely cold, it is important to drink a lot to replace the fluids you lose, as exercise costs you so much more effort under such extreme conditions.

Are the manufactured drinks beneficial for you? Dr. David Costill of the Human Performance Laboratory at Ball State University in Muncie, Indiana, has told me he does not believe most of these drinks are of value. He thinks orange juice is every bit as good to drink, perhaps even better. It may be so, and maybe it's my placebo, but I like the added peace of mind I get from taking ERG. I also like the taste of the product, although it sure doesn't hit home like a nice, cold Pepsi.

I believe that ERG is the best of the electrolyte products. Others, from what I understand, have too high a concentration of sugar and take a longer time to leave the stomach and pass into the bloodstream to the muscle tissue. If you are going to use any one of these drinks, you should dilute it so the consistency of the solution isn't too thick. Whatever the manufacturer recommends, I dilute by half again as much.

When Garry Bjorklund had trouble in the 1977 New York City Marathon, it occurred just a short while after he had taken a drink of a too-thick solution, and he became sick to his stomach and vomited. That knocked him out of the race, in terms of winning.

Garry and I were running together in the lead at about the twelve-mile mark in the 1978 New York City Marathon and I offered him one of my drinks. He later passed me one of his drinks after he had taken a sip of it. I took a sip and found it was too strong. I instantly thought, "Is Garry trying to sabotage me?" Of course, I say this kiddingly. Runners have too high a respect for each other and their sport to consider such a trick. Winning isn't that important. In addition, Garry and I are good friends. However, at the time, I was seriously amazed that he would be drinking so concentrated a drink.

I quickly gave the drinking bottle back to him and he soon ran into trouble. He later said he was dehydrated. It may have been that the solution he was drinking was staying in his stomach too long and was never getting to his muscle tissues in time to be of any value. If you dehydrate early in a race, it's difficult to repair the damage already done to yourself in the later stages of a race.

I later heard someone mention that Garry was experimenting with a different drink. Even though he hasn't run in a lot of marathons, he's an experienced Olympic-caliber competitor and I doubt that he was experimenting with drinks in the course of a major competition. If you're going to experiment with anything in the way of accessories like new athletic drinks or racing shoes, you'd better do it during your training.

When I run marathons, I usually have some ERG in the first half of the race. If ERG is unavailable, I will drink water. Water gets to your tissues more quickly than anything; I believe it takes thirty minutes for a good electrolyte product to leave your stomach and get to the tissues. Over the final miles of a marathon, I just take water for that quick kick, that quick replacement.

DIET SUPPLEMENTS. There are many accessories, so to speak, that can be utilized in the interest of running improvement: vitamins, steroids, drugs. I feel that most of these are not very useful for most athletes, apart from some of them actually being illegal. Vitamins may have something of a placebo effect and, psychologically, this may be beneficial. I guess that's one of the reasons I take a small amount of extra vitamins—that and the fact that my mother introduced me to the habit of taking a multi-vitamin daily.

I am aware of the many field-event competitors in track and field who use steroids to enable them to train at higher levels. I have mixed feelings about the concept. My gut reaction is that these athletes aren't doing it on their own ability with just their desire to excel, improving and progressing "naturally."

Yet, I can't criticize these athletes because I know relatively little about the effects of steroids; perhaps, in fact, they are simply a form of "vitamin," a supplement to ensure that your strength will be properly maintained should your diet be insufficient for whatever reason at some point. Furthermore, steroid use is widespread internationally and does not appear to be on the wane, even though athletic officials at major competitions require tests to see that competitors have no traces of steroids in their system. If they do, they punish them with temporary suspension from athletic competition and withdrawal of any honors won in the immediate competition. I ought to add that the suspensions are generally so short as to constitute a mere slap on the wrist.

DRUGS? I personally know of no athlete who uses them or has ever used them. I do know of world-class athletes taking sleeping pills so they could be assured of getting their rest during the hectic European track season. Such a practice leaves me feeling uncomfortable. I'll never forget how amazed I was at the length of the list of artificial aids that are banned from use by athletes at the Olympics. Some of the illicit aids were so mild and are utilized by so many people in everyday life, I was shocked to see they were considered taboo by the International Olympic Committee. Rick DeMont, one of our swimmers, once had to forfeit his gold medal because he took an allergy pill prescribed regularly for him by his physician. I remember taking aspirin for the minor pain in my foot, and wondering if aspirin was also considered an illegal aid.

The top six finishers in many major competitions have to submit to blood and urine tests to determine their "purity" from steroids, drugs, and other aids. When I unexpectedly placed third at the 1975 World Cross-Country Championships in Rabat, I was asked to submit a urine specimen right there on the spot in an open field before several big grandstands full of people. I was so excited about my unexpected bronze medal, that I could not produce the sample until some six or eight hours later—too late for the test results to have much validity, I think. Yet, the formality had to be observed.

I have added a vitamin-B complex and sometimes, usually in the summer, a magnesium pill. This is something Ellen picked up after I had dehydrated and cramped very badly at the Montreal Olympics—a factor contributing to my poor race. From what I understand, magnesium is a most important electrolyte. If your body has insufficient magnesium, cramping will often occur during exercise. It can be found in leafy vegetables and even in peanuts. When I travel to Fukuoka, Japan, I often eat gobs of peanut butter in my room in the days before the marathon. It's easy to digest and doesn't fill you up.

Something else I take to guard against electrolyte imbalance is vitamin C. I take one pill a day, probably five hundred to a thousand milligrams. I frequently take an iron pill as well. You want a high level of hemoglobin in your blood, and this is particularly true for women runners.

Many vitamins and diet supplements have appeared in

recent years with the growth of public interest in running. Bee pollen is one of these products on the market. Sometimes, prior to a race, I'll pop two or three bee-pollen tablets. Again, this possibly does no more for me than enhance the placebo effect. How important is the psychological factor? It has yet to be explored to a great extent in this country. I know that a number of European athletes take bee-pollen pills and some top American sprinters, like Steve Riddick, use them.

Several members of the Greater Boston TC took big doses of bee pollen prior to the American trials for the International Cross-Country Championships in Atlanta in January 1978, and they all ran well. Whether this was a direct result of taking the bee pollen, or whether they were just in such superb condition from their training, is debatable. I tend to believe the latter was the case, but I feel anything you can do within reason to encourage a positive mental attitude before an athletic event will benefit you. That's essentially why I take these minimal doses of diet supplements like vitamins and, occasionally, bee pollen.

ALCOHOL.   There will always be controversy when the subject of alcohol comes up in relation to athletic performance. There probably never will be any unanimous agreement. From my own personal experience and from watching world-class athletes, I would say that you can get away with a modest amount of alcohol consumption and still perform at as high a level as anyone else.

All of this is in direct relation to what you are used to, how much you drink and how you handle it. Frank Shorter may have had a liter of beer the night before he won the gold medal in the marathon at the 1972 Munich Olympics. If I ever tried that, I would have awakened with a hangover and finished eighty-third. Frank is simply more of a beer drinker than I am.

On the other hand, Frank might have said good-bye to the gold medal had he pounded down four or more liters of beer. He simply knew what he was used to and that the fluids and carbohydrates in the beer suited him. There is a certain amount of magnesium in beer. In moderation, it can't harm you. On the whole, however, I wouldn't recommend it as something to add specifically to your training program. For purposes of relaxation, yes. As a diet supplement, I'm not impressed with beer as a food.

Before the 1978 New York City Marathon, I saw Dr. George Sheehan, one of the "gurus" of running, warming up with a beer in each hand. I'm sure they were not there to balance his body as he ran along. I'm sure he ran with them and drank them. He was fifty-nine at that time. He knocked off a 3:15 or 3:20 marathon. He did it under trying conditions—mid-to-high seventies and high humidity.

So, as this example illustrates, if you drink in moderation, it's OK, even during a marathon. On the other hand, I've never heard of anyone drinking gin or whiskey during a race. Perhaps that'll be assessed as acceptable in the future. Part of the beauty of running is that you can probably drink a little more and get away with it. Not only in drinking, but in your diet in general, you have a little more latitude than most sedentary persons. You are going out and burning off the excess in your training run.

When I did a clinic in Ohio, a radiologist in the audience who was involved in preventive medicine said one ounce of alcohol was injurious to your heart muscle. He said that the heart muscle was the only major muscle that helped eliminate lactic acid, that any consumption of alcohol was dangerous to the body, and that athletic performance, at least, would be impaired. But Dr. David Costill told me it was ridiculous to worry about minute things like that. As long as moderation is the key to your program, a little alcohol is not going to mean your downfall.

STRESS TESTING. With the growth of running, the stress test has been in the news. From my own experience, a resting stress test is not of too much value in determining how strong your heart is, or if there are any deficiencies or weak spots in your heart.

Only an active stress test during which you are striding on a treadmill, and your pulse rate goes up fairly high, is a relatively effective method of determining how hard you should exercise, or how hard you should run. Such stress tests are administered at most hospitals or where there are sports-medicine clinics set up for the purpose. But Dr. Sheehan has told me that stress tests are really of little value in determining the risk an individual runs in beginning a regular aerobic exercise program. Family history in relation to illnesses, such as heart disease, is a better guide.

They put a few electrodes on you in a stress test, monitor your heartbeat, and catch your pulse. Research has indicated that these tests do not pick up everything. The value of a stress test can be limited but, for someone who has not been involved in exercise on a continuous basis for some time, or is overweight, there is value. Your cardiovascular and muscular system has deteriorated, and it will take time to build it up again. Stress tests can provide a guideline for some people.

DIET. To maintain a sound level of cardiovascular fitness, a well-rounded diet is imperative. I have found I'll eat more when my mileage is up. In fact, I recently discovered I average about 3900 calories per day. Before the 1977 Boston Marathon when I was doing around 155 miles per week for seven weeks prior to the race, I was eating more food. I didn't gain weight, since the mileage neutralized it.

I've received some publicity about the junk food I eat: a pizza at Shakey's before the Fukuoka Marathon, a cheese-burger at McDonald's after the 1976 Ohme thirty-kilometer race in Japan, and bacon and eggs the morning of that race. I ate the breakfast, although I knew it was a mistake from a physiological point of view, for several reasons. One, I was hungry; and two, I did it for strategic purposes.

I knew Tom Fleming, the only other American and a contender to win, was very cautious with his diet, especially before racing. His room was across the hall from mine and Tom just happened to be in my room as I ate. He kept saying, "How can you eat all that stuff? Yech!" I knew Tom had to be a little psyched out by my apparently casual attitude toward the race. My stomach did bother me a little, but I won the race. Tom suffered severe blisters, yet pulled off third place.

On another occasion, Tom was staying over at our place for an afternoon or so and I had just returned from my teaching job. It was about three o'clock in the afternoon when I arrived home. I greeted Tom, went to the icebox, grabbed a cold potato, lathered it with a healthy covering of Hellman's mayonnaise, and popped it into my mouth. Then, I nonchalantly dressed for my ten-mile training run. Tom was all shook up. I do admit to being a ham sometimes, but it's all in fun.

So I do eat some junk food, but it's impossible to train twenty miles a day on a rotten diet. In addition to the vitamin pills I take, I try to eat foods that are high in potassium and magnesium: bananas, tomatoes, oranges, cantaloupes, spinach, peas, fruit juices, green beans, nuts.

The end result of it all is translated into performance. If everything has gone well and my training has included high mileage, one speed workout with some intervals, and I am free of injury, I go into a race with confidence. When one aspect of your training is off, everything is thrown off. Whoever has everything going for him and is most hungry for a race victory will be the guy who wins it. Your drive or focus of concentration for that victory cannot falter in the slightest, or the whole carefully constructed plan may tumble about you.

15
Running Gear

Hopkinton, Massachusetts, 1975. A cold, bleak April morning. The start of the Boston Marathon was less than half an hour away, something like twenty minutes to the sound of the gun on Hayden Rowe. All I had on was a cheap sweat suit, no hat, and no gloves, and I was shivering and trying to loosen up in the cold.

"Do you need some gloves?" asked my brother, Charlie. I responded, "I guess so," and off he went to a nearby drugstore in Hopkinton. Charlie bought me a pair of white workman's gloves, which I kept taking off and putting back on throughout the race that day.

When my hands starting sweating after five or ten miles, I simply carried the gloves. When my hands got cold again, I slipped them back on. I was used to training with gloves, so it seemed a perfectly natural thing to be racing with them. Even when Jock Semple leaned out of the press bus and yelled, trying to be helpful, "Bill, give me the gloves," I yelled back and said, "No."

It was a comforting thing to be able to run with them, as if it were a part of my training routine. When I trained in the winters of New England, I became accustomed to taking my gloves off and putting them on as I ran. I made the race sort of a training run, a conscious effort to simulate what I went through every day. I figured if I was more relaxed, I'd run without tightening up. I was more than a little excited about leading the whole Boston Marathon!

Being a New Englander and a person of Northern European background, I think I can handle a cold-weather climate better than a warm-weather climate. For that reason, I'm used to wearing gloves a lot. Actually, my hands normally tend to get cold very easily. I don't even have to be outdoors in the cold. I can be inside a warm building.

After I won the race that day, someone stole my gloves. Or else, I just put them down somewhere and forgot them. Since that day, I have always worn gloves, when it is cool outside, for any thirty-kilometer race or marathon. Even in shorter races, I'll sometimes wear them. Physiologically and psychologically, it helps me. The gloves are extremely light, inexpensive, and serve their function admirably.

For these reasons, the white gloves have kind of become my trademark. If I've got the gloves on, I feel I'm ready to race; if the weather is cool I have a feeling that all systems are go and that I will race well. I wore them in Fukuoka in 1977, when I won. I didn't wear them in Fukuoka in 1978, when I lost. It was too warm.

Somebody called me and said Frank Shorter had jokingly commented at a clinic that I could never win a race without my white gloves. Yet, I did win the New York City Marathon on hot days in October 1978 and 1979 without the gloves. I finally have two hot-weather marathons I can point to and say, "Well, yeah, I can win a race without those gloves." And I can successfully race marathons in the heat even if I don't like heat.

But it's true. The white gloves have become sort of a superstition with me. Even if I used them purely for functional reasons, when I walked up to the starting line wearing them or holding them in my hands, it was an indication I would be tough to beat. Somebody asked Tommy Leonard at the Eliot Lounge who he thought would win Boston in 1978 and he answered, "Billy White Gloves." A crazy nickname, but it made the newspapers. It made me feel like an ass, though. Tommy Leonard's a great friend, but he can sure embarrass you. I was similarly embarrassed when a woman told me I looked like Mickey Mouse. What a figure to emulate! Chuck Riley, a Greater Boston TC teammate, was in Singapore that week and he told me the newspaper headline the day after the Boston race said, "Bill Rodgers, wearing Mickey Mouse gloves, wins Boston Marathon."

Conversely, when you're running in the summer or in hot weather, the wrists and hands are one part of the body you want to keep cool. If you're running along and people offer you ice cubes, take them, run with them in your hands, and rub them along your wrists where the veins are close to the surface of the skin.

You want to keep your body temperature down. Pour water on the back of your neck and on your head. These areas are where the body's temperature can be controlled to a great degree. Pour water on your neck. But in winter, you want to keep those areas of your body warm. Put up the collar on your all-weather suit. Wear a hat.

Several times in my career, I've worn headbands. When I won the 1975 Boston Marathon, I was wearing a New Balance headband, which had been given to me by Ken Mueller, the top masters runner. I had fairly long hair, so I put it on and I wore it most of the race. After the halfway point in the race, it became uncomfortable and I threw it away.

I never wore a headband again until a marathon race in Kyoto, Japan, in 1977, when a group of musicians named

Ondekoza gave me one. When I had been in Japan before on a small island named Sado, I had worn a headband in a marathon race. The one they gave me had my name on it, indicating I was sort of an unofficial member of the Ondekoza team. Ondekoza play the feudal or classical music of Japan, and a group of them perform on the Prudential Plaza every year after they run in the Boston Marathon.

I won the race, so it became somewhat symbolic to me. It epitomized for me the Japanese approach to the marathon, an intensely competitive focus. Not everyone would take an unusual strip of brilliant red cloth from strangers, tie it around his head, and wear it for twenty-six miles. It was as if I were going into combat, and that's what it symbolized to me. I am a bit eccentric at times, I suppose, and I don't care what others think. Even though I felt a little queer about it, I was proud to wear it.

When I went to Fukuoka for the 1978 race, some Ondekoza members again gave me a headband to wear. Here were the top runners from all over the world and there I was on the track before the race wearing this headband. Japanese writers asked about the significance of it. I told them of Ondekoza. Wearing it did psych me up some. Watch Ondekoza perform and you will understand the intensity I'm speaking of.

Unfortunately, it didn't work for me that time. About halfway into the race, it seemed to be too tight on my head. I guess you start looking for ways to relax. I took the headband off, but I carried it with me until the end. I never thought of taking it off until three runners passed me and I found myself in fifth place. Perhaps this caused me to notice feelings of being uncomfortable or tight. That's when I look for ways to respond, to relax.

When the runners went by me, I suddenly became very tired. I had this feeling that something was wrong. Maybe if I took the headband off, I would relax a little more. I knew it was going to be a tough final thirteen miles. I wasn't going to win, but I had to run "honorably," to the best of my ability. This is part of the reason for racing this race, the marathon, to fulfill your expectations as well as you can, to leave yourself satisfied. If things had been different that day, I would have loved the sensation of running up the final hill and into Heiwadai Stadium wearing this headband with the fire-crackers going off in the background. Just for effect.

Because runners are somewhat unique athletes, they must cope with the environment on a year-round basis, both in training and racing. My entries in my schoolboy diary indi-cated how I passed up training because of rain and cold weather. That is no longer the case. The elements may conspire to keep a runner indoors, but he can learn to adapt to different weather conditions and train comfortably in adverse weather by dressing properly.

Very often in summer, I train in a pair of briefs, shorts, socks, and shoes. I generally don't wear a T-shirt. Comfort is an important factor in leading to relaxation, and you will run more efficiently if you are relaxed. I've seen beginners out there wearing rubberized suits, figuring if they sweated enough they'll lose some weight. You may lose a lot of fluid and a few pounds during that run, but when you return from the run dehydrated, you drink and you put it right back on. You can't lose weight on a long-term basis that way.

When you race in the heat, it's important that your running gear be well ventilated and light, not only in weight, but also in color. When it is bright and the humidity is high, you want a vest that has perforations so your skin can breathe and the sweat can rise to the skin and evaporate. That cools your tissues and your skin.

You also want something light in color to reflect the sun. You don't want a dark jersey on a hot, sunny day, because that absorbs the heat. You would then heat up externally, adding to your high internal temperature, which is the last thing in the world you want to happen on a hot race day.

For running briefs, you want a pair that will permit freedom of movement in your thigh area. Only recently has running gear been made with the needs of the runner specifically in mind. Lighter-weight racing shorts are available from a number of different manufacturers. Nylon tricot shorts seem best because they are soft and evaporate perspiration very quickly, which minimizes chafing. Generally, I prefer nylon briefs, since they are not cut too low. If they are, I experience chafing.

Never try out a new pair of briefs, a new shirt, or a new vest in competition. You don't want to experience chafing for the first time in a race. If it is going to happen, it should happen during a training run when you can learn from the experience and go on to a different product. You have to experiment. Try things on and see what fits most comfortably. Talk to experienced runners, store clerks, and study the different products.

Cold weather presents a different problem. Two of the most important items to own are thermal underwear and an all-weather training suit. The thermal underwear should be lightweight to allow for heat retention and permit the perspiration to be absorbed by the material. This is also accomplished with the venting in a rain suit.

Ventilation is important. You should allow the air to cool your skin through an evaporation process. Until recently, I'd never worn an all-weather suit that was very effective in keeping the rain out. You can take with a grain of salt any claims made by manufacturers that you are not going to get wet if you wear this particular suit in the rain. There is a point when you are going to get wet underneath the suit, and it's going to cling to you. It generally happens pretty early on in your run. The only all-weather suits that can lay claim to this advantage are those made of a new material called Gore-tex.

What makes a rain suit attractive is that you can use it on a twelve-month basis, except when it is over sixty degrees in the summer. They are lightweight, they cut the wind very well, they flex easily. When you want knee-lift to jump over something, you have it. It's not a heavy, bulky garment, and though it may retain water it will not retain so much that running becomes awkward, as often occurs if you are caught in the rain in a warm-up suit. You can fold it, tuck it away in a small area, and take it with you when you travel.

One of the things to avoid in winter is overdressing. Overdressing leads to more extensive effort in training, increased perspiration, which then saturates the clothing, and your normal running form can be thrown off by adjusting to the weight of too many clothes. You want to wear light layers of clothing under an all-weather suit. You can still work out at a decent pace, even in the cold, and you may have as many as three or four layers of clothing on. What I do, when it is around twenty degrees, is put on two light T-shirts, briefs, shorts, a thermal underwear shirt, and an all-weather suit.

You don't want to put on so many layers of clothing that you start to perspire very early in your run. When the sweat soaks through, the wind hits you and the sweat freezes on you. Or worse, you can suffer hypothermia, which means you get very cold and your body temperature drops and it can drop to dangerous levels. It invites colds. If you are a bit chilly in the first few minutes of a training run, disregard it. You will warm up soon enough. Run out into the wind, return with it at your back. Toward the end of your run is when you are perspiring. Don't stop to chat or for anything else after running and building up a sweat in cold and/or wet weather. Head straight to a warm place, a shower, and dry clothes.

Since up to 40 percent of your heat loss during a run is through the head, a tight knit, woolen cap that you can pull down over your ears is essential. Your ears are a very sensitive part of your body in the cold. If you keep your head warm when you run, not only will you be more comfortable, but you help to keep the rest of your body warm too.

Running at night is something I have tried to avoid. Yet, I'm often in situations where I end up running after dark, particularly in the winter months when the days are so short in New England. I know many runners who have been hit by cars, have stepped in potholes, and have injured themselves by running at night.

If you are forced to do it because of your working situation, try to pick out a spot where you have good footing and it is going to be relatively safe. One possibility is an indoor track, if you are fortunate enough to gain access to one. It's safe, you can see where you're going, and you minimize the chances of injury.

On some of those brutal January and February days, nothing is sweeter than a warm indoor track. Of course, most of my career, I have trained through the New England winter. You either adapt to it, or you quit running at that time of year, or you go to a warm climate.

Failing any of these, I generally try to stay on sidewalks with a lot of streetlights. During the winter, I'll often run on small back roads because there is less traffic to worry about. Do make sure you run in a high-visibility area. Sometimes the head-lights of cars enable you to see better when you are running at night. When Boston was buried under snow in February 1978, I was in Puerto Rico for a race. For those who stayed home, as I was informed, running at night was a delight. There was no traffic for a week due to a ban—only foot traffic.

Visibility is essential, primarily because most of us train "with the cars" and we want to be sure their drivers see us easily, well before they're near us. You can get vests that are highly visible and you can wear them over your rain suits. They are a bright red or orange and reflect the headlights of approaching cars. The suits we manufacture at Bill Rodgers and Company have a strip of material on the front and back that serves the same purpose as a reflectorized vest and makes you more visible at night.

Cotton warm-up suits or suits made of rayon or polyester fabrics are good under certain conditions, but they are inap-

propriate for cold-weather training: They absorb moisture and
that creates added weight and discomfort. Also, the looseness
of the fabric enables wind to pass through, and the net effect is
enormous heat loss. When it is raining, a warm-up suit soaks
up the water and if it doesn't have a drawstring, it will tend to
fall down. You don't need that when you're running. A nylon
suit may absorb water to some degree, but it doesn't fall off and
at least it's light enough so it won't become a burden. I've gone
on training runs wearing a heavy warm-up suit, and I swear
it's accumulated several pounds of water. It's not worth the
aggravation. The main point is that warm-up suits are only
appropriate on relatively nice spring and early fall days.

I never knew anything about how to dress properly for
running when I was starting out in Newington in 1963. It
wasn't until I entered Wesleyan in 1966 and met Amby
Burfoot that I started running in adverse weather conditions,
and that's where I learned what to wear.

Of the approximately twenty-five million runners in the
United States, many still fall into the "fair weather" category.
They'll only go out and run when conditions are ideal. They
adhere to the conventional belief of a decade ago, that you
can't run comfortably in poor weather. But you can, if you
dress correctly and have made running a part of your life style.

If it is raining and warm, go out in a T-shirt and shorts, or
other light clothing like an all-weather suit. If there is lightning
or any evidence of an electrical storm in the area, it is sensible
to skip your run. I have been out when there was lightning in
the air and even though, in some ways, it's made me run faster,
all the time I think of stopping, hiding under a bridge, or
ducking under a car. It's a frightening experience to be out
there. I'm a bit compulsive about my training, yet lightning
makes me think seriously about whether I want to go out for a
run.

Tom Fleming has told me how he doesn't run at all when it
rains. It freaked me out. I'd say, "Tom, there must be thirty

days a year, at least, when it rains. Do you miss that many days?" I'm not sure what he does to compensate for it, but it automatically makes me feel I have a little extra advantage over him.

Some of the Kenyans, I've read, have made similar statements. They don't run when it rains. You look at Henry Rono, setting three world records within the span of two months, and Fleming himself has run a 2:12:05 marathon. Maybe you don't need to run when it rains. And animals don't go out in the rain. I suppose it's a bit unnatural. All I can say is try, experiment in the rain, and dress for the conditions. It's quite possible you'll enjoy a run in the rain, or you may feel a certain nostalgia for those times as a kid when you didn't care about the elements. Remember when you actually searched out puddles to splash and roll in? A *cold* rain can be a bitch, though.

Running in the rain is particularly dreary in the early spring and late fall, when it's warm enough to rain and cold enough to be uncomfortable when you get wet. If you are going out on a long run, reconsider. Ten miles is the most I'll do on a rainy day, unless I'm actually in a race and simply have to go on. In the summer, though, it's not that bad in the rain, and it actually cools you off. It's fun splashing through the puddles.

When winter arrives, I sometimes enjoy it. It's pleasant to run over snow where no one else has been, and it has a cushioning effect. It's a unique sensation. You feel as if you're lighter on your feet when you land on a snow-covered surface. You must beware of how deep the snow is, however, and if there is a light crust or not. When the snow is of a certain consistency, you can run well on it; but there are other snow conditions when the opposite holds true.

Once when I was running around Jamaica Pond before the roadways were plowed, there was a light crust over the snow that was more than a foot deep. I'd break through every time my foot landed, resulting in a shock. That was hard running.

The top of your foot can catch on the crust and you may well fall. But, conversely, you acquire a feeling of perseverance. It can be a satisfying workout. You work up a good sweat, which never hurts you. When I do particularly unusual runs like that one, I often conjure up visions of great runners of the past. That tough run in the snow brought to mind the great Paavo Nurmi, who surely traveled through considerable snow in Finland. And I thought of Emil Zatopek, who would occasionally wear combat boots as running shoes. Sometimes I remember certain photographs of famous runners during my runs. I'll never forget a photograph of Jim Ryun running up a long, winding Kansas road with no one, and nothing else, in sight. Or of Steve Prefontaine leaping along the green Oregon mountainsides.

You learn how to run according to how deep the snow is, how slippery the surface tends to be. If it's icy, you want to avoid it. If you are on an icy surface, try to take short steps in order to keep your balance and escape injury. I slow down, take my corners really wide, and proceed with caution.

When you do run on snow, you often build up more than normal fatigue. Also, the cold weather zaps your energy just as much as does intense heat. When these two factors are combined, and added to bad footing, your pace will be a little slower. Be aware of these points and adjust the duration and intensity of your runs accordingly. I run less on "bad" days, more on "good" days.

There are a couple of different tricks you can use when running in the winter. One is to put petroleum jelly on your face when it is really cold and the wind is whipping up. Your face is generally the only part of your body exposed to the wind, and it can cut. Sometimes a ski mask will help, but even that is not sufficient if it is a really cold day. If the application of petroleum jelly makes you feel grubby, remember you're going to shower immediately following your run. Using it is a recommended way to cut down on the wind chill.

Ointments such as petroleum jelly can also be useful in competition and training when applied to areas of your body that tend to chafe when you run. I generally haven't had much difficulty, mainly because the materials I wear are those that cause less chafing and are properly fit. Experiment with the clothing you're going to wear before you race in them.

One of the recent outgrowths of the running movement has been the manufacture of running gear for women. Unisex styles do not work well for women. Our people tried to make one unisex training suit but found that some of the functional features such as the high wind collar and the front vents did not work for women because of a poor fit. Now we make a separate suit cut specifically for women.

FOOTWEAR. The shoe is an individual product, something you have to pick out by yourself. Forget what certain magazines or individuals say about the shoe that is best for you. Go to a store that is staffed by experienced runners who can offer their advice about the better shoes available. After that, experiment with several pairs. Walk around in them, see how they fit and judge for yourself. The clerk may have a helpful opinion, but in the end you are the only one who will know best.

The most important thing is the fit. Do not buy basketball shoes, tennis shoes, or cheap imitations of the higher-quality running shoes. Such choices lead to injuries and excessive muscle fatigue. Also, inferior shoes will wear out sooner. Go to a store that is stocked with Tiger, Adidas, Nike, New Balance, Etonic and the other major running shoe companies.

Training shoes and racing flats should both have good heel support. Your heel should be cupped snugly so that it doesn't move in the shoe. There should be very little room for movement of the heel. Your foot is thereby kept in a neutral position. I believe a thumb's width of space between the end of your big toe and the end of the shoe is adequate room for foot movement in the shoe. If your foot slides around in the shoe, you're bound to develop blisters and other injuries.

The shoe should have good fore-foot and rear-foot cushioning. Test under the ball of your foot and under the heel. That's where the constant pounding from running is.

If you land on a rock or a pebble, you don't want to feel that sharp pain that can shoot right through you. That happens particularly after you've run a number of miles and you start aching a little in the area. If you hit a pebble then, you really notice it. So, purchase a shoe with a ratio of three to one, heel thickness against fore-foot cushioning. It takes pressure off the posterior part of your foot.

The shoe should be flexible under the ball of your foot. If you press it with the front of your hand, it should bend easily when you press it back. This allows for proper movement of the foot in the sole on your pushoff after landing.

When you're running, try to avoid large amounts of wear in an isolated spot. Most people tend to land on their heels. It's unimportant how you land. What is important is to be sure that no one spot in your shoe wears down, creating an imbalance that could lead to injuries. For that reason, you can have your shoes resoled or you can buy shoe glue, a gooey substance that is put on areas of wear on the shoe. Left to harden overnight, the shoe is again structurally intact and balanced. This is cheaper than buying a new pair of shoes.

I can remember when I was getting back into running, I foolishly thought I was saving money by wearing my shoes until they virtually fell off my feet. I remember one early training run when I actually threw my shoes away and finished the run in my bare feet. Those shoes were doing my feet more harm than good.

I had another experience when I was running and I developed an arch problem. I had my foot bandaged by Buddy Evans, the trainer at Bentley College in Massachusetts, and I tried whirlpools. Nothing seemed to help. I tried icing, heat applications, but it persisted.

Finally, Buddy said, "Let me see your shoe." He put his hand inside my shoe and then told me to put my hand in the shoe and feel the sole area. There was an incredibly deep indentation on the bottom of the shoe. I had virtually pounded the bottom out of the shoe. I had indented it so much I was getting absolutely no support. I went out, bought a new pair of shoes, and the problem ceased to exist. So make sure your shoes do not wear too much. Take care of them and when you do, you'll also be taking care of your feet, your legs, your back, and so on.

Generally, a racing flat is lighter than a training flat and is a snugger fit. I have my racing and training flats made for me by Tiger and, at least for me, I feel they make the best racing flat in the world. I have cushioning built up in those areas where I land most heavily. I have had one pair of racing flats, which I've worn in five or six marathons and in perhaps twenty-five or thirty road races in one year, and they showed little sign of wear. I wore those shoes in frequent practice runs after I determined it was time to break in a new pair of racing shoes.

It's important to find the shoe that's best for you, which means more experimenting and buying different pairs of shoes. Sometimes you can't tell in a store if a pair is ideal for you, but don't race in a pair of shoes you picked off the shelf the day before. Break them in first. Save your new shoes at first for shorter runs, and not your weekly longer runs.

The spikes I use are made by Onitsuka Tiger in Japan. They have a bit of a heel lift, perhaps three-quarters of an inch, because I generally run the longer distances on the track. Sprinters are more up on their toes and need no heel at all. Do racing flats or spikes give better traction on the track? It's open to debate. Some runners wear flats with a waffled sole. I ran with spikes in my college and schoolboy days, so that's what I've stuck with when I go on the track. You have to be your own judge.

16
Inspiration, Sportsmanship, and Coaching

Tommy Leonard is an Irishman, yet the English have a word that best describes him: They'd call him an Original. I once called him the Guru of Road Running in New England and, when we were in Japan, they picked that up as "Ondotori." Take your pick because, in any language, Tommy is something special, something Original.

I've told you how I first met him in 1974, at the Falmouth Road Race he organized on Cape Cod. He is a bartender at the Eliot Lounge in Boston and his favorite expression is, "I just want to be known as Tommy, your friendly bartender. Nothing more, nothing less." Of course, the impact he has had on road racing in New England and the people he has inspired are quiet contradictions of his own evaluation of the effect he has had on so many lives.

He is the ultimate promoter, the guy who could put on a road race anywhere at any time and attract a crowd. He dreamed up the idea for a race on the day following Thanksgiving one year as he was driving home to Westfield, Massachusetts. "Why not have a post–Turkey Day Trot?" he asked. He phoned a newspaper in Springfield and an article appeared the next day inviting all runners in western Massachusetts. There was one flaw. He invited them to show up on the front lawn of his brother's house and his brother knew nothing about it. "I was banished from the house," Leonard said. Some thirty runners showed up, the race went off through the fields, and Leonard proclaimed, "We'll make it an annual event."

The only flop I've heard of that Tommy was associated with was a lobster feed he put on one summer when he was working at a place called the Beachcomber in West Falmouth on Cape Cod. "We ate lobster for a week," said Leonard. "Lobster pies. Lobster popsicles. What a flop. Nobody came. Hey, Mike Todd was my idol. One year he was a millionaire, the next year he was broke. He and P.T. Barnum were my idols. Showmen. If I hadn't been a runner," he has said, "I'd be in that Great Road Race in the Sky." He was an orphan, adopted and raised by a family in Westfield. "I ran away from the orphanage," he said, "and I jumped over the wall into a snowbank up to my neck." He was proud of the family of Frank Tierney, his adoptive parents. "I had gotten a tattoo in the Marine Corps and, for about six years, I wore a long-sleeved shirt in the summer so they wouldn't see it."

Tommy loves to drink beer. One time, when he was going home, he stopped in a shopping plaza in Westfield, waiting to be picked up. "I had too many beers," he said, "and I passed out in a bowl of fried rice. I had soy sauce in my mustache. They sent an ambulance. They thought I had had a heart attack. I saw the blue lights and I sat up on the stretcher. 'I've got the strongest heart of any man in Westfield,'" is what Tommy told the startled ambulance drivers.

"That which is used develops. That which is not used

wastes away," Tommy said, quoting Hippocrates. "I used to read Socrates, Plato, Aristotle when I was in the Marine Corps," he said. Those were the days when he was running on railroad tracks—moving from tie to tie—before the running boom. "The element that is coming in now is the Rocky-disco element," he said.

We all stopped off at Honolulu after the 1977 Fukuoka International Marathon. Friends had thrown a party for Tommy and raised the money to send him to Japan. "Not a day goes by," said Tommy, "when I don't think of that trip." He planned to run in the Honolulu Marathon the following Sunday. He entered, picked up his number on Saturday afternoon at Kapiolani Park and, in typical Leonard fashion. . . disaster.

He overslept. He was supposed to board a bus at 4:30 in the morning to go to the starting line. We were staying at the Sheraton Moana on Waikiki. I heard a knock on my door. It was Tommy, looking for a pin for his number. It was 5:45, the race was set to start four miles away at 6. He left, started running to the starting line and, all of a sudden, some four thousand runners started coming at him. "I wasn't going to run thirty miles," he said. "That's more than I did in training. I had sake'ed myself to death in Japan. But it was worth it." We watched the Honolulu Marathon.

The Eliot Lounge is the meeting spot for runners on the weekend of the Boston Marathon. Tommy hangs up flags of all the countries of the official runners. He receives requests from writers from around the country for press passes to the Eliot. "It's the runner's shrine," he said. "A tabernacle. It's not Carnegie Hall. But it's a slice of Americana. Nothing more, nothing less."

Tommy likes the simplicity of running, the way it was at an earlier time in the sport when he was alone with his thoughts. "I like to run through the woods, listen to the babbling brooks and whispering hemlocks." He lives running and, all the time through the various stages of my own post-collegiate career, he has been behind me. He is not only an athlete—not that fast (3:17 is his best) but mighty consistent (twenty-four Bostons)—but also, to runners like me, the Source of Inspiration—putting up all the different flags and the pre-marathon spaghetti dinner at the Eliot, personally greeting Jack Foster, Kevin Ryan, and all the foreign and out-of-state runners, welcoming them to Boston and to the company of those against whom they would be competing. He is The Guru, an enthusiast of life and a promoter of the sport. He is a friend, a guiding spirit.

As much as any other figure, he has helped promote the sport of running in the New England area: Falmouth, the Boston Freedom Trail, the Holyoke St. Patrick's Day Road Race. They are his fantasies, his creations. They are three of the biggest and most successful road races in the Northeast, if not the country. And he adds a hell of a lot to the Boston Marathon. More than any coach, runner, AAU official, or sportswriter in New England, he has helped develop the sport—because the truth is that road running is bigger than track in New England, always has been.

What differentiates Tommy Leonard from so many who are involved in the road running movement is that he has never tried to make money from the sport. In fact, he has often dipped into his pocket to help runners and to buy prizes. He does it for the love of running and he has no money. He is completely unselfish. He once wound up with sixty-five cents when his bar tab for himself and friends was settled. That's sixty-five cents he had left for the next week.

The athlete receives inspiration in many different forms and from many quarters. You receive inspiration when you conjure up an image in your mind or you hear something on radio or television or read it in the newspapers. You receive a more personal source of inspiration from the people around you. To be successful at a high level, you need all types of inspiration.

I was never very impressed by the traditional figures of American sports such as Babe Ruth, Mickey Mantle, or Bob Cousy. I never collected baseball cards. I played all of the team sports, but just for the fun of it. The first individual athlete who ever made a real impression on me was Abebe Bikila, and the image of him running the marathon is something that will never be erased from my mind. It was an inspirational point in my development. I was in junior high school when he was winning Olympic gold medals, and I can still remember the tremendous effect of watching this superhuman individual running the marathon at a 5:00 per mile pace with such seeming ease.

The sports for which I have a particular affinity are cross-country skiing, gymnastics, and running. I could never become inspired by a softball pitcher, a roller skater, or a yachtsman. I may find these pursuits entertaining, but totally uninspiring and lacking something in the real drama of athletic achievement.

Ron Clarke, the great middle-distance runner from Australia, was an inspiration. I admired his attitude toward running. He experienced the frustration and disappointment of never winning an Olympic gold medal. He never made excuses when he lost—and that was rarely. He was always up front about the sport. He raced frequently at a high level, traveled a lot under difficult circumstances, and always did the best he could. He was a great sportsman.

Gerry Lindgren, who set so many age-group records as a schoolboy, was an American who was an inspiration to me. We're about the same age. He still ranks as one of the best high school and collegiate runners ever in the United States and the world. He ran a 13:17 three-mile in high school. Some of his achievements may never be matched. He went out and competed against the Russians as a high school kid and he beat them. His achievement was meaningful to a young schoolboy of the same generation growing up in Newington, Connecticut.

I never forgot it. What I liked so much about Gerry was his youthfulness, his attitude, his personality. He seemed to laugh and joke a lot while at the same time remaining a fierce competitor.

I have mentioned Amby Burfoot before, the influence he has had on my career. What he was able to accomplish as an athlete amazed me. He combined it with a personality that was, at once, casual, disarming, and infectious. He was so incredibly gracious and friendly, so informal. He had a good sense of humor, a feeling for what he was doing.

Frank O'Rourke, my coach at Newington High School, was the first person who took a sincere interest in me as a runner and realized that I was trying to be good and that I had some chance at success. For this reason, he was the first person who inspired me to excel, and that first person is one you remember. If I'd had a bad experience in high school, who knows? I might have turned against running. I will never forget the Saturday mornings Coach O'Rourke would spend with us in our workouts, the extra effort, the time spent with everyone on the team.

Art Dulong, who ran for Holy Cross College in Worcester, Massachusetts, was the guy who overshadowed so many of us in our college days. Even in high school, Coach O'Rourke told me to stay with Art Dulong in the New England Cross-Country Championships. By the time we were one hundred yards into the race, he had opened up fifty yards and he just kept increasing it. He was my age, yet wildly ahead of me in ability. It seemed inconceivable that I could ever be as good as he was. It didn't make me mad, vindictive, or aggressive. It made me wonder. Could I ever be as good as he was? Because of injuries, his career was cut short. If not, he would have been on at least one of two Olympic teams, aiming for a medal at ten thousand meters.

When I was at Wesleyan and Dulong was at Holy Cross, Frank Shorter was a two-miler at Yale. He turned a particular motivation into the marathon gold medal in the 1972 Munich Olympics. To see an American do it was inspiring. It had a major impact on distance running in this country and on my career. He is such a great competitor, twelve months a year when he is healthy. For six years, he was on top. Runners emulate Shorter. I've seen them holding their arms as Frank does during a race. Competing against Frank for several years has taught me a lot. I believe I have a similar affinity for and understanding of competition and running in general.

I think of so many great distance runners: Buddy Edelen, Jim Peters, Emil Zatopek, Paavo Nurmi, Lasse Viren. I have beaten Viren several times since he won gold medals for the second time in the five-thousand and ten-thousand, but I still hold him in awe. I feel apprehensive about going near him. Is this man for real? He's a superman, almost. Yet he doesn't act that way at all. He's a very earthy sort of person. He's friendly, quiet, and almost shy. He speaks truthfully, never trying to put you on.

Tom O'Hara was another runner I admired, the way he used to put on that finishing kick. My attitudes and inspirations toward running evolved out of my high school days. I'd see these athletes on television. O'Hara seemed to be always winning in the indoor meets.

There was also the late Steve Prefontaine (killed in an automobile accident in 1975), who was not only a great athlete but someone who spoke out for the runner against the Establishment of Athletics. He was a lonely voice at the time, trying to agitate against the inhibiting policies of our AAU. He was trying to improve the climate for athletes, to be a voice for them all. He was an admirable person.

I admire anybody who is out there trying to improve himself, people with motivation. Such people usually cooperate with others, too. I'm not keen on those who want someone else to do their work. Scott Graham, my Greater Boston TC teammate and former Melrose neighbor, has also been an inspiration. As much for my sake as his own, he has been out there on so many training runs with me over the past few years, innumerable hours over the streets and roadways of our area.

That's what has remained with me about my experiences with the members of the Greater Boston TC. People like Vin Fleming, Bob Sevene, Don Ricciato, Chuck Riley, Jack McDonald, and Dick Mahoney were unselfish with their time. They helped me in my training, they were friends. They harbored no strange feelings about who I was, about the success I had. They treated me just as they would any other guy on the team. They let it go at that.

It's important, even for beginners, to have someone to train with, to have someone to relate to. Form these contacts and help each other. Running is more fun when you train that way. Your immediate friends are the most important influences. Waldemar Cierpinski of East Germany may have had a network of coaches, doctors, lab researchers, and psychologists, and the assistance of a national team to guide him to victory in Montreal. I had Ellen, my family, and friends. They guided me and were the companions who helped me win.

Even if my parents did not quite understand what I was doing as a runner, they still supported my efforts and were never critical of what I was doing. That's important. The people who work at the Bill Rodgers Running Centers make it possible for me to train, to race, to travel, to talk about running at clinics, and do work for different organizations. If I bomb out, it's been my own fault. In turn, everyone from our Running Centers has the opportunity to train, and often with a co-worker.

I hope, ten or twenty years from now, someone will look back at his or her career and say that I played some kind of a role in it and motivated him or her to be a good runner. That would be one of the major satisfactions I'd get out of life and of running in general.

Of all the inspirations, Ellen has been the most profound. It's not always easy, since runners can sometimes be difficult to live with—particularly before the big races, or after a race when you've done poorly, or when training conditions are bad, or when you have an injury. Ellen has always been there to help me out. We've always had fun at it. She's made sacrifices with her time at the store, sorting out the opportunities and the offers and dealing with a fair share of con men, geeks, and wolves in sheep's clothing.

SPORTSMANSHIP is the essence of athletic competition. Perhaps because of the classic background of running that is rooted in the Olympic tradition, the highest ideals of sports have always been ingrained in our approach to competition. You are a gentleman, or a gentlewoman. You are a true champion, whether you win or you lose. This is one element of the Olympic tradition I admire greatly.

Frank O'Rourke, my coach at Newington High School, always sent us over to shake hands with the opposition *after* the competition. Frank Shorter, who taught us how to win in the 1972 Olympic Marathon and how to lose (if a silver medal can be called a loss) when he finished second in the 1976 Games, brought it up in his remarks in a Diet Pepsi Guide to Running. "Runners," he wrote, "feel a sense of kinship with one another. It's like being a member of a club where there is a common outlook on life, as well as a common goal."

The unwritten rule is you do your best on your own against your competition, but you never try to physically hinder your rivals, touch them, or come into contact with them in any way. You have the room, generally, to maneuver in a road race, yet you frequently are penned in on a track, even in a cross-country race. Often it is wet, slippery, and very hilly in cross-country, and you are unable to avoid bumping someone.

Even under such high-stress situations, it is very rare for a runner to become involved in a fight, or even to exchange heated words. I remember running next to Garry Bjorklund in the 1977 New York City Marathon about fourteen miles into the race and, when we took a sharp corner, my elbow hit him in the side. "I bet you didn't expect to find that in a marathon," I said apologetically to him. He might have encountered elbowing on the indoor track circuit, or even on an outdoor track, but this was his second marathon and there was no way he should have expected an elbow on the wide thoroughfares of New York.

Strangely enough, marathoners tend to group together in a race. Partly it's for psychological strength, but partly for drafting purposes. Because the distance is considerably longer than in a normal road race, runners sometimes have the feeling that they have to stick together to achieve their goals. They sometimes feel the goal itself is the main opponent. To win is the other major achievement and, to achieve victory, it is often necessary and wise to help each other out. It's almost an involuntary impulse of marathoning: You stick together for the psychological strength to run the race well.

Generally, runners are apt to apologize and say, "I'm sorry," or "Excuse me," if they bump each other during the course of a race. This is common from junior high school all the way up to the upper echelons of marathoning. There have been exceptions, of course. One Irish runner told me how a teammate of his was running in the British Triple-A Championships on the track, and an English runner was very close on his heels, often nearly tripping him. The Irish runner simply turned around, swung his elbow and nailed the guy in the face. I've seen runners at New England Cross-Country Championships finishing with bloody noses. But that sort of thing is extremely rare.

I tend to be a runner who prefers to run right on the shoulder or heels of another runner, and this irritates some of them. I ran in Oslo, Norway, in a five-thousand-meter race in the summer of 1978, with Kenyans Josh Kimento and Samson Kimombua. They were being followed by an English runner named Mick MacLeod, who followed them even closer than I ever would. The Kenyans complained. Kimombua did trip, although I'm not sure it was the fault of MacLeod. It's ironic. Al Salazar has said that some Kenyans, particularly Kimento, practice the same tactics. You can't throw stones when you live in glass houses.

It takes a very pointed, very specific case for an official to rule a runner out of the race. Unless a runner is obviously pushed or shoved, the race goes on. Such was the case when Jim Ryun fell in the 1972 Olympic fifteen-hundred-meter run. When Shorter, Bjorklund, Craig Virgin, and myself were locked up in the ten-thousand-meter Olympic trials in 1976, there was some contact during the first five miles. Each of us was almost tripped once or twice. When you're trying to maintain such close contact, it's hard to avoid it entirely. Bjorklund even had his shoe ripped off, finishing barefoot and in third place to make the Olympic team. I was the guy half a second behind.

On the indoor circuit in the United States, strategy becomes important. Knowing when to make your move, when and whom to cut in on, when to start your final sprint, and how to run on the different surfaces are all a part of it. The experienced runners are the ones who make the moves at the appropriate time. Some of the top runners know the right way to "cut a runner off" so he can't be passed in the last few yards of the race. It is not grounds for disqualification, just sound strategy.

CHEATING. This is not to say the marathon hasn't known occasional episodes of cheating. Some French runners were accused of cutting the marathon course short in the 1928 Olympics in Paris. They unexpectedly did so well, it followed that they had disappeared somewhere and subsequently reappeared on the course. A runner from Colombia ran a marathon in Israel, jumped into a first-aid truck on the course, rode for a while, jumped out, and finished the race. He was later disqualified.

That sort of thing is anathema to most runners, who would never entertain the thought of cheating and who refuse to tolerate it when it is done by others. They take their racing seriously. Such intrusions by imposters jumping in are frowned upon. It happened to Shorter in his great win at the 1972 Olympics, when some guy jumped into the race ahead of him just before the victory lap in the stadium. Another guy jumped in after five miles in the 1978 New York City Marathon and ran with the leaders for a quarter of a mile. A protestor joined my finishing sprint at Boston in 1978, and a woman ran up and took part during the final mile in the 1979 Boston run.

If the crowd is aware of what is happening, the response is generally negative. The top runners don't buy the acts at all. George Plimpton, who writes books about his acted-out fantasies, was on a speaking program with me at a day school in Massachusetts. He told how, at a Boston Marathon, he jumped in with three hundred yards to go and the runner who was winning turned around with a look of terror on his face. I know, from personal experience with Jeff Wells in 1978— when he was so close at the end and finished only two seconds behind me—how it fatigues you, frightens you, and throws you off balance to see someone bearing down on you. Here was Plimpton glamorizing his act. I suggested to Plimpton that, maybe the next time, he might summon up the courage to run the entire marathon. As far as I know, he hasn't.

This idiotic grandstanding seems to be increasing in road running, as the sport grows and merchandise prizes and T-shirts are items to stockpile. It happened on a large scale in the Maryland Marathon of 1978, when runners ran the first third of the marathon, cut back in, and finished, just to get the jacket for completing the distance. One runner felt so guilty about it, he returned the jacket.

We also have the Oscar Miranda incident, courtesy of

Boston, 1979, and a TV station in Tampa. He was sent by the
station to run Boston. He ran and finished in 2:16:31. He was
fifty-three, so he was recognized, at first, as the first master to
finish. The officials later disqualified him, saying he showed
up in no checkpoint counts and, because he finished twenty-
second overall at his age, there were legitimate doubts that he
had run the distance.

SPECTATORS, for the most part, encourage the runners. Yet
there are the few who can spoil it. I was running next to Josh
Kimento in San Blas, in 1978, when a spectator suddenly
threw an ice cube in our direction, which actually bounced off
Josh's eyebrow. Sometimes spectators get carried away, reaching out to slap your hand, grab your arm, or talk to you.
Occasionally, when they try to give you water, they end up
obstructing your progress.

Spectators differ, perhaps according to environment or
society. European spectators at track meets are very knowledgeable, applauding performance, and aware of the significance of the effort and the potential time. They start chanting if
a runner shows the courage to break to the front and put the
race away. Reactions vary.

The key word in Japan is orderliness. There is an intense
interest in what is going on and a very real sense of understanding. Everybody stays well back from the competitors and
applauds with enthusiasm. They are aware that they are
watching the best athletes in the world. It is a controlled
enthusiasm, but one that reflects a keen appreciation of the
race.

I can remember certain incidents and situations in the
United States that reflect a different side of the spectator. I was
alone in the lead in the 1976 New York City Marathon and
someone yelled out, "Go back to Boston!" I remember running
Boston in 1973, when I had a long ponytail, and several
discouraging cries were directed at me: "Get a haircut!" Isn't it
wonderful to see people so deeply involved in athletics?

When I sat out the 1976 Boston Marathon because of its close proximity to the Olympic trials, I watched it from a Greyhound bus in order to gather some observations for an article for the *Boston Globe* on the race. The majority of the sportswriters were unaware of who I was and had a very casual, flippant attitude toward the event. They had a total lack of understanding of who these athletes were or what they were trying to achieve.

Contrast this with what happened when I ran on Sado Island off the East Coast of Japan in 1976. It was a setup in which I ran a marathon against a group of Japanese runners who were part of a relay team. They were part of Ondekoza and they ran to build up their cardiovascular systems so they could perform better in their dance and musical performances.

There were five different legs to the relay and, after I took the lead on the second leg, I can remember running through several small villages on the sparsely populated island and, even though I was the only Westerner in the race and I was beating the Japanese relay team, people were out there with Japanese and American flags, cheering me on as if I were an astronaut in the United States being driven down Fifth Avenue in New York City. I spent half the race waving to these people. It was a sunny, crisp, clear day on an easy, flat course out in the countryside. I really left with a good feeling for the people.

Something similar happened when I ran the thirty-kilometer Ohme race in February 1976. Tom Fleming and I were the only American representatives, invited as part of a reciprocal agreement the sponsors of the Ohme race have with the organizers of the Boston Marathon. There were more than eight thousand Japanese runners over the course that went out from the city and returned over the same route.

Tom and I agreed that we would cross the finish line together. We figured, "Why make it competitive between us?" Tom had pulled on a pair of Tiger shoes he had received from the Onitsuka Tiger people only the day before the race. The result was that he developed a bad blister, and, after twenty kilometers, the blister started to bother him a lot. He started to slow down, a Japanese runner passed him, and he placed third instead of tying with me. But my best memory of Ohme was my fondness for the people who continued cheering us both on the way back when we were in the lead by ourselves.

Runners appreciate what is going on in the race. We were in the Baltimore Marathon in 1976 on a cold December day. I was in a small pack with Fleming, Ron Hill, Barry Brown, and a few others. Fleming put on his normal surge about five or six miles into the race. He's a runner who loves to go out and take the lead. We'd been out there chatting with each other, not feeling competitive at all. All of sudden, Tom put on his surge and Barry and Ron start shouting, "Tom, Tom, don't leave us!" He just kept on going.

I caught up to Tom midway into the race on the out-and-back course. There were about two thousand runners in the field. It was much like Ohme as we returned. Some runners would yell to Tom, "Go get 'em, beat 'em. You can win." Some would yell the same things to me. We were having a lot of fun, joking and trying to sort out how many runners were pulling for me and how many were pulling for Tom.

Sometimes crowds and your companion runners can have no effect on you, when you are totally exhausted. You've used up all your physical and mental energy. You are totally drained. When that happens and you "hit the wall," you run through a valley of physiological despair and mental fatigue. I've certainly had my share of that.

KYOTO, 1977.   I had a knee-problem for two weeks prior to the race, so I had cut back my training. I found myself winning the race but, at the twenty-five-kilometer mark, I was so tired I came to a halt. Thousands of Japanese were shouting at me to try to break the record, and I was within striking distance. I calmly walked over to take a drink and just sat there and looked around. I started to get back a little of the psychological and mental energy I needed and I carried on to the finish. They shoot off firecrackers and flares as the runners approach the finish, and that gives you an extra lift.

I stopped outside Heiwadai Stadium in Fukuoka, in 1977, to take a drink of water. I sensed the spectators were a little freaked out because I stopped. They stared at me in stunned silence. This is universal, I guess. Spectators simply don't expect to see one of the leaders stop. They don't get angry, as they might at other athletic events. They just sort of stare at you in quiet disbelief.

When I dropped out in Boston, in 1977, at the top of Heartbreak Hill about five miles from the finish, I walked into the crowd and nobody said anything. Some people just looked at me. Finally, somebody came and offered me a big bottle of Pepsi. I guzzled that. Somebody else came up, quietly offered me a ride, and drove me to Kenmore Square so I could meet Ellen at the Eliot Lounge. This man was, I discovered later, the coach at nearby Winchester High School. He must be a good coach. He didn't pester me with annoying questions about my defeat that day.

Something I always remember when I think of running and sportsmanship is the visit of Ron Clarke to Emil Zatopek. Here were two of the greatest distance runners in history, meeting in Czechoslovakia. The one great athletic achievement that always eluded Clarke was the Olympic gold medal. When he left, Zatopek gave him a small package at the airport. Clarke unwrapped it on the plane and discovered one of Zatopek's Olympic gold medals with a message inscribed on it, "To a great runner and fine friend." It was his way of recognizing that Clarke was one of the greatest runners in the world and, simply because he had never won an Olympic gold medal, some people had downplayed his career. Zatopek, a great Olympic champion, was fully aware of the talents of Ron Clarke.

There have been some ungentlemanly actions on my part in my career, I regret to say. In 1975 I ran a twenty-kilometer

National AAU race in Gardner, Massachusetts, and I felt I was going to win it. Dave Babiracki, a California runner, was giving me a run for it. I pulled away from him eight miles into the race, but he caught up to me two miles later and we were neck and neck.

As we rounded the last turn to the finish, he put on an incredible sprint. He was a first-rate miler, whereas my best was an ordinary 4:18. I sprinted, went after him, and fell short. I was handed a marker indicating I was second. I threw it on the ground, walked away, and started ranting and raving about how I was going to quit my job so I could train and rest more frequently. I was working at the Fernald School. I was looking for any excuse. Why hadn't I won? Blame my job, even though it wasn't the real reason. It was Dave's day to win and I couldn't accept that.

There are sometimes moments of stress. When you don't win, it's a difficult time. That's when you have to watch yourself more carefully than when you win. You learn humility when you lose. You should practice it when you win. Competitors resent it when someone carries on about a win. Victory in a race is something that is earned, something you fought for. It is also yours to some degree by virtue of Lady Luck, Fate, by chance, by good fortune. The runner who fails to understand that is due to experience some severe disappointments in his career. That's why I always say the marathon can humble you, no matter who you are.

Etiquette is also a part of it, in training as well as in racing. You don't race when you are training. It isn't the thing to do. If you feel exceptionally strong, you tell the other runners, "Hey, I feel really good and I want to push it ahead a little." They'll understand. Part of running with other people is the camaraderie. It's a social occasion. You help each other through the workout. It's not the time to do your flashy training. Save that for when you're off by yourself or when you have made prior plans with other runners to do a hard workout.

Similarly, on training runs it is "good etiquette" not to leave someone behind if he begins to slow down, no matter what his reason for slowing down. At the very least, one other runner will usually stay back to encourage the fellow who's having trouble maintaining the group pace.

I was out running one day with Scott Graham, Vin Fleming, and George Hirsch, the publisher of *The Runner*. We went out for a twenty-four-mile run on a snowy day in January. For George, it was his first long run in some time. He kept up but, after fifteen miles or so, it became apparent his pace was a little too slow for the rest of us. Vinnie and I were too impatient to hang on. We started to push ahead and, even though George was my friend, Scott was the one who stayed back and helped lead him in. I was too impatient. I had to get the run over with and I ignored George because of it.

I'm often in the lead in a marathon, but sometimes I find myself trailing Bob Hall, the wheelchair athlete. He's also a front-runner, a leader. The wheelchair competitors start ahead of us, so I occasionally catch Bob about twenty miles into the race. I pat him on the back, he shouts out words of encouragement. He usually doesn't repass me, except in the 1977 Boston Marathon when I dropped out.

I heard of an incident involving Amby Burfoot that tells you something about Amby. He was in the lead in an NCAA Division II Cross-Country Championship along with Bob Fitts. Fitts started veering off the course as they approached the finish. Amby is such a generous and noncompetitive soul that he called out to Fitts and redirected him back on the course. Fitts outkicked him at the finish and won the race. Amby will never be confused with Vince Lombardi.

The heat of upcoming competition rubs people different ways. I still remember Frank Shorter coming into the dormitories of the American athletes at the Montreal Olympics. He came up to me and offered me an extra ticket to the opening ceremonies. Do you realize how hard these were to come by?

We were competitors. I even had a faster time going into the Olympics, and he had to view me as a dangerous rival. But here he was showing what a sportsman he was.

TYING. AAU rules prohibit a tie. I think it's an absurd rule. It's perpetuated by administrators, in keeping with their mentality. They are generally not athletes, people who are unaware of what the runner is doing. I think it's up to the athletes to determine if they want to tie, if the race should be termed a tie. I ran in three races in 1978 when I tried to tie with someone else, and in only one of them was it allowed to stand. That time it was simply because the race officials were happily unaware of the ridiculous rule.

I tied with Greater Boston TC teammate Randy Thomas twice in 1978. We tied in a half marathon in Cleveland and they gave the win to me. Possibly that was because I had won it the previous year, but we had agreed to tie. We each had the same time and it was understood, by us, that we'd jog across the finish together and make it a tie.

What *is* unfortunate is when an official intervenes out of petty vindictiveness. It happened in the Freedom Trail race in Boston in October 1978. Randy and I crossed the finish line together in a deliberate tie and, all of a sudden, an AAU official ran up and started yelling, "Give it to Thomas, give it to Thomas!" He hadn't seen the finish, I was told. I felt, in my gut, that he was out to get me, simply because I had won a lot of races and I wasn't on his dance card. He's an AAU official and I'd expect him to be impartial.

I think the concept of tying is the right of the athlete. If athletes want to tie, let them tie. They compete throughout most of the race, and then they may feel there are good reasons not to compete any more. They are pleased enough with their effort and are friends and possibly teammates with their rival, so they forget the rivalry. To have some AAU official muck it all up is nauseating. It's a regulation that's indicative of how the AAU has failed to comprehend the feelings of the athlete. It's one rule that should be changed.

John Parker, in his book *Once a Runner,* talks about how the running world is divided into a hierarchy, virtually a class system. You have the fastest, the world-record holders, and the Olympic gold medalists. You step down to the national-record holders, the local champions, the college and high school champions. Runners are very aware of the different levels of the ladder. They know where they stand as far as rankings are concerned.

They forget it once the race is history. They often go out together for a warm-down run. They go to a bar for a drink. They go to a private home for a party. They go out to dinner. It becomes a social occasion. The competitiveness tends to subside. There are very few runners who really dislike each other. Such feelings are not fostered in running.

The essence of sportsmanship is understanding what you are doing in your sport, how you got there, where you are going. Being an athlete is not a one-way street. It is not just you, the athlete. You must have people helping you out, the input of friends. You must appreciate the support, or ultimately you will really "fall." I recently discussed the Lombardi "winning-is-the-only-thing" ethic on a training run with a friend. We agreed that the concept of winning is important to an athlete but, if you are unaware of the people around you who have made sacrifices and contributions, you are lacking in something, and it will all catch up with you in the end.

COACHING—THE GOOD AND THE BAD OF IT. I have mixed feelings on the subject. In general, my experience with coaches over sixteen years has been a positive one. Yet I also have witnessed incompetence and greed by people in the coaching profession, traits that sometimes turn up at all levels.

When I first joined the cross-country team in Newington in

1963, it was strictly intramural. The coach was the regular gym teacher. He knew nothing about running, but he had a simple idea: "Let's get cross-country started." It sufficed. Out of three intramural cross-country meets, a varsity program was born a year later. That's the way some truly good things are started, when one person has a dream and has the imagination and energy to realize it.

I can't even remember his name, but I remember he didn't have too much time for coaching because of his regular physical education duties. Of course, he wasn't paid to coach cross-country. We simply went out and ran our two, three, or four miles every day, or three or four times a week. There wasn't much input on his part. We simply did it. He had the idea, though, and I credit him for that. I didn't expect any more, but I remain in his debt.

They hired somebody who was an industrial-arts teacher to coach indoor track. His name was Joe Bajek, and he brought an enthusiasm for the sport with him. I don't believe he was that knowledgeable about track and field, but he did have enthusiasm and a good sense of humor. We always had fun. We had a weight man as our captain and we did an hour or two of calisthenics every day and spent the rest of the time on our specialty. We would occasionally run time trials, a concept I've never believed in, whether it was taught by Arthur Lydiard or Mr. Bajek.

Bajek coached only one year. It wasn't because he was unsuccessful. The job paid very poorly. It was not worth it in terms of the amount of time and energy he had to invest. He had a family and, when your salary is one hundred dollars a week and you have to be there five or six days a week and traveling to meets, it's not worth it. Isn't it typical of our American approach to amateur sports? We place the emphasis and focus on the sports that are played by professionals: basketball, baseball, football. It annoyed me then, it almost sickens me today.

Frank O'Rourke, a gym teacher at the junior high school, became the new coach: an intense, dedicated, knowledgeable man who had a background as a half-miler. He possessed an understanding for what we were trying to do. I took running pretty seriously, became fairly good at it, and O'Rourke and a few other people motivated me to excel.

There was a math teacher, Don Grant, who was a track nut and who came to our "away" meets. One or two parents would also come. One lady would always bring a big container of orange juice for the competitors. That was about it. Nobody showed up to watch a track meet in that era and, as much as any reason, it is why I continue to condemn the excess money and support given to the sports of baseball, basketball, and football. The public has perceived of these sports as superior, worth the investment. I disagree.

You always knew it if you were loafing when Coach O'Rourke was around. He had the second loudest voice in the state of Connecticut. The loudest was Irv Black at New Britain High School. You'd hear O'Rourke during a race, letting you know your standing. We had dual meets twice a week and, in a certain two-mile race, or "deuce," I was dead tired. It was windy. I could hear Coach O'Rourke yelling, "Pick it up" from the other side of the field. I flipped out and started swearing at him in the middle of the race, but I kept running.

We had a 12–1 record in my first year. We discovered interval workouts. They'd be posted on the wall every day in the team room. Coach O'Rourke was amenable to modifying the workouts. He didn't have a closed mind and he was interested in his athletes and their futures. He cared for you as a person. When I started getting letters and offers from different colleges, he'd offer advice and counseling and tell me I should be concerned about the academic program as well as the athletic one.

He spent a lot of time with me. He always had some words about how a workout was going or how a particular race went.

He was a positive influence on my life. He wrote in my yearbook about how some day I would be a great runner. I just laughed and sloughed it off then, but I have him to thank for the early inspiration and for pointing me in the proper direction.

Wesleyan was a different experience. The emphasis was to do well academically, not necessarily athletically. Since I was not into the intellectual life style that much, I adopted a somewhat lackadaisical approach to college, and my running and studies both suffered as a consequence. Still, it was a healthy environment for a runner.

Elmer Swanson, the coach, was active. He'd go out every day, time us, work with us on our running form, and instruct us how to run the hills in all types of weather. He'd give us tips, talk to us about our competition and how we ought to approach a certain race. He followed me wherever he could after graduation. He didn't push anybody too far during our college years, something that has enabled me to compete at a high level for a long time. He didn't burn you out. How many runners are burned out in college? Too many. I learned to enjoy my running more at Wesleyan.

I left the influences of Bajek, O'Rourke, and Swanson and ventured into the land of emptiness, of no coaches, no clubs, no future in running. That's what I thought, at first. I finally wound up in the Greater Boston Track Club, four years and a lot of miles later. I came into contact with Bill Squires, the coach, and Bob Sevene, one of the founders.

Squires, who also coached at Boston State, had a boundless enthusiasm. He's hyperactive. He had a great influence on me, revised my training, added more long intervals, and built up my base for the marathon through anaerobic work. I credit him with playing an important role in my American record run in Boston, in 1975, and my early growth as a marathoner.

Coaching, in the United States, is at a lower level, in general, than it is in Europe. It's not that difficult to become a coach in this country. You can contrast this with a Valeri Borzov of the Soviet Union getting a Ph.D. and writing a thesis on sprinting. He learned everything there was to learn about the event he participated in at a world-class level.

I often see situations in which one coach gets possessive, tries to accumulate all the top runners. It brings up the age-old question: Does the runner make the coach or does the coach make the runner? Who makes whom great? It works both ways, to a degree, but when a coach becomes too authoritarian and too dictatorial toward an athlete, it's time to break away.

The athlete knows himself better than any coach does, simply because the coach is unaware of everything going on in the mind of the athlete or of how he feels physically. If there is a conflict, it becomes a limiting factor. You can't race and train for two people. You have to be doing it basically for yourself. I realize there are some people who work best under a coach and, to some degree, I am one of them. But I also have a streak of independence and, because of it, I often prefer to operate alone and rely on my experience.

The late Percy Cerruty, the great Australian coach, personified the authoritarian approach. His philosophy of running revolved around a total life style approach, including a training camp around which the athlete's life revolved. It makes sense, to a certain extent, but it demands a tremendous commitment by the athlete. Cerruty based his central concept on the belief that there was a certain way to live in order to achieve superior performances. He is correct. But I do believe it would be mighty difficult to live in a "camp" of the sort he had for very long!

He also believed there were specific running styles that would enable you to realize these performances; there I am in complete disagreement. He compared humans to horses, talking about gaits, trots, and canters and saying you should run naturally and free. I used to run with a friend around Jamaica Pond who'd read that Cerruty said you should express your emotions when you run. Act freely, without restraint. There are no formalities. Don't be afraid to show facial strain as you run, for example. If you want to run hard, run hard. Shout out as you run. This Cerruty-fan friend of mine would start shouting, totally freaking out people.

Coaches of some of the top women runners, in particular, seem to adopt a dictatorial approach. In March 1975, we were at the World Cross-Country Championships in Rabat, Morocco, and the coach with Julie Brown was guarding her, keeping her apart from the male members of the team. This was true both prior to the race (which, incidentally, she won) and also afterwards. I had the impression he didn't want anyone talking with her, and breaking her concentration, her momentum, or her allegiance to him. We went out for an early morning run and some of the women joined us. Some of them commented about a coach on the team who had the attitude the men were going to corrupt the women, lead them astray, or cause them to deviate from their training or racing schedule. Absurd.

Norm Higgins, who coaches Jan Merrill, is like this in some ways. He's protective. Yet Merrill and Julie Brown are two of the top women runners in the United States. Part of it is due to their natural talents, their motivation. Part of it, I suppose, is due to proper guidance. I would find it unfortunate, though, if I were in their shoes, being ruled the way they are. I admit they are younger and, at this stage of their careers, experienced guidance is probably a positive thing. After all, it's hard to criticize what may well have helped Jan and Julie to their success.

Mihaly Igloi of the San Fernando Valley TC is this way, dominating the athlete and controlling the workout. So is Harry Johnson at Athletics West. This kind of a relationship would be impossible for me to endure. I'd chafe under such a set of circumstances. That's probably because I think I have too much experience of my own for any coach to have that kind of controlling influence over me.

People make much of the fact that Rolf Haikkla coaches Lasse Viren, travels with him, and has a close relationship with him. I have been with them in Japan and, in my mind, Haikkla seems more of a friend, comrade, and masseur than a coach. He speaks the same language, of course, but how much of a coach is he, in the sense of one who adjusts workouts, life style, rests, and so forth? Not too much. It's important, I guess, to have someone there to take the detached, objective look and perhaps pass along a tip or two. Haikkla acts much as Viren's aide, an attendant, supporter, and pre-race strategist.

I remember some of the early little things. Coach O'Rourke taking my flats during cross-country season, examining them, and putting in a special heel lift to enable me to win a race—in fact, my biggest high school win in the Class-A Cross-Country Championships in 1966. Sam Bell, an Olympic coach in Montreal, making sure everything was OK with our uniforms, our water bottles, and our peace of mind. These are seemingly small things, yet they grow in importance when juxtaposed with some examples of indifference I know of through my international experiences.

Too many of the coaches in Montreal were along for the ride, people who coached at large universities who did little to promote the development of the sport in this country. At their schools they had the power and money to bring in a lot of good athletes, stage a track meet once a year, and get appointed an Olympic coach. It's no secret about the politics involved, and most athletes I know feel this way. And many coaches are also upset about such a system. A better alternative? Perhaps coaches and athletes could come up with one if our athletics system were organized and cohesive enough for any harmony!

Ed Mendoza, my roommate at Montreal, shocked me when he told me how one of the American coaches had been caught selling our tickets at the games. Each of the athletes was supposed to receive a limited number of the very scarce tickets to events at the Olympics. Here was this coach selling them for personal profit. He was arrested and put in jail for a night. Of course, nothing about this even leaked out in the newspapers.

Incidents like this strike home when I talk about how no team coach came up to me after I finished the 1976 Olympic Marathon and tried to help me analyze why I did so poorly. It left me with an empty feeling for the Olympics and the Pan-American Games. I don't feel I have to be told I should be at the Olympic Training Camp because, "We're a team." I do have feelings of patriotism, to an extent, but the feelings are for the athletes, not for many of the coaches. I left Montreal with the feeling that I was there mostly on my own, except for Ellen, of course. However, my friends from the Greater Boston TC were helpful and supportive at Montreal, as was my then coach, Billy Squires.

When a runner leaves college and seeks out a club, he or she should try to find the club with experienced coaches and runners. You'll know soon enough if what they're doing is the right thing. If you feel any physical, emotional, or psychological conflicts with the coach, get out. No coach is infallible. When a coach starts talking about his infallibility, watch out. Walk away.

Of the noted coaches, my favorite is Arthur Lydiard of New Zealand. He believes in building up an aerobic base over a long period and then sharpening. I disagree with him and his feeling that you should peak for one or two races a year. I like to race more frequently at a high level then he believes you should. But his training techniques remain valid and he's worth reading and getting to know.

Percy Cerruty, who coached Herb Elliot in Australia, had some good ideas in terms of the general overall life style and attitude that is necessary to be a great runner. He'd be considered eccentric by the beginner who listened to him talking about what foods to eat, but to the top level competitors, many of his dietary concepts and training techniques are very valid. He would permit the athletes at his training camp to have only specific foods such as grains, beans, fruit, with little red meat, fat, or sugar. He also evolved a number of different concepts in regard to the runner's form at different paces based on his observations of animals.

Squires preaches moderation. He believes in developing an anaerobic base for distance runners and in doing fairly heavy mileage on the roads. He also incorporates light interval work and some long intervals that aren't too fast or too intense. Hill work is also an integral part of his training method. He believes in peaking for certain races. He aimed me for the World Cross-Country Championships in Morocco. I finished third and won Boston one month later. He's since influenced top American marathoners like Randy Thomas, Vin Fleming, Bobby Hodge, and Dick Mahoney.

Bill Bowerman, the former University of Oregon coach, studied what Lydiard preached in New Zealand and saw how many people in that country were running. Not just the college students and the high school kids, but everyone! He brought back the concept of jogging and light running, and promoted that, and he made Eugene, Oregon, an early jogging capital in this country.

He also became a proponent of running form, emphasizing the importance of a certain most efficient style. He promoted the concept of hard and easy days for running. If you were a top-level marathoner, he might recommend thirty miles one day, six the next to recover. Go back to your normal twenty the next day. Or you might have two easy days of six and ten, then step up to twenty. It depended upon your maturity, how far along you were in your training program.

I think the concept of the hard and easy days is generally valid. Still, I don't feel you tie yourself into any system and automatically go by anything that is axiomatic. If you run thirty miles one day and feel good, why not do twenty miles the next day instead of just six? That's my approach. My own training is based on a little bit taken from each of these different coaches, from that and from my own personality.

You can't plug yourself into a particular coaching system. What you do is try to study and learn about different coaches, different concepts, and different ways to improve. You experiment. Try a little bit of one, a little bit of another. You soon find out which ones appeal to you and work, and which ones don't.

Part of it is psychological. Do you enjoy interval workouts? Do you enjoy twenty-mile runs? What appeals to you? These are the factors that will determine which way you're going to head as a runner, which coach you're going to rely on more. Pick and choose. Suit yourself. You are running for yourself. You're not running for your coach. Never kid yourself. Don't run for several conflicting people or goals.

It's good to have the support of a coach, but he should understand his role. He is there simply to help you excel. If you feel exploited or your workouts are too difficult, speak up. If your coach doesn't listen to you, move on, leave the coach, and seek out someone else. It's interesting that many people have regarded Cerruty, Bowerman, and Lydiard as eccentric, whereas others rate them as geniuses.

Squires also fits the mold. He gets so carried away at track meets and clinics, he's apt to jump up on a table and start shrieking at the top of his lungs. One thought will suddenly intervene in the middle of another. He'll completely lose himself and may lose you before he makes the point. Cerruty was critical of most civilizations and the attitudes most people had toward themselves. Perhaps, as I once heard someone say, eccentricity is the mark of genius.

17
Politics and Athletics

Baron Pierre de Coubertin, whose foresight and persistence were responsible for the rebirth of the Olympic Games in 1896, enunciated a basic precept that became a backdrop to the competition. "The most important thing," he said, "is not to win but to take part, just as the most important thing in life is not the triumph but the struggle. The essential thing is not to have conquered but to have fought well."

By reviving the Olympic Games, the Baron believed he might stem what he felt was a disturbing tide of commercialization in international sports. The concern remains a part of the eligibility code of the International Olympic Committee. "To be eligible for participation in the Olympic Games," it reads, "a competitor must not have received any financial rewards or material benefit in connection with his or her sports participation."

When we begin to fuse the ideal with practicality and twentieth-century reality, we enter into a vast gray area.

"We're all professionals," Frank Shorter told a Senate committee. "Making money is common throughout amateur sport," Dwight Stones told *Sports Illustrated*. "Success," reads the final report of the President's Commission on Olympic Sports (1975–77), "reflects on the ability of a sports system to permit individual athletes to reach the limits of their potential."

I find myself, an amateur athlete, an Olympic hopeful, and a businessman with heavy obligations to the people who are in my employ, walking the fine line between amateurism and what somebody has categorized as "shamateurism." It is a broad, complex subject, one that has never been properly examined. What is amateurism? Judges in federal district courts have sidestepped attempts at definition in the interest of uneasy compromise. I am not about to define the term, merely to touch upon a few points involved with the political issues that are related to it in the United States.

Although I believe in the essential thinking behind the sentiments of Baron de Coubertin that "the essential thing is not to have conquered but to have fought well," I am in disagreement with his basic concept of amateurism. Again, what is amateurism? Different federations in different countries provide completely different interpretations. American skiers view it in a different light than American boxers, swimmers, gymnasts, or road runners. There are barriers and obstacles limiting what each athlete can do when he or she seeks to coexist as an athlete and a businessperson.

The American AAU puts out a booklet listing the rules and regulations that all amateurs are required to adhere to in order to remain amateurs. The rules are constantly changing, constantly being modified. The athlete has trouble keeping pace with the changing nature of the rules. Since the system itself is so complex and inefficient with regard to the administration of amateur athletics in the United States, all the rules never adequately filter down to the athlete.

Perhaps the public, in general, simply does not care what

happens to the amateur athlete. A Dwight Stones slips out of sight and, who cares? The modern history of amateur sports is laced with examples of people being punished because of the ludicrous interpretations of the rules. Jim Thorpe, the American Indian who was stripped of his medals after the 1912 Olympic Games because he had played a few games of baseball as a semi-professional, is the classic example. Wes Santee, the top American miler of the 1950s, was banned from amateur competition because he allegedly accepted something like thirty dollars too much for expenses.

Such rules are a farce. They are basically written by the officials of the International Amateur Athletic Federation. The American AAU is forced to comply with these rules and inform us what we can or cannot do as amateurs. We have to direct any change through our own association. Ollan Cassell, executive director of the AAU and the American representative on the international board (incidentally, a gold medalist on the sixteen-hundred-meter relay team in the 1964 Olympics at Tokyo), has promoted a general softening of the rules in recent years that has enabled amateur athletes in this country to exist better in a business world.

When Frank Shorter wanted to break the ice in the United States by opening up a store with his name on it, he first had to contact the American AAU and they went to IAAF for approval. There was an international precedent set by English marathoner Ron Hill, who had a running gear store and a clothing line. I came along and asked to open the Bill Rodgers Running Centers and it was approved. But only provided I own 51 percent of the company, which is something that limits me considerably in terms of franchising the stores. I must also own 51 percent of the clothing line. I can advertise it but I am prohibited from using a picture of myself or listing my athletic accomplishments in the brochure. Isn't that somewhat hypocritical?

The reality of inflated expense money and under-the-table

payments to athletes in track and field has been with us since the revival of the Olympic Games in 1896. Nobody denies it. Paavo Nurmi of Finland was guilty of it in the 1920s. I know a story of an American runner who participated in the 1928 Olympics. He had an open expense account at Brooks Brothers. He was taken care of that way. Hypocrisy? Until there is a modification of the rules on an international level the situation will continue to exist in one form or another.

Why shouldn't the athlete be compensated for an honest performance? I remember going to a race in Newark, New Jersey, a few weeks before I finished third in the International Cross-Country Championships in 1975 and a month and a half before I set an American record in the Boston Marathon. I had to haggle with the people there to get thirty-five or forty dollars for expense money. I had driven from Boston to Newark, spent a night there before the race, paid all my food, hotel, and gas bills, and placed second to 1974 Boston champion Neil Cusack. I still found it difficult to get reimbursement for any of my expenses. For that reason, I have never returned to that race.

It's important for runners to remember those races where they treat you well and to boycott races where the runners are shabbily treated. There's a notorious race in Massachusetts that's sponsored by a car dealership. They put on a marathon, offer no protection from traffic, set up no water stations, put out no refreshments, provide no shower facilities, and keep awards to a minimum. Amby Burfoot won it one year and won a set of tires. They may have been retreads.

All of it becomes further complicated when certain AAU officials stick their noses in. I happened to see a letter written by a New England AAU official to a director of the Falmouth Road Race in 1975. The official indicated that if he found out Shorter was receiving too much expense money he would "like to be the first person to put the nails in his coffin." In other words, he'd like to be the one to terminate his amateur career. It's attitudes such as this that are at the heart of holding back the development of track and field and distance running in this country—or any country, and there are others with similar problems. The sooner that type of official no longer plays any kind of active role in the administration of athletic policies, the better it will be for all of athletics.

Similar circumstances have enveloped the Springbank Road Race in London, Ontario. There are two cliques involved. One believes in bringing in the top runners, treating them well, and giving them adequate expense money. All of the top runners I know feel the same way about what constitutes a quality race. The second group is opposed to the concept. I know of many races that have been inaugurated and quietly discontinued because of a lack of adequate financial support.

The first marathon I won was the Bay State Marathon in Framingham, Massachusetts, in 1973. I can still remember the race directors telling me how they had to work to get any financial support in order to buy merchandise prizes and supply refreshments for the runners. It's difficult for the small track clubs to survive, so there is no longer a Bay State Marathon.

We encountered similar financial problems in our early years of the Greater Boston TC. We had no money to send top athletes to perform at higher levels of competition. Many of us in the club suggested a road race. We started a race called the Gurnet Beach Classic in Duxbury, Massachusetts. It's a fun run on the beach that was directed by our club founder, Jack McDonald. It's grown from one hundred to seven hundred or eight hundred, and we've made money out of it through entry fees and the sale of T-shirts. It is still held, but is no longer run by the Greater Boston TC. Yet it was merely a beginning.

The next step was to put on a major road race, and the result was the Freedom Trail Road Race in the fall. It's interesting that the initial sponsor for the race was Labatt's Beer, a Canadian company. It was a sad commentary on American beer companies who at that time opted to advertise their product on TV telecasts of professional football, baseball, and basketball. The American companies finally realized that the sponsorship of a road race would contribute to a positive image for their companies, and H. P. Hood, a Boston dairy-products concern, is now the sponsor.

I used to point out how runners were the rare exception, athletes who had to pay to be athletes. But the running boom finally produced the corporate sponsor. Perrier, the French mineral water company, sponsors Falmouth, the Cherry Blossom Road Race, and races in Fort Lauderdale, Florida, and in Louisiana. Pepsi has established a national series of ten-thousand-meter races, leading up to a national championship. Winners in regional finals win trips to the nationals. I believe in these and other instances both corporations and the runners benefit. I think of officials who fought against corporate involvement, and all I can say is that they were trying to perpetuate ignorance.

Within this climate, I participate, work, and wonder. I feel, as so many do, that many of the rules are a joke and drastic modifications are imperative. The central concept of amateurism is highly impractical. Nobility should be redefined. The nobleman of the nineteenth century could afford the luxury of having competition as his hobby. Nobility of performance in the modern world requires sacrifice and an intense effort. The top-level amateur athlete is as highly dedicated as any professional athlete. The amateur hockey team from the Soviet Union may well have received the sort of support that amateurs here can't enjoy, but they did qualify officially as amateurs. And they dominated and embarrassed the best group of professionals the National Hockey League could assemble in the winter of 1979.

It's not a problem I'm going to solve, or attempt to solve. I'm simply putting forth my own thoughts on the subject. I'm opposed to the present setup of amateur sports in the United

States. Athletes don't have enough voice nationally and internationally. Inadequate money is appropriated for amateur sports and insufficient interest is shown by the media. In particular, American television has failed miserably in this respect. I think the general public is sick of the saturation coverage of professional sports, to say nothing of celebrity "nonsports"—I mean someone like Rod Stewart's a fine singer, but let's skip it when it comes to his athletic skills—"trash" sports like refrigerator-pushing contests, frisbee and skateboard competitions, and the massive amounts of time, energy, and money pumped into the professional superstructure.

I was asked by President Carter about the state of affairs for the amateur athlete when I attended a White House state dinner after winning the 1979 Boston Marathon and I said the situation was improving—slowly. Congress passed an amateur athletic bill that was an outgrowth of the President's Commission on Olympic Sports. The outlay was sixteen million dollars for the United States Olympic Committee and the American AAU to utilize in promoting the development of amateur sports. Unfortunately, as of late 1979, this money has not been allocated, owing to the never-ending quarrel between the NCAA and the AAU. Of course, both our athletes and American prestige suffer.

One of the recent steps taken was to set up an Olympic Job Program, aided and organized by Howard Miller of the Canteen Corporation. Athletes could apply to the U.S. Olympic Committee for a job with a variety of corporations that had indicated interest in the program. The athlete would be placed according to his or her interests and abilities, and the background he or she would acquire would be useful for future employment and career development. While the athlete was training for the Olympics, adequate time off would be granted and the salary would continue.

It's a positive step, a contrast to the situation I was in when I had my pay docked as a schoolteacher for taking time off to compete for my country while I was working in Everett, Massachusetts. The Olympic Job Program has been successful, to a limited degree. There haven't been enough athletes placed in the past two years to warrant calling it a complete success, but it could be significant if it is broadened a great deal.

One method to fund sports federations might be for a large corporation, say Exxon or General Motors (there are, of course, many to choose from), to become the sponsor for a specific federation for a given number of years. In return they could use the federation in their advertising and promotion. The commitment will have to be undertaken sooner or later if Americans expect any kind of positive results in international sports competition.

Where the shortcomings are magnified to the greatest degree is at the grass-roots level. More work has to be done with younger athletes, more adequate training provided, and the best facilities and coaching made available. Young athletes should be sent around the world to meet the best competition in other countries. That would translate into world-class performances when they step up from the junior ranks.

What is good about the corporate approach is that it keeps the government out of athletics, at least to a degree. Politics and athletics often become inextricably intertwined. The Olympic Games have become an unfortunate stage for political expression. Nationalism is a dominant force of the twentieth century, and the athlete often becomes the innocent pawn. National federations also frequently dictate when and where top athletes can compete. It is a fact that before an American can compete anywhere internationally, he or she has to acquire permission from the AAU.

The United States Olympic Committee took one significant step in the right direction when it set up a National Sports Festival in the summer of 1978 in Colorado Springs. It brought together people of all ages and both sexes from most of the

Olympic sports, and that had a national impact. The approach was similar to that of Spartakiad in the Soviet Union and East Germany. It's useful in building interest and enthusiasm among the athletes and the general public. It attracted six hours of national TV exposure in its second year, when competition was conducted in 31 sports.

Why it was held at a high altitude is a mystery. I guess it was because the offices of the U.S. Olympic Committee had been moved there and it was the site of one of the training centers for the Olympics. That made everything centralized. Still, it is poor thinking to have athletic events at high altitudes. The majority of athletes in the United States (and the world) live at or near sea level, and forcing them to perform at high altitudes is absurd. This was the Mexico City Olympics revisited. All it did was feed the egos of those athletes who were accustomed to training at high altitudes.

The subject of sports medicine is a controversial one. Since the Montreal Olympics, there have been considerable improvements in the implementation of a sports medicine program through the Olympic Training Centers. Before all of this, the athlete had to go it on his or her own. I went to an orthopedic specialist after Montreal and I paid for the visit. I could probably go to a national center now, although I'd still have to pay for the air fare. Recently, a podiatrist friend, Lloyd Smith of St. Elizabeth's Sports Medicine Clinic in Brighton, Massachusetts, has treated me gratis. I am deeply appreciative of his interest, attitude, and help.

I hear disquieting talk from medical people that some of the individuals on the National Sports Medicine Committee are realizing personal gains. I've been told that one member of the committee displays an Olympic emblem as a sort of advertisement in his personal office near the headquarters of the U.S. Olympic Committee. Isn't this somewhat shoddy? Doesn't this show why I feel that the amateur athlete is basically a slave, a servant? Aren't certain promoters, politicians, architects, bankers, and medical people making a lot of money because of major competitions and the Olympic Games? We all know this is true. We don't need to look far to see it. Montreal and Lake Placid are wonderful examples. How does their expense money compare with ours? Why aren't they castigated and penalized by the people who administer the sport? I wonder.

I've also been told that one of the directors of the U.S. Olympic Sports Medicine Committee has been filling jobs on the Committee with old cronies, setting them up for financial gain. It's this sort of corruption, individual greed, and absence of a general overview of how to best help the athlete that damages the Olympic cause. Too many coaches, officials, and medical people in many countries are ignorant and/or uninterested in the fate of the athlete. If they live in East Germany they are out to promote the policy of their government. They are out to make money if they live in the United States.

If you are an athlete who lives in East Germany, Russia, Cuba, Finland, Japan, or Ireland you are a member of a certain national team. If you live in the United States, you are on your own. We have a national track team for just about a week or two each year. When the Olympics roll around, it suddenly becomes imperative for you to get to a training camp in the interest of national interest and patriotism. It's a sad joke. If they want you there, they ought to help take care of it beforehand.

It's easy to sift through the horror stories involving the American AAU. The organization desperately needs fresh blood, new ideas, and more input from the athletes if it is to improve its performance. After one race in Massachusetts, an AAU official suspended several individuals because the race wasn't sanctioned. After a long, arduous process and a lot of bickering, fighting, letter writing, phone calls, and news articles, the runners were reinstated. All it did was point up how asinine the suspensions had been in the first place.

Some officials within the AAU thirst for the power to control and dominate the lives and careers of athletes. What is it Lord Acton said? Power corrupts, absolute power corrupts absolutely. There are certain regulations all card-carrying AAU members are required to live by, and if they don't they are suspended. These are vague rules, rules that are often unfair and that do not reflect the needs of the athlete. They are being changed, to a degree, but such changes are too slow in coming.

Some of the changes being implemented as a result of the President's Commission on Olympic Sports may eventually enable us to compete on a fairly adequate level internationally. If more changes aren't forthcoming, we will continue to slide backward. The Moscow Olympics of 1980 will show us how far we have slid since the period lasting from the early decades of the century right through the 1960s, when the United States was the dominant power in track and field.

The Olympic Job Program should be enlarged. Knowledge should be imparted through qualified coaches and publications to reach a broader base of potential world-class athlete. Information concerning the latest training methods, diet, dates of competition, sports medicine, and where to go for assistance should be disseminated to the athlete.

I dwelt on the inadequacies of coaching at all levels in a previous chapter. It's worth repeating. We need more than the high school coach who goes up in the stands and puffs on a cigarette while the kids go out for a run or to put the shot. Without the proper coaching and an educational system that recognizes the need for it, the disparity between amateur and professional sports will continue to be too wide.

Big changes have to be made, but they are not going to be if only one or two dozen people raise their voices in protest. It must come about through concerted action. The sixteen million dollars appropriated is a pittance. The National Football League kicks in twenty thousand dollars per year to the U.S. Olympic Committee, and I laugh when I contrast it to the

amount spent on professional football in this country. With so
many people presently involved in improving their cardiovascular systems, the spin-off may be more of an emphasis
on the amateur-related sports.

I received travel money from the AAU once in my life, to go
to the American trials for the International Cross-Country
Championships in 1975. I received two-thirds of what I
needed. The women's cross-country team was denied full fares
and uniforms on another occasion. It's a disgrace, and something should be done to rectify such situations.

I think there should be a network of sports medicine
committees on a national basis. There should be more Olympic
training centers, and I don't think we need any more at a high
altitude! They don't have to be as elaborate as the ones
currently set up in Colorado Springs, Lake Placid, and Squaw
Valley. Dr. David Costill of the Human Performance Laborato-
ries at Ball State had all sorts of difficulties getting funds from
the Olympic Sports Medicine Committee. Here is one of the
top physiologists in the United States and he can't get the
proper assistance from a source that should help him to
continue his work.

The politics of picking coaches has to end. Why not form a
small committee and search out the top coaches on a quarterly
basis, bring them together for conferences on the progress
being made, and avoid the cronyism that has been a part of
picking national coaches for Olympic and Pan-American
competition? Identify the coach with innovative ideas by
communicating with the athletes and the top track clubs.

Such an overview committee should have the power and
teeth to decide which AAU and Olympic committee officials
are standing in the way of progress of amateur athletics. If they
are fingered, they should be removed. The athletes should
have a majority voice in it. If certain officials are incompetent,
the athletes should have the right to have them removed.

Why doesn't the AAU kick back some of the money it

receives from all of its new members throughout the United States to the various clubs and organizations which are promoting athletics and putting on road races and track competitions? It could be used for developing age-group running, interclub racing, clinics, and masters competitions. Wherever this is being done, it's not to as great an extent as it could be done.

If I have a question about my amateur status and how it may be altered or affected because of my business, I can go to one man in the AAU house in Indianapolis, Ollan Cassell. But he's rarely there. He's generally traveling, attending meetings of the IAAF in some foreign country, or occupying himself with other matters. Why is there only one man to answer all the questions on a national basis for so many athletes?

I also think there is an obligation to be prompt and consistent when dealing with the athlete. These people are supposed to be providing a service, aren't they? I can't buy the popular argument of many AAU officials that they are above criticism because they are volunteers. We can do without volunteers who do an incompetent job. We want paid workers to do a professional job. That's what is happening in other parts of the world. People who are intent upon helping their athletes succeed are working for the federations.

Government subsidization is the way it is done in the Eastern European countries and in the Soviet Union. There is a semi-subsidization in a country such as Japan, where an athlete may work for Nippon Steel and receive the time to train, or in England where an athlete may work for a newspaper, or have a job that gives him the free time. The Finnish federation often pays for an athlete to go to a warm-weather climate in order to train in winter. Esa Tikkanen of Finland trained for the 1979 Boston Marathon in the Canary Islands and Toshihiko Seko of Japan trained in New Zealand.

The concentration in Rumania is on gymnastics. They seek out the kids who seem to have the potential at an early age, provide them with the proper coaching, and put them through a demanding program to ensure excellence in their individual events. That's why the scores of ten go to Nadia Comaneci instead of to an American or British girl. All of it comes down to how much each nation wants to put into specific sports. It's the amateur sport that suffers in the United States.

I have mentioned the contrast between a Waldemar Cierpinski of East Germany winning an Olympic gold medal in the 1976 Marathon and Frank Shorter of the United States winning one in 1972. I think the situations in which an athlete wins an Olympic gold medal on his own are going to be fewer and fewer. Shorter used his own guts and initiative to pull it off. Someone may do it in 1980, but, as you travel farther into the future, science and the supportive society are going to play a larger part. The countries that are willing to go the route of scientific medical approach to events such as the marathon are the ones that will be picking up the gold medals, and the ones that will produce a runner who will break Australian Derek Clayton's 1969 world record of 2:08:33.

The answer? Given the American situation, I feel the best concept is one of open sport. It has worked in golf and in tennis. Eliminate the difference between the professional and the amateur. There will still be the Olympic Games. Open them up. The individual with the most desire, talent, training, coaching, financial support, motivation, and help from his friends, teammates, and country will win the competition without the artificial aid of drugs, stimulants, or cheating. With the proper funding of organized clubs and programs, the United States could do well once again in Olympic and other international competition in *any* sport. Or, at least, to paraphrase Baron de Coubertin, we will have fought well and conquered.

18
The White House

It was Tuesday, April 17, 1979, the morning after Boston and my new American record of 2:09:27 in the chilling rain and gloom. I was at my store in Cleveland Circle, about to take a hot bath. The telephone rang and I heard Ellen talking to somebody. She said, "Who's calling? The President? The President of what?"

When we found out it was the President of the United States, Jimmy Carter, we all went into a state of shock. A presidential aide had called Joe Notar in our downtown store. He called the store and said, "Clear the lines." Lois Dowd had answered the call when it came. She called to Ellen who picked up the phone and said, "This is Ellen Rodgers, can I help you?"

When I picked up the phone, the aide was on the other end. He asked me my name, and where I was situated; then the line went quiet. I waited about a minute or two and suddenly President Carter came on the phone. He congratulated me on my race and we started talking about running the marathon. He said, "I grind out five miles a day, and I really admire marathoners."

He asked how Frank Shorter did and I told him he hadn't done all that well, as he was still recovering from surgery. I told him Americans did very well throughout the field, considering that it was an exceptionally strong international field. I mentioned that Joan Benoit, a senior at Bowdoin College in Brunswick, Maine, set an American record for women. We talked about several things. He said he reads a lot of running magazines. I told him I thought he was doing a good job as a runner and as a President.

He ended the conversation by saying he'd like to get together some time. I said, "That sounds neat with me." He said, "Well, how about May second?" That sent Ellen sprinting off to get my appointment book to see if I was doing anything on May second. It was a Wednesday. I knew I was heading out to San Diego for one of the Diet Pepsi ten-thousand-meter series races that weekend. But there was some time before that race, so we said, "Definitely. We'd love to head down."

It turned out to be a state dinner for Japanese Prime Minister Masayoshi Ohira. We received the printed invitation in the mail a few days later. It was black tie. I would have to go out and rent a tux. When it made the newspapers, Massachusetts Senator Paul Tsongas heard about it and invited Joan Benoit and me down for a luncheon the day before our dinner at the White House.

We met a lot of Senators: Senator Proxmire, Senator Strom Thurmond, Senator Baucis of Montana. We put on a little "clinic" at the luncheon. Senator Thurmond asked me if I ate the white or the yellow part of eggs. He asked me if I did stretching exercises. He told me how he did sit-ups and push-ups and how he has run as far as six miles recently. He's over seventy. I could tell by shaking his hand that he's a pretty fit guy. There were a lot of questions like that. We received a little introduction to politics and politicians.

We were interviewed by some reporters and we posed for pictures with some of the senators. Joan and I pretended we were jogging on the Capitol steps with Senator Tsongas. He runs and he indicated he was planning to run the Falmouth Road Race in 1979. Senator Baucis said he was going to run a marathon in his home state of Montana. They all seemed pretty knowledgeable and looked pretty fit. They had a lot of practical questions.

We were also introduced to House Speaker Tip O'Neill of Massachusetts and I mentioned how I had to get a cab to get to the Capitol and to go out and rent a tux. We were paying all our expenses for air fare and hotel out of our own pocket. So they figured the least they could do for us from then on was to give us the courtesy use of a chauffeur and a limousine. We were driving when I saw a sign for fireworks. My father collects them and I'm something of a fanatic myself. You can't buy them in most cities, so we loaded up.

The next evening we all headed over to the White House. We drove up to the gate and an aide met us. He checked our invitations. He recognized me and he happened to have his own Boston Marathon number there. He asked me to sign it. Right there at the White House gate. Later, after the State Dinner, he gave us a tour of the White House.

We parked the car, walked up to the entrance, and went inside. There were all these aides in formal military uniforms. They ushered us into a reception room. We met another aide who briefed us and told us what the steps to follow would be, the protocol. You'd go through a reception line, he said, and you'd be assigned to a dinner table.

He told me a funny story about how he was walking up to the White House one day and suddenly all these men were darting behind bushes and trees nearby. He didn't know what was going on. An instant later, Jimmy Carter went running by on his daily run. The Secret Service agents were jumping from tree to tree and bush to bush on the White House lawn, keeping an eye on Carter while he was running.

The White House dinner was an interesting, unique experience. I was nervous. I'd never been in this kind of situation before. Secretary of State Cyrus Vance was there. Actor Peter Falk was a guest. I responded by drinking a lot of champagne— American champagne. Finally we were escorted to the receiving line to meet President and Mrs. Carter and Prime Minister Ohira and his wife.

As I walked through, President Carter recognized me. We shook hands and exchanged greetings. He was very friendly. He kissed Ellen. He asked a photographer to come over and take a picture of Mrs. Carter, himself, Ellen and me. He introduced me to Prime Minister Ohira, who understands English, and I told him the Japanese runners were very tough marathoners. He smiled.

We went to our tables. Joan Benoit and I were assigned to the same table. No one else was at the table when we got there. We were wondering what the situation would be. Would we sit with President and Mrs. Carter? I walked up to the table and I saw a name card for Joan next to mine. Peter Falk was to my right. We all sat down.

Sure enough, the next thing I knew, President and Mrs. Carter and Prime Minister Ohira and his wife showed up at our table. Joan and I kind of scrunched down in our seats before my manners caught up to me and I stood up. It was a bizarre moment. There was President Carter sitting directly across from me. I just sort of went into shock. I'd seen President Ford when he spoke to the athletes at the 1976 Olympic training camp, but I'd never met a President before. Plus I wasn't politically that much in tune with President Ford. I'm more in tune with Carter, and I was before the invitation. I still like him. Maybe I like him a little more now. He impressed me as tremendously sincere, straightforward, and honest.

We had a great dinner. We started off with avocado with a sea food salad. It was followed by a regular salad and a choice of chicken, buffalo, or suckling pig with Georgia or Texas barbecue sauce. Of course, I tried everything. It was a beautiful night and it was the first time a dinner had ever been held on the west terrace of the White House. There were 180 people, with soft violin music floating in the air.

I heard President Carter talking to Peter Falk, saying that I ran a marathon at a sub-5:00 pace and that Joan Benoit ran at a sub-6:00-per-mile pace. Peter Falk was nodding. "Yes, yes," while he was smoking Kool cigarettes. He even offered me a Kool. I said, "No thanks, only Winstons." I used to be a Winston smoker. Falk, apparently, is a golfer and I think running is a little foreign to him.

Quite a bit of the conversation centered on running. President Carter asked me a question about an adductor injury he had. He asked how many breaths per stride it is normal to take. He said he starts off taking maybe three breaths per stride, then gets up to four when he's tired. He told me he'd run as far as ten miles and he wasn't any more tired than he was after six or seven. Mrs. Carter said she has trouble on the hills. She runs two miles with the President sometimes.

We also discussed some political issues. Joan Benoit commented that solar energy ought to be explored more before we put all our eggs in the nuclear energy basket. Mrs. Carter talked about the city of Davis, California, where people bicycle a lot, thus saving energy and becoming more fit. After a dessert of whipped cream cake, President Carter gave a talk about how the relationships between Japan and the United States have changed. We're no longer enemies; we're allies. Prime Minister Ohira also spoke. They had worked out some trade agreements to eliminate restrictions on getting American products into Japan. It was a happy occasion, and President Carter was in a very good mood. We went inside, listened to pianist Bobby Short entertain, received a tour of the White House from the marathoner who worked there, and that was it. It was time to call it a day.

I was still on a high after my American record run in Boston. It was something I had focused on since my difficult race at

Fukuoka the previous December. I knew that had not been an accurate representation of what I could do on an average day in the marathon. So I was one of the first people to file my application for Boston. For a time, in January and February, I had considered not running Boston. One or two additional marathons had popped up. I'd run Boston in five out of the last six years and I thought maybe a brand new marathon with a big name would be appealing—just as New York City was in 1976. There was one being planned in Washington, D.C. It never materialized.

I was in Phoenix, Arizona, for a race and a "training vacation" and I told one reporter that I might not run Boston. I also said there were many races where the runners were being exploited and ripped off. I mentioned the 1978 Chicago Marathon where runners were charged ten dollars and weren't given much in return and the administration of the race was reportedly poor. I mentioned a few other races like that.

The comments were reported inaccurately and distorted when they went out over the wires and were picked up all over the country. They took two separate statements and put them together. So the final statement was different from what I had originally said. They were combined to say I would not run Boston because I felt Boston was a rip-off.

I took a lot of heat for that. One race director in Massachusetts tried to nail me in the press. Will Cloney and Jock Semple criticized me. This one race director made some unwarranted comments about expense money I allegedly received. There are some people who are new to the sport who don't understand it. They don't understand amateurism. They don't understand the position of an amateur athlete. They primarily want to make their own reputation. They don't really care about the top-level athlete or about any athlete, for that matter. Unfortunately, they're speaking from positions of ignorance.

I tried to fight back against all of this as well as I could in the media. I tried to clarify the situation. The real truth is that an amateur is in a very vulnerable position in a lot of ways. You have to be careful. My only response could be to run in Boston and run really hard. There were a number of individuals to whom I wanted to make my point by how well I ran my race. Then they might get off my back and leave me alone. A number of my friends, world-class runners, have had the same feelings.

I also had plans to break 2:12 in Boston. I had missed it by twelve seconds in New York, when it was seventy-eight degrees. I was recovering from the flu at Fukuoka. So circumstances had prevented me from getting under 2:12, but that's a significant mark to break. If you are under 2:12 in a marathon, you are hitting the nitty-gritty of world-class marathoning. Times somewhat over that are good, but not what I would call excellent. I also had in mind using Boston as if it were the Olympic trials. I tried to imagine that it was 1980 and I was preparing for the Big One and this was how I was going to do it.

Everything had started out pretty well. I went out to California and trained high mileage for awhile. Eventually, all that fell apart, mostly because of business reasons. My mileage dropped. I knew I was in good shape. In sub-2:12 shape. But I didn't think I had been able to follow through completely enough on my plan. I also knew there were ten sub-2:12 marathoners in the Boston field, making it the strongest bunch of Boston starters in history.

I hadn't raced as much before Boston in 1979 as I had in 1978. I tried to do a little more speed work. I did five repeat miles at about a 4:41 pace with a quarter-mile jog in between. If I didn't run a race, I'd be sure to do a workout like that once a week. But my mileage was lower than it'd been in the past. I averaged only about 125 miles per week. I had pulled back, in a sense. I was very busy trying to handle business difficulties. I was tired. Still, I hadn't traveled a lot to races so, conversely, that gave me a little extra rest.

I looked over the competition. At Boston, there is always a

strong American field, and 1979 was no exception: Randy Thomas, Garry Bjorklund, Tom Fleming. Even more to the point, there was an exceptional foreign field: Toshihiko Seko, the Fukuoka champion, arrived early; Kevin Ryan of New Zealand; Trevor Wright and Chris Stewart of Great Britain; Esa Tikkanen of Finland; the South African contingent which was running unofficially. I expected Seko would be my top competition. He has the ten-thousand-meter speed and, besides that, the top Japanese had not run Boston for ten years. They certainly wouldn't send one of their top marathoners to run the Boston Marathon unless they thought he could win it. It would be a waste of time and they simply wouldn't do it.

I also had this feeling, as usual, that many people, particularly Americans, still had the impression that I wasn't here to stay. People thought, and perhaps still do think, that I'm vulnerable. It wasn't that way with Frank Shorter. He used to be considered invulnerable. You couldn't beat Frank. For some reason, people have this belief that I'm easier to beat. Some of the marathoners talk like that. Maybe Nike West would send in a crew. An organized team effort. That's something that always gets me going. When I read comments by individual runners about what they expect to do, it gets my adrenaline pumping. I also get pumped up when someone has just defeated me. Trevor Wright did at Fukuoka, as did Seko, and at Boston I hoped to rectify that situation. All of these factors affected me during the race.

The day started out pretty well in terms of weather, except for the light rain. As I was about to leave the house, Ellen yelled to me and suggested I ought to take a wool cap. I went back in and grabbed my best, thickest wooly training cap. There was no wind, but it was forty-two degrees and a light rain was falling at the start of the race. I felt very chilly. I kept my hat on after I took off my gear, and I ran practically the whole race wearing it. I didn't take it off until the last quarter mile, when I started waving with it to the crowds. I also wore

my white cotton gloves. This helped to keep my body temperature regulated. I later deduced that, by wearing the hat, I didn't
become as tight and my body stayed a little warmer in the
cold. One loses a lot of body heat through the head. I figured
my hat helped me retain it.

About two minutes before the gun went off, one of my
contact lenses must have been hit by a raindrop. It was
knocked to the side, and slid off my pupil. I couldn't see out of
one eye, and I'm incredibly nearsighted. So I needed a mirror. I
asked the crowd, "Does anybody have a mirror?" A girl came
up with a camera, unscrewed the camera lens, and I used the
mirror inside the camera to adjust the contact lens.

For a frantic moment about one minute before the start of the
Boston Marathon, I couldn't see. I had this vision of running
the entire Boston Marathon virtually with one eye, semi-blind.
I suddenly felt how the blind runners must feel and how the
handicapped people in wheelchairs feel. That's what I thought
of. "How am I going to run this intense competition with just
one eye?" Fortunately, I got my contact lens back in.

I first bought contacts during my freshman year in college.
Part of it was vanity. One girl told me I would look much better
if I bought contact lenses. That did the trick. I also had run the
New England Cross-Country Championships the previous year
in the pouring rain during my senior year in high school, and
one of the lenses in my glasses fell out. The same thing
happened in my freshman year at Wesleyan. That's when I
decided to wear contacts.

I've lost a lot of lenses on training runs, particularly in the
winter. You'll lose the fluid under the lens and it will become
dry on your eye. Then if you touch the skin near your eye, or if
a snowflake hits it, the lens can just pop right out. I've had
branches swing up and hit my eye. I've had the strings from
my sweat suit flip up and knock the lens out. I've lost
countless lenses that way.

The only incident during a race was in my first race coming

back after three years of inactivity. It was a thirty-kilometer race. Some grit went into my eye at sixteen miles and, if you wear contact lenses, you know how much that hurts. I staggered along, holding my face for about fifty yards. The grit flew out and I finished. I can wear glasses and compete but, even when I used eyeglass holders, I used to get a headache. If I didn't wear the holders, the eyeglasses would slip off my nose. I do need some kind of help. I'm probably legally blind without contact lenses, a hopeless case.

I figured the Boston race would not be decided until as late as the twenty-two-, twenty-three-, or twenty-four-mile mark— or when we started down Beacon Street. It turned out that it broke up a little before that. But I knew that the name of the game would be to hold back, use my head, and conserve energy. I was just going to space out that energy very conservatively all the way, and it turned out I really had no choice in the matter. Tom Fleming went out really hard, as he always does, and we always had someone to chase and pace ourselves on.

All along the course, I had help getting water. It was a cool day, consequently I didn't need much. Ellen and people from the store were out there. There were also people from New Balance shoes, passing water to people on their team. That included my Greater Boston TC teammates, Bob Hodge, Dick Mahoney, and Randy Thomas. They happened to be up front for a good part of the race. They shared water with me. Then I'd share it with them. It was a real cooperative effort. There we were in the lead of the Boston Marathon passing cups of water back and forth to each other as we ran at a sub-5:00 pace.

As the race developed, an Olympic-sized pack of twenty-five runners ran together for the first eight miles. After ten miles, it started to thin out. Tom Fleming had about a two-hundred yard lead as early as eight miles. We all tried to keep our eyes on him. We knew he was running close to a world-record pace—something like 2:10. I figured, on a day this cold, Tom had to buckle. Maybe, if there was a wind at our backs and with no rain, he could have kept going. I had to gamble that things would catch up with him.

I never saw Seko until the fifteen-mile mark. He stayed right behind me the whole way up to then. At about eight miles I was in the lead with Bjorklund, Thomas, Hodge, Mahoney, Bob Varsha, Kevin Ryan, and John Halberstadt and Kevin Shaw of South Africa. Don Kardong went flying by me at about twelve miles into the race. I thought it was a replay of Montreal and he was going to run a fantastic race. He disappeared and I never saw him again. I later found out he dropped out.

Bjorklund passed me after fifteen miles. He took off on this downhill section of the course. He obviously wasn't too familiar with the course design and Boston terrain. He had a big uphill section coming up, the Newton Hills and Heartbreak. I was just freaked out that here was Garry pouring it on as he went over this downhill.

We headed into the hills and I caught my first glimpse of Seko. He came up right next to me. I was feeling pretty bad at this point. My stomach was upset and I had to go to the bathroom. We'd been running hard for fifteen or sixteen miles and all I could think of was, "Geez, I've got another ten miles to go. Two guys are ahead of me." It looked like Bjorklund was going to take the race and suddenly Seko appeared. He was running the same race he ran at Fukuoka. Lie back for fifteen miles, then make his appearance. Shock everybody. He'd conserved his energy. Make the big push.

For an instant, I was wavering. He surged ahead of me. I watched his stride. I analyzed his form, tried to study this individual. I even adapted my stride to his. A much shorter stride. I suddenly felt more comfortable. I felt "gung ho." I thought of how I lost at Fukuoka to him, but I had no flu this time to bother me. I decided it was the time. "I've got to run hard now." You don't think about later in the race. You run hard when that person's there with you.

We chased after Tom and Garry. Garry had passed Tom by then and was in the lead. We pulled up next to Tom and he said, "We'll catch him on the hills." We stayed with Tom for a quarter of a mile and pushed on. We chased Bjorklund up the first hill. We caught him after we finished the hill and, by this time, Seko had fallen in right behind me. Just shadowing me. He was right on my heels. A Fukuoka replay.

What was good was that I had Garry to chase. If he hadn't been there, I don't know what would have happened. It might have been a different race. When I have someone to chase, I can run hard. I'll just keep on running hard. I don't feel the fatigue as much if I have someone to chase. I didn't think of Seko as much as long as I had this other person to go after. As I said, I completely forgot Seko was in the race for fifteen miles. There was always this other person. I just focused on him.

I caught up to Garry and he said, "Go for 2:08." We just zipped by. We kept running a steady pace. Seko was behind me. He never came up to me again. As I went up Heartbreak Hill, I noticed that, for the first time, I had a little lead on him. Five to ten yards. I couldn't believe it. I said, "Good grief." It was the first time the awareness hit me. "Maybe," I said, "I can win." For twenty-one miles or so, I didn't think I was going to win. When this awareness hit me and I had this big downhill coming up, I knew I had a shot. When I think I have a shot, after I have felt all was lost before, I can be tough.

We were in an area of the course I knew really well, approaching my store in Cleveland Circle. Seko didn't know the course. It was totally unfamiliar terrain. It was all to my advantage. The crowd was for me. I felt stronger over the last four miles than I ever have in a marathon in my life. I ran hard. I really felt the little hill just before Kenmore Square near Fenway Park. This was the toughest part of the final four miles.

I couldn't see Seko for most of the final five miles. There were a couple of official vehicles behind me, and the streets were narrowed by spectators pressing in as close as possible to see better. I didn't know how close Seko was. Was he 20 yards behind? Or 120 yards? I knew I'd been moving fast, but I thought he might be staying with me. I didn't want to lose by ten seconds. I didn't want another Jeff Wells incident to occur. The thought that I could lose it haunted me. What happened in 1978 was a nightmare. Two seconds faster than Wells!

I finally caught a glimpse of Seko. He was about two hundred yards behind. I knew I had won the race. I passed the Eliot Lounge and, just before I went up Hereford Street to the finishing stretch, I looked behind one more time to be absolutely sure. When you're in a race such as Boston, you absolutely want to know. I took off my hat, began to wave to the people, and started to savor the win.

I turned down the hill to the finish line and I saw 2:09:22 on the clock. I knew Ron Hill had a 2:09:28. I wanted to break that. I pushed hard the last thirty yards and I ran 2:09:27. To get a personal record was almost as important to me as winning the Boston Marathon. It had been four years since I had improved on my marathon time. That's a long time and I had run a lot of hard marathons. It was as if I was caught in a rut. People never expected me to run faster. But this was it. This was what I could do. I think I changed the thoughts of a few people about me.

The inevitable decline caught up with me after Boston, brought on in part by the fact that I had already accomplished much of what I had set out to do in 1979. I had set the world record for twenty-five kilometers on the track, and I had lowered my American record in the marathon in Boston. I was also swept up by the escalating demands on my time for interviews, clinics, speaking engagements, and business affairs. The clothing line was busier, and dealers who carried my running gear wanted me to make appearances at their stores.

I was also committed to a fairly heavy schedule of road races. Just twelve days after Boston I ran in the Trevira ten-mile race in Central Park, and I was second to Craig Virgin, who went on to set an American record for ten thousand meters on the track and to win the Atlanta Peachtree and Falmouth races. I didn't realize it at the time, but it was an ominous sign for the summer. Virgin was merely one of many who would leap from the track to the roads with great hopes and subsequent success.

After a major win such as Boston, there is an almost inevitable psychological and physical decline. You lose the sharpness and the edge that you had. You fall off a little. I made up my mind when Boston was over that I wouldn't run any track races during the summer, even though I had enjoyed the European experience the year before. I'd stay with those road races I had committed myself to, and leave it at that.

If there was a grand plan, it was simply that there were two races left that mattered. The Olympic trials and, hopefully, the big one that would follow. Oh, I'd run more races and run some of them to win, but the Olympics were lodged solidly in the back of my mind as I headed into the summer. What I didn't realize was that there were so many quality five-thousand- and ten-thousand-meter runners and stee-plechasers, such as Virgin, Herb Lindsey, Greg Meyer, Ric Rojas, and Frank Shorter, who were gearing up and getting into the best shape of their lives for the summer.

Take Meyer, whose eyes were on making the U.S. team in the steeplechase. He was one of the new breed. He works at my store in Cleveland Circle and trains with me. I knew what kind of shape he was in, and he proved it when he ran to an American record on the roads (28:24) to beat me in the Boston Diet Pepsi run in June. He was new to the roads, but he was in peak shape for the AAU steeplechase and easily beat me at ten kilometers. I was in the lowest form I'd been in the entire year.

I went to France on what amounted to a vacation trip to visit

the Perrier plant. I ran the lowest mileage I'd run in four years.
Forty miles. I felt terrible physically, and when I came back
from France on July 1, I immediately went out and did a 140-
mile week, a crash program. For the next month, I averaged
between 130 and 145 miles per week. We also were living
through a stretch of hot, tropical weather. It toughened me. I
got back into shape quickly. I did some pretty high-quality
track work as well, probably the best I've ever done.

The intention in my July training program was to reap the
benefits in late August, when I planned to run the Falmouth
Road Race and follow it up the next Sunday by running the
first Montreal International Marathon, which was an adjunct
to the World Cup. I was left at the start in Falmouth, made up
some lost ground, but finished third (32:39) to Virgin (32:19:7)
and Lindsey (32:27), which still left me with three of the five
fastest Falmouth times. I was far from displeased with my run.
In fact, given the circumstances of a crowded and delayed
start, I was very pleased.

I went up to Montreal, where the organizers had set up a
marathon that attracted the talent you normally find only in
Boston and New York on the North American continent. I
went up hoping for decent weather, only to find intense heat.
It was eighty-five degrees on the morning of the race and,
when I went up to the starting line, I knew it was not to be.
Perhaps it was a combination of being tired and the heat of the
day, but I dehydrated, hit the wall, and finished fifteenth in
2:22:12. It was my slowest completed marathon since the 1976
Olympics, which, ironically, were in the same city.

It was a depressing experience, and the talk intensified that I
was slipping. Some people thought I wasn't in decent shape.
I'd been beaten on the roads in Denver, Milwaukee, Falmouth,
and Montreal. Some people were advising me to pass up New
York. What if it was hot again? It might be too much effort. I
might get injured. Concentrate on the Olympic trials. Forget
New York. It wasn't worth it.

I ultimately decided to run New York. It wasn't so much that I wanted to defend my title. I'd done that before, and, let's face it, I wasn't having much luck defending my titles on the roads. What I was thinking of was my world ranking for the year as a marathoner. This is my race, the distance I'm best at. If I could win New York, coupled with my Boston record, it could solidify a number-one world ranking by *Track & Field News*. I felt I had been slighted a year ago, when I was rated second. I felt that, even if I didn't win New York, a solid performance would do it. I figured I'd try to run conservatively and cautiously enough to ensure a decent, more than respectable race.

The New York City Marathon was built up as a duel between Frank Shorter and me at the marathon distance. The *New York Times* headline asked, "Will New York Become a Rodgers–Shorter Showdown?" The teaser on the cover of the *New York Running News* when it put out its special marathon issue asked, "Frank Shorter and Bill Rodgers: Have they come full circle?" The significance of it all struck me as I headed to New York. I was viewed as being in a state of decline, and Shorter was viewed as someone on his way back from surgery who was about to return to the top.

He had beaten me twice on the roads during the summer, once at ten kilometers at the altitude of Denver and once in Milwaukee over ten miles, when he ran the fastest time of his life (47:34) and I came in third (47:58). He still had to qualify for the American Olympic Marathon Trials. He had missed it by two seconds when he finished seventy-fifth (2:21:56) in Boston. So this was an important race for him as well.

What upset me was that Fred Lebow was supporting Frank again. It's symptomatic of the people who feel that Frank, simply because he won the gold medal in 1972, is inevitably number one. No matter what I or any other marathoner has done since 1972, Frank is number one. I've held the American record since 1975. I'd won New York three straight years. I had the three fastest times on the course. But the article in the *New York Running News* talked about my "dismal loss in Montreal" and my string of setbacks on the road.

If you had examined my races which included a second to Alberto Salazar in the Boston Freedom Trail and a second to Herb Lindsey in the Lynchburg ten-miler, you'd find my times were comparable to my 1978 times, when I was winning these races. I ran my best ten-miler (47:14) ever at Lynchburg, one of the fastest ever run in the United States. I knew I wasn't that badly out of shape, despite the observations of some runners, fans, and writers. I was running up against guys who were generally better geared to the shorter, faster races than I was. It hurt to lose. There's a sense of pride involved, even if the distance is not your specialty. But things had been easier, in the past, on the road-race circuit. Today it's getting brutally tough, too tough for anyone to dominate it. Even Virgin, who had a superb year, ran fourth in the Diet Pepsi ten-kilometer race in Purchase, New York.

So I seized upon the New York City Marathon as an opportunity to make a couple of points. You should evaluate a runner in terms of the distances he's best at. And you can't write someone off after one, or even a few, losing races. That's ridiculous. You certainly can't dismiss a marathoner because of one off day and think that someone is through. Marathoners, if anything, are the epitome of athletes who bounce back.

I arrived in New York with the impression that people in the sporting press wanted to see a Shorter victory, to see if his comeback was complete, to return him to the pedestal. New York would be the setting. I also arrived as the temperatures were starting to play tricks. Ellen had brought her heavy winter jacket and I had brought a leather jacket. I figured it would be about forty-five to fifty-five degrees and dip lower at night.

Indian summer intervened. It's something the New York City Marathon is going to have to contend with in the future.

Probably about one third of their races are going to be in warm weather, similar to Boston. That's exactly the way it turned out to be. I couldn't believe it when I heard it was going to be close to seventy-five degrees. It seemed impossible. Two weeks earlier it had been thirty-four degrees and we had had a blizzard in New England. February weather. Now we're going up to seventy-five? A forty-degree jump? I was prepared for the worst, aware that training in the tough-weather environment of New England helps me as much as it hurts me.

I looked out from my suite of rooms at The Sherry Netherland on the morning of the race and saw the city enveloped in a dense fog. It was still there at the 10:30 A.M. start, preventing the normal gaggle of helicopters from getting off the ground, which was something of a relief. As it turned out, the hazy fog helped the runners, cutting the rays of the sun out for about the first fifteen miles of my race. The sun came out as I was going over the Queensboro Bridge.

The start was a page out of a European race, with runners jumping the gun and taking off before the final countdown to zero. I'd say there was a five-second gap between the time the first runners started and the time the cannon went off. There were people as much as twenty yards in front of me. I started to inch out. I looked around a couple of times. I thought they'd stop but when nobody did, I knew I had to go. If I didn't, I'd be crushed or trampled.

Everybody went out so unexpectedly fast that the trucks and buses for the press and photographers couldn't get into first gear fast enough. The runners had to stream around the vehicles, and they, in turn, had to weave their way through the runners to get out in front. I found myself behind a lot of runners who didn't belong up front. They were 2:40 to 2:50 marathoners. They were ahead of me for the first mile. It's an uphill mile going over the Verrazano Narrows Bridge. I was forced to go out right away at a 5:00 pace.

I wanted to run cautiously. That was my whole feeling about

the race. I was pretty confident that the haze was going to burn off, and as I've said, it eventually did. I went by the three-mile mark at 14:44, just under a 5:00-mile pace. I knew if I could keep that up, I'd do about a 2:10 marathon. When I hit the ten-kilometer mark, I was 30:55. I estimated that fifty to sixty runners were still in front of me. I was one minute behind the leaders, and I later saw that stretch out to a wider gap.

I was running steadily with Steve Kenyon of Great Britain, who was running his first competitive marathon in six years. I'd run against him a lot at shorter distances before and had never beaten him. We ended up running together for seventeen miles. He had a watch, so I took a couple of splits from him. We just worked our way up, keeping our eyes on certain runners as key points. We first focused on Lasse Viren and aimed for him. He was running comfortably, but we had developed a certain kind of momentum. It wasn't very fast, just very steady.

We started to pass people who had taken it out too fast for the hot weather, people who were running the course for the first time. Dick Mahoney, my Greater Boston TC teammate who had finished tenth in Boston, was lured into going out too fast. He probably wasn't aware that it was so humid, because it had been so overcast at the start. We met him about twelve miles into the race at the Pulaski Bridge, and the leaders were about one minute ahead.

I caught up to Shorter at the same point, and I asked, "Who are all the people ahead of us?" He shook his head and said, "I don't know." There were so many of them that we were both a trifle shocked. Kenyon and I continued on, starting to move a little quicker as we approached the Queensboro Bridge.

Earlier in the race, at perhaps the 10,000 meter mark, I'd seen a runner limping along with a bandaged leg. Steve Kenyon told me it was Gerald Tebroke of the Netherlands, a top ten-thousand-meter runner and pre-race contender to win. I had considered him a threat to win. The same was true of Dave Black of Great Britain. I asked Steve, "Where's Black?" He pointed him out, and I said, "Let's move up on him."

We pushed the pace hard as we reached the center of the bridge, and we swooped down on Ian Thompson of Great Britain, Benji Durden of Atlanta, Jukka Toivola of Finland, and Zakaria Barie, a marathoner from Tanzania. I caught up to Ian and asked, "Who's ahead of us?" He said Kirk Pfeffer, an American age-group record holder at seventeen and eighteen who had run a 2:11:50 in Enschede, Holland, in August. He was 1:30 ahead of us.

We came off the bridge and made the turn up First Avenue. I really ran hard. I broke away from Thompson and Kenyon. Durden was the only one who went with me. I was trying to move into second. I instantly surged really hard. The crowds are so great on First Avenue, they carry you along. It's a great place to break away in the race. Benji and I had been in a real duel in Wheeling, West Virginia, in a twenty-thousand-meter race. I had done the same thing then, and I beat him that way. He responded this time, and we went back and forth. He stayed ahead of me along most of First Avenue. I finally caught up to him between nineteen and twenty miles. We talked a little bit and I moved ahead.

People were telling me I was about 1:20 back of Pfeffer at the twenty-mile mark. I could finally see the lead runner. For the first time, a photographers' truck was in front of me. It's the way it had always been in New York, the photographers in front of me. I always had that truck to focus on and chase. I didn't until twenty miles of the race this year. It was as if I was finally getting into the race.

I was afraid I couldn't win, but I thought I should get second. I was concerned that Pfeffer was going to get my American record. I figured I was running a 2:11 or a 2:12. I didn't want to lose the race and the record too. I could see Pfeffer as I moved up to the twenty-two-mile mark. He'd run the half-marathon in a course record 1:03:51, pretty quick on a hot day. But the pace

and the heat were beginning to get to him, and I could sense he
was starting to slow up.

It helped me. I was constantly narrowing the gap, and the
longer I went, the more I kept getting hints from the crowd that
I could catch him. He was probably twenty-five seconds ahead
of me as I went onto Fifth Avenue. Now I knew I could catch
him. It was similar to the feeling I'd had in Boston in April,
when I knew I could win. As I said, I can be very tough when
that happens.

I knew I had to keep moving steadily, since I was feeling
very tired myself from pushing so hard. As I went up the hill
into Central park, the trucks were almost right in front of me. I
could see Kirk struggling, and as I came up the hill to the
twenty-three-mile mark, my brother, Charlie, was there with a
bottle of water. He yelled, "He's got five seconds on you." he
had timed the interval distance between us.

I came up behind Kirk, turned to say something, and he was
so tired he could hardly respond. All we said was "Hello." I
tried to move away from him as quickly as I could. I kept
looking behind me to see if he was trying to come after me. I
didn't want to have to confront anyone any more. I just wanted
to run hard until the twenty-five mile mark and cruise in.
That's what I did, winning my fourth straight New York City
Marathon in 2:11:42. Pfeffer held on to take second in 2:13:08
and Kenyon came in third in 2:13:29.

I had proved my point, and it was time to sip some
champagne and enjoy the rest of the day with Ellen, Charlie,
and some friends. We went to the awards ceremony that night
at the Sheraton Center, and in the middle of it, someone came
up to me to say-I had a phone call from President Carter. He
invited Ellen and me to Camp David. He had had some
problems running in a road race in Maryland, when he
collapsed, and I told him the next time he enters a road race
just to try to finish. And that was the end of my year, my last
marathon before the Olympic trials.

I said, in 1975, I knew I could run faster. I finally proved it at

Boston. I still think I can go better than 2:09. I'll never break 2:08. I have no illusions about that. I think if I'd had a wind at my back on that day in Boston, I'd have run in the 2:08s. I might have had a shot at the world record. But there are no ifs in this sport. You take what you get.

To win Boston was important for all the reasons I have brought up, and to set a personal record was immensely gratifying. I wanted to win Boston for another reason. It would put me up there with a small group of people who have won it twice or more. Now I'd won it twice. Johnny Kelley had won it twice. Some top runners had won it twice or more. Leslie Pawson of Pawtucket, Rhode Island, and Eino Oksanen of Finland have three Bostons. Gerard Cote of Canada has four. Clarence DeMar of Melrose, Massachusetts has seven. I think I can get Cote. I have no illusions about DeMar but, in marathoning, you have to aim high.

Bill Rodgers

When Bill Rodgers won the 1975 Boston Marathon in the American record time of 2:09:55, he slipped quietly back into a private life one day later, eating pizza during a solitary interview in a basement apartment in Jamaica Plain, Massachusetts. When he won the 1979 Boston Marathon and lowered his own American record to 2:09:27, he was personally invited by Jimmy Carter to a state dinner at the White House and he was besieged the day after for interviews by television, newsmen, wire service reporters, and the national news magazines.

As the marathon, in general, and running on the roads, in particular, have become an American obsession, Rodgers has personified it for the estimated twenty-five million running devotees. He has stamped his imprint on the running movement with an engaging personality, an availability, and a consistency of performance that has been unmatched on the roads.

Starting with his Boston win in 1975, he has run nine sub-2:12 marathons, four more than anyone else on the world list. He has run the four fastest marathons by a United States citizen, and his 1979 Boston Marathon time of 2:09:27 is the fourth fastest marathon time in history. He has won Boston three times (1975, 1978, 1979), New York four times (1976, 1977, 1978, 1979), and the Fukuoka International Marathon once (1977); and, within one time span of less than six months, he won all three of the major marathons in the world open to him in a non-Olympic year.

During one stretch from January 1, 1977, through October 23, 1978, Rodgers ran fifty-five serious races on the roads from distances of 10 kilometers to a marathon and he won fifty of them, extending an unbeaten streak to nineteen by winning the New York City Marathon. On the track in Boston, he also set American records for 15 kilometers (43:39.8), 20 kilometers (58:15), and for the one-hour run of 12 miles, 1351 yards and 2 feet and a world record (1:14:12) for 25 kilometers in Saratoga, California.

A native of Newington, Connecticut, Rodgers attended Wesleyan University and, after running a 8:58.8 two-mile in December 1969, at the Coast Guard Academy, did not run another competitive race until February 1973. He received a Master's Degree in Special Education from Boston College and taught emotionally disturbed children in Everett, Massachusetts, for two years before opening the first Bill Rodgers Running Center on November 14, 1977, in Brighton, Massachusetts, on the Boston Marathon course at Cleveland Circle. He now has two other Running Centers, one in Boston and one in Worcester. Rodgers and his wife, Ellen, recently moved to Sherborn, Massachusetts.

The Rodgers Record

Bill Rodgers

Birth date:	12–23–47
Birthplace:	Hartford, Connecticut
Residence:	Sherborn, Massachusetts,
Raised:	Newington, Connecticut
Height:	5'9"
Weight:	128 lbs.
High School:	Newington H.S.
College:	Wesleyan, B.A., Sociology
	Boston College, M.A., Special Education

AWARDS

National AAU—Di Benedeto Award—Best Athletic Performance of 1975

Nominated—Sullivan Award—1975

Track & Field News—All-American Marathoner—1975

AAU All-American Long Distance Running Team—20Km—1973

Special Needs Citation—from superintendent of Boston public schools

James Francis Thorpe Award—from Dr. Franklin Perkins School—1976–77

AAU All-American Track & Field Team—10,000M—1976

AAU All-American Long Distance Running Team—30Km & Marathon—1976

Voted Best Marathoner in the World by Runner's World and Track & Field News—1977, 1975, in 1976 ranked #6, in 1978 ranked #2

Nominated—Top 10 Finalists—Sullivan Award-2nd in balloting.

Won Will Cloney International Award for U.S.A. at Boston in 1978 and 1979

Robert De Celle Award for Long Distance Running—1978

RECORD

BEST MARATHONS
Boston—1st place—1979—2:09:27 (American record)
Boston—1st Place—1975—2:09:55
New York City—1st Place—1976—2:10:10 (course record)
Boston—1st Place—1978—2:10:13
Fukuoka, Japan—1st Place—1977—2:10:55 (fastest time in 1977)
Fukuoka, Japan—3rd Place—1975—2:11:26
New York City—1st Place—1977—2 :11:28
New York City—1st place—1979—2:11:42
U.S. Olympic Trials—2nd Place—1976—2:11:58
New York City—1st Place—1978—2:12:12
Amsterdam, the Netherlands—1st Place—2:12:47 (course record)
Fukuoka, Japan—1978—2:12:51
Baltimore—1st Place—1977—2:14:22 (course record)
Kyoto, Japan—1st Place—1977—2:14:26

NATIONAL CHAMPIONSHIPS
20Km Road—1st Place—1973—1:03:58
30Km—1st Place—1976—1:29:04 (unofficial world record)

BEST ROAD RACE MARKS	BEST TRACK MARKS—OUTDOORS
1978—10Km—28:36	1 Mile—4:18:8 (1968)
1977—20Km—1:00:24	2 Miles—8:53:6 (1975)
1977—30Km—1:29:04	5000 meters—13:42:00

3 Miles—13:25.4 (1976)

1978—½ Marathon—1:03:08

10,000 Meters—28:04.4 (5th fastest American)

15,000 Meters—43:39.8—1977 (American record)

20,000 Meters—58:15—1977 (American record)

1-Hour Run—12 miles, 1,351 yds.—1977 (American record)

10 Miles—46:40—1977

25 Kilo—1:14:11.8—1979—world and American record

30 Kilo—1:31:50 American record

INTERNATIONAL COMPETITION

San Blas ½ Marathon—7th Place—1:08:28—1974

San Juan 450 (20 miles)—1st Place—1:45:04—1975

Ohme, Japan, 30Km—1st Place—1:32:06—1976

International Cross Country, Rabat, Morocco (12Km)—3rd Place—34:20

Sado, Japan Marathon (200 meters short)—1st Place—2:08:23—1976

Springbank International—12 miles—1st Place—54:31—1977 (course record)

RECENT ACCOMPLISHMENTS

1979—30Km—1:31:50—American record on the track

1979—25Km—1:14:12—world record on the track

1979—Marathon—2:09:27—Boston Marathon American record

1979—Marathon—2:11:42—fourth straight New York City win

COMPLETE MARATHON RECORD

Terminology:
PR—Personal Record
AR—American Record
DNF—Did Not Finish
*—200 meters short

	Marathon	Date	Place	Time	Location
1.	Boston	4/16/73	DNF		Boston, Mass.
2.	Bay State	10/28/73	1	2:28:12	Framingham, Mass.
3.	Boston	4/15/74	14	2:19:34	Boston, Mass.
4.	New York City	9/29/74	5	2:36:00	New York, N.Y.
5.	Philadelphia	12/1/74	1	2:21:57	Philadelphia, Pa.
6.	Boston	4/21/75	1 AR	2:09:55	Boston, Mass.
7.	Enschede	8/30/75	DNF		Holland
8.	Fukuoka	12/7/75	3	2:11:26	Japan

	Event	Date	Place	Time	Location
9.	U.S. Olympic Trial	5/22/76	2	2:11:58	Eugene, Oregon
10.	Olympic	7/31/76	40	2:25:14	Montreal, Canada
11.	New York City	10/24/76	1	2:10:10	New York, N.Y.
12.	* Sado Island	11/7/76	1	2:08:23	Japan
13.	Baltimore	12/5/76	1	2:14:22	Baltimore, Md.
14.	Kyoto	2/13/77	1	2:14:26	Japan
15.	Boston	4/18/77	DNF		Boston, Mass.
16.	Amsterdam	5/21/77	1	2:12:47	Holland
17.	Waynesboro	10/8/77	1	2:25:12	Waynesboro, Va.
18.	New York City	10/23/77	1	2:11:28	New York, N.Y.
19.	Fukuoka	12/4/77	1	2:10:55	Japan
20.	Boston	4/17/78	1	2:10:13	Boston, Mass.
21.	New York City	10/22/78	1	2:12:12	New York, N.Y.
22.	Fukuoka	12/3/78	6	2:12:51	Japan
23.	Boston	4/16/79	1AR PR	2:09:27	Boston, Mass.
24.	Montreal	8/26/79	15	2:22:12	Montreal, Canada
25.	New York City	10/21/79	1	2:11:42	New York, N.Y.

Joe Concannon

Joe Concannon has covered the Boston Marathon for the Boston *Globe* since 1967, when his first story was about Kathy Switzer, who entered as K. Switzer because women were barred. He first wrote about Bill Rodgers when he won the Falmouth Road Race in August 1974 on Cape Cod and, subsequently, he may be the only person to have witnessed the eight big marathon wins by Rodgers. Boston, 1975. New York, 1976. New York, 1977. Fukuoka, 1977. Boston, 1978. New York, 1978. Boston, 1979, New York, 1979.

A native of Litchfield, Connecticut, he received a degree in political science from Boston University, and before joining the Boston *Globe* staff, worked as a sports information aide at Harvard University and as sports information director at Holy Cross College in Worcester, Massachusetts. He presently writes a weekly column on running for the *Globe* and his favorite event is the Litchfield Hills Road Race, which starts and finishes by the village green in the center of his hometown. Rodgers has won it twice.